Fforde, Jasper.
The Eyre affair

MIDNIGHT ON THE MAVI MARMARA

MIDNIGHT ON THE MAVI MARMARA

The Attack on the Gaza Freedom Flotilla and How It Changed the Course of the Israel/Palestine Conflict

Edited by
Moustafa Bayoumi

HAYMARKET BOOKS
CHICAGO, ILLINOIS

Published by Haymarket Books
P.O. Box 180165
Chicago, IL 60618
773-583-7884
info@haymarketbooks.org
www.haymarketbooks.org

Trade distribution:
In the U.S., Consortium Book Sales and Distribution, www.cbsd.com
In Canada, Publishers Group Canada, www.pgcbooks.ca

Library of Congress Cataloging in Publication Data is available

ISBN 978-1-60846-121-9

This book was published with the generous support of Lannan Foundation and
the Wallace Global Fund.

Printed in Canada by union labor on recycled paper containing 100 percent
post-consumer waste, in accordance with the guidelines of the Green Press
Initiative, www.greenpressinitiative.org

10   9   8   7   6   5   4   3   2   1

CONTENTS

5. OLD FRIENDS, NEW THINKING

6. PALESTINE ON OUR MINDS

INTRODUCTION

Moustafa Bayoumi

There were 581 passengers on the *Mavi Marmara*. The Turkish vessel named for the blue waters of the Sea of Marmara was by far the largest ship in the Freedom Flotilla, a convoy of ships full of volunteer humanitarian workers and aid for the beleaguered people of Gaza. Although this was not the first attempt to break the siege of Gaza by the sea, it was easily the biggest. In fact, there had already been eight voyages before. The first endeavor was in August 2008, and it had been successful, as were the four following it. The sixth mission was launched at the end of December 2008, during Israel's punishing war on Gaza, and the small boat carrying medical supplies and three volunteer surgeons was in the high seas when it was rammed by the Israeli Navy. Taking on water, the boat crawled to the coast of Lebanon and, after a second attempt, eventually reached Gaza. The seventh mission was menaced by Israel. The eighth was boarded by the Israeli Navy. Neither reached Gaza.

All of these previous missions, however, were dwarfed in size by this, the ninth attempt. The Freedom Flotilla consisted of the *Mavi Marmara*, along with two other vessels from Turkey, two from Greece, and individual ships from Ireland and Algeria. (Some of the ships flew different nations' flags. The Irish Ship was the *Rachel Corrie*, which sailed to Gaza later, and an eighth Greek ship, which was American-flagged, failed to launch due either to technical difficulties or possibly Israeli sabotage.) On board the flotilla was 10,000 tons of humanitarian aid, all of it desperately needed and cruelly disallowed by Israel's blockade (with the Egyptian government's collusion) of the Strip. A sense of what the aid entailed can be grasped from what was loaded on the Defne Y, a smaller Turkish vessel: 150 tons of iron for reconstruction, ninety-eight power units of all kinds, fifty precast homes, sixteen children's playgrounds including seesaws and slides, medical equipments such as ultrasound scanners, X-ray machines, electric patient beds, dentistry units, Doppler echocardiography devices, wheelchairs, electric mobility scooters for the disabled, stretchers, mammography equipment, microscopes, dialysis machines, radiology monitors, crutches, ENT Units, operating beds, and gynecological couches.

The ships had been carefully inspected at all points of departure for any weapons, and none were ever found. The participants on the flotilla included artists and academics, doctors and lawyers, activists and journalists, and lawmakers from dozens of countries, including parliamentarians from Israel, Egypt, and Sweden, and two members of the German Bundestag. Volunteers had come from over forty countries, united by the simplicity of their mission: to publicly deliver aid to Gaza in order to challenge Israel's illegal blockade on that small, densely populated strip of land on the Eastern Mediterranean. These were not thugs, brutes, or terrorists. A terrorist, after all, is one who kills innocent civilians to advance a political cause. (Just as George Orwell observed with the word *fascism* long ago, the word *terrorism* today has virtually no real meaning except to signify the complete inhumanity of your opponents, especially if they are Muslims.) Rather, these were ordinary people trying to help other ordinary people.

What happened next is now well known and, especially after reading the testimonies in this book, should also be in little dispute, even if the Israelis confiscated all recordings of the event in a desperate attempt to control the narrative. (Importantly, some people did smuggle out recordings. More importantly, you can't confiscate people's memories.) At around 4:25 a.m. on May 31, 2010, Israeli commandos attacked the *Mavi Marmara* while the boat was in international waters. They had been trailing the convoy for hours and harassing them for about ninety minutes prior to this by circling the ship with Zodiac dinghies full of Israeli commandos. Immediately following the morning prayer, the Zodiacs moved quickly alongside the *Mavi Marmara*. They shot at the ship with paintball rifles and attempted to board. The ship then turned, heading away from Gaza at full speed. Israeli helicopters descended minutes later, and the commandos began firing smoke and percussion grenades on the ship, followed almost immediately by rubber bullets and live ammunition. Meanwhile, those on the ship were not about to be boarded in international waters, and they resisted the attack with slingshots, bare hands, water hoses, and various objects from the ship. Three Israeli commandos who had dropped from helicopters were overpowered, their weapons disabled, and were taken below the fifth deck, where they were searched and then provided with basic first aid. The other commandos continued to fire live ammunition rounds, shooting dozens of unarmed civilians, including an Indonesian doctor.

By the time the attack was over, nine people—eight Turkish citizens and a dual American-Turkish citizen —were dead. Autopsy results later revealed that those killed in the attack where shot a total of thirty times. *The Guardian* reported that sixty-one years-old, "was shot four times in the temple, chest, hip and back," and that nineteen-year-old Furkan Doğan, "was shot five times from less that 45cm, in the face, in the back of the head, twice in the leg and once in the back. Two other men were shot four times, and five of the victims were shot either in the back of the head or in the back.") Footage released by Iara Lee and analyzed by Ali Abunimah shows that the Israelis fired indiscriminately into a crowd of unarmed people huddled behind a cabin door, disproving the claim that the commandos were merely defending themselves against an onslaught. According to Kevin Ovenden, an organizer of the Viva Palestina solidarity group and a volunteer aboard the ship, the attack lasted for twenty-eight minutes. Jamal Elshayyal, a reporter for Al Jazeera and also a survivor of the raid, writes that after the initial attack concluded and the ship's passengers had surrendered, the Israelis refused the passengers' increasingly desperate pleas for medical assistance to the wounded, leading to three more men bleeding to death. Both Elshayyal's and Ovenden's testimonies, along with seven others, are included in this book.

One of the dead was the tae kwon do coach of the Turkish national team, himself a former European champion of the sport. Another was a sixty-one-year-old electrical engineer. Also killed were a Kurdish telephone repair shop owner, a former newspaper journalist who traded in that job to work for the Humanitarian Relief Foundation (IHH), a firefighter with four sons, a thirty-two-year-old aid worker with a young daughter, two family men, and the nineteen-year-old American-born high school student from inner Anatolia. Their ages ranged from nineteen to sixty-one, and their names are Çetin Topçuoglu, Ibrahim Bilgen, Ali Haydar Bengi, Cevdet Kiliçlar, Fahri Yaldiz, Necdet Yildrum, Cengiz Songür, Cengiz Akyüz, and Furkan Doğan. It's important to remember their names. The dead are easily maligned and even more easily forgotten. What we need to recall most is that these were ordinary men, shot to death in a middle of a humanitarian mission.

The attack on the *Mavi Marmara* was not only brutal. It was criminal. Not only did the Israelis have no legal right to forcibly board the boat in international waters, as legal scholars George Bisharat and Ben Saul explain in this volume, they also had no justification for their use of lethal force. As Saul writes in another essay, "one cannot illegally attack a ship and then claim self-defense if those on board resist your attack. The right of self-defense instead rests with the passengers." The degree of unarmed resistance the Israelis met is also immaterial. Leon Wieseltier, a stalwart supporter of Israel, explains that the civilians on board "were 'armed' with metal bars and a knife, but still they were civilians, and soldiers are trained to respond unlethally to the recklessness of a mob."

By the viciousness of the raid, the Israeli government seemed to be delivering a deliberate and deadly message to future humanitarian missions: Fear not for the lives of others but for your own. The American media largely reported the attack with evident sympathy for the attackers, not for those who had been attacked, but this is perverse. Imagine for a moment that the *Mavi Marmara* had been sailing to Iran in support of the Green movement, and Iranian commandos raided the ship in international waters, killing nine along the way. Those offering resistance would immediately be lionized as heroes, the dead remembered as martyrs to the cause of freedom.

Unsurprisingly, the US government responded (in yet another display of a double standard) by shielding Israel from condemnation in the United Nations Security Council at roughly the same time it sought to cajole China into isolating North Korea over the sinking of a South Korean military vessel. Israel established a dubious panel of inquiry (see Yousef Munayyer's essay in this volume). But the reaction of the Obama administration notwithstanding, international outrage was swift, and spontaneous. Demonstrations quickly broke out in Istanbul, several Arab and European capitals, major American and Canadian cities, the Gaza Strip, Israel (10,000 demonstrated in Tel Aviv), the West Bank, and elsewhere. Egypt finally opened the Rafah border crossing, and Greece ended military exercises with Israel. Turkey's long relationship with Israel was damaged, perhaps beyond repair. Belgium, Norway, Denmark, Spain, Greece, and Sweden summoned their Israeli ambassadors; Turkey, Ecuador, and South Africa recalled theirs; and Nicaragua suspended its diplomatic ties with Israel. Dockworkers in Oakland, California, Sweden, South Africa, and Norway refused to unload Israeli ships for a time in protest of Israel's actions. The Pixies cancelled a scheduled concert in Tel Aviv.

Israel's self-inflicted isolation, in other words, was—and is—on the rise. By killing nine unarmed civilian humanitarian aid workers,

Israel's actions have pricked the conscience of many around the globe. The result is a growing global movement ready to stand up to Israel's brutal rule of its Palestinians, which has, in recent years especially, been marked by a series of "strategic blunders," in the understated words of Anthony Cordesman, a chief analyst for Center for Strategic and International Studies (and hardly a friend to the Palestinians). Together, these "blunders" have a cumulative force if only because of their grotesquery.

Before the attack on the *Mavi Marmara*, there was the siege on Gaza, which is described in harrowing and tragic detail here in an essay by Sara Roy, and which, despite an announced relaxing of its lines of strangulation (still far less than what is needed), continues to decimate the economy, livelihoods, and health of more than 1.5 million people. (Without freedom of movement and open borders for exporting—not importing—goods, the Strip cannot develop economically and is doomed to a deliberate and cynical present of aid dependency, corruption, and pauperization.) The siege is connected to the war on Gaza in January 2009, dubbed "Operation Cast Lead" by Israel, where the territory was sealed shut and bombed ruthlessly, killing, according to the Israeli human rights organization B'tselem, at least 1,390 Palestinians, mostly civilians, including 344 children, 110 women, and 117 men over the age of fifty, as well as 248 police officers who were inside police stations. Thirteen Israelis were killed during Operation Cast Lead, three of them civilians and four soldiers killed by friendly fire. Palestinian casualities, in other words, were on a scale of 100 to 1 in this war. "The Biblical injunction of an eye for an eye is savage enough," wrote Oxford University's Avi Shlaim at the time of the war, "but Israel's insane offensive against Gaza seems to follow the logic of an eye for an eyelash."

The war in Gaza was launched two and a half years after the 2006 war in Lebanon, which killed over 1,000 Lebanese, many if not most of them civilians, compared with about 160 Israeli dead, including forty-three civilians. In the final three days of that war, the Israelis carpet bombed southern Lebanon, dropping more than four million cluster bombs (equivalent to about one for each Lebanese). Since this ordnance often does not explode upon impact, the south of Lebanon was effectively mined. To date, at least forty-six civilians have been killed and more than 300 people (mostly children and farmers) have been maimed since the end of that war. Large swaths of valuable Lebanese farmland are now also uninhabitable.

Hamas and Hezbollah are also guilty of targeting civilians, albeit to a lesser degree, and they are accordingly and correctly ostracized by much of the international community for it. Israel, on the other hand, has repeatedly violated the principles of international law, including the laws of war, with extraordinary impunity, until now at least. But maybe that is beginning to change.

Even those at the epicenter of the American and Israeli political establishments are recognizing the unsustainability of Israeli policy. Commenting on precisely these wars and the Gaza flotilla attack, Anthony Cordesman writes that the US's commitment to Israel "does not justify or excuse actions by an Israeli government that unnecessarily make Israel a strategic liability when it should remain an asset." General David Petraeus, former Commander of Central Command and currently Commander of NATO forces in Afghanistan, testified in March 2010 to the Senate that the Israel/Palestine conflict jeopardizes US foreign policy interests (and, in another report, that Israel's intransigence in peacemaking endangers American lives). And the head of the Israeli Mossad, Meir Dagan, told the Knesset in June 2010 that "Israel is gradually turning from an asset to the United States to a burden."

And as the Gaza Freedom Flotilla and its subsequent fallout makes clear, average citizens around the world increasingly view Israel's actions as indefensible; and with greater frequency and in larger numbers, these ordinary people are becoming motivated to put an end to such violence themselves.

For more than sixty years, the Israel/Palestine conflict has dragged on seemingly without end, and as if change is rarer than peace. Yet, in terms of global public action at least, the Israel/Palestine conflict may be heading into a new phase.

* * *

Midnight on the "Mavi Marmara" is the first book about the attack on the *Mavi Marmara*, but it will likely not be the last. As Philip Weiss and Adam Horowitz write in their contribution here, the attack on the *Mavi Marmara* will probably be understood as this generation's "anti-1967" moment for Israel. Immediately following that war more than forty years ago, Israel was seen by many in the Western world as the "scrappy underdog beating the odds." Today, according to Weiss and Horowitz, that image "is gone forever, and the ongoing siege of Gaza has caused many to consider what Zionism has built in the Middle East."

In these pages, you will find testimony, analysis, history, and poetry from activists, novelists, academics, analysts, journalists, and poets, all of which tackle the events of that night and their meaning: for the struggle for Palestinian rights, for the state of Israeli society, for American Zionism, for the history of the conflict, for the role of resistance strategies in today's world, and more. The attack on the *Mavi Marmara* is particularly significant because its impact will be felt along three significant and related lines, the understanding of which is necessary if we are to see where the Israel/Palestine conflict is headed and possibly find a way out of our current impasse.

The first line concerns the internationalization of the struggle for equal rights in Israel/Palestine. There was a time not too long ago when most college students interested in the Israel/Palestine conflict were either Jewish or Arab, but this is no longer the case. The Palestinian cause for equal rights is increasingly recognized as today's moral question in a similar manner to the way campus activists approached the struggle to end South African apartheid in the 1980s. In fact, the two struggles are frequently compared, and for obvious reasons Israel's supporters are made nervous when the apartheid label is applied to Israel. Former US President Jimmy Carter, for example, was excoriated for his book, *Palestine: Peace Not Apartheid*, mostly because of the last word in its title.

Often left out of this discussion is how the Israeli political establishment already speaks in these terms. Both former Israeli Prime Minister Ehud Olmert and former Prime Minister (and current Defense Minister) Ehud Barak have warned that Israel is headed toward apartheid. (The difference between them and many campus activists is that the activists would say Israel is already there.) Barak told a national security conference in the Israeli city of Herzliya in March 2010 that "as long as in this territory west of the Jordan River there is only one political entity called Israel, it is going to be either non-Jewish, or non-democratic." He continued: "If this bloc of millions of Palestinians cannot vote, that will be an apartheid state." Olmert, for his part, warned in 2007 that the collapse of a two-state solution will mean Israel will "face a South African–style struggle for equal voting rights."

Palestinian civil society groups and international campaigners have known this for some time. In 2001, a group of Palestinian, Israeli, and American activists organized the International Solidarity Movement (ISM), an organization "committed to resisting the Israeli apartheid in Palestine by using nonviolent, direct-action methods and principles." (Adam Shapiro details the organization and its strategies in his chapter in this book.) The ISM's methods are powerfully simple. They involve witnessing and documenting Israeli military occupation. Their volunteers come from all over the world and participate in civil disobedience against Israeli military rule. They also frequently come under Israeli fire, and several have been wounded, including Kate Edwards (Australia), Caoimhe Butterly (Ireland), Brian Avery (USA), Tristan Anderson (USA), and Emily Henochowicz (USA). The American student Rachel Corrie and the British student Tom Hurndall were killed by the Israeli military (One ISM member, Akram Ibrahim Abu Sba', was killed by members of the Islamic Jihad.)

Similarly, in 2005, hundreds of Palestinian civil society groups came together to issue a call to the international community that it boycott, divest, and sanction (BDS) Israel until is fulfills its obligations under international law. In these pages, Omar Barghouti, a BDS leader, details the success of the movement and its growing imperative in the wake of the attack on the Freedom Flotilla. Several major performing artists have cancelled their concerts (Elvis Costello being the latest before the Pixies), large institutions such as the Norwegian State Pension Fund have divested themselves of companies that do business in the West Bank, and campus groups (including at Hampshire and Evergreen Colleges—the University of California at Berkeley came close) are increasingly seeking to divest their university portfolios from businesses that profit from the occupation.

The BDS movement is also significant for being able to unite disparate Palestinian groups along three basic principles toward reaching a just solution to the conflict: an end to the Israeli occupation of the West Bank, Gaza Strip, and East Jerusalem; recognition of the fundamental rights of the Arab-Palestinian citizens of Israel to full equality; and respecting, protecting, and promoting the rights of Palestinian refugees to return to their homes and properties as stipulated in U.N. resolution 194. The road to liberation here is not armed struggle but nonviolent resistance. The respected independent Palestinian lawmaker Mustafa Barghouti explained BDS in the *New York Times* in December 2009: "A new generation of Palestinian leaders is attempting to speak to the world in the language of a nonviolent campaign of boycott, divestment and sanctions, precisely as Martin Luther King Jr. and thousands of African-Americans did with the Montgomery bus boycott in the mid-1950s. We are equally right to use the tactic to advance our rights. The same world that rejects all use of Palestinian violence, even clear self-defense, surely ought not begrudge us the nonviolence employed by men such as King and Gandhi."

BDS and ISM are not alone in their efforts. They often work closely with Israeli organizations like Anarchists Against the Wall or other international groups like Code Pink. Solidarity also comes in the form of guerilla art, as when the British street artist Banksy beautifully transformed Israel's inhumane and illegal (according to the International Court of Justice) separation wall into a canvas of subversive graffiti. What all of this points to is that, as with the Freedom Flotilla volunteers, there is an ever-expanding chorus of ordinary people from all over the world who are motivated by the principles of unarmed resistance and their honest desire to see long-delayed justice for the Palestinians finally fulfilled. And they are willing to act on their convictions.

Alongside the internationalization of the conflict comes a debate about Zionism in the United States that Norman Finkelstein has explored for years and that was put into sharp focus by a recent article by Peter Beinart in the *New York Review of Books*. Titled "The Failure of the American Jewish Establishment," Beinart's article describes why American Jewish college students have a diminishing attachment to Israel and to what he terms the American Jewish establishment. (In this book, Daniel Luban writes as "a member of the 'younger generation' whose attitudes have become the subject of so much discussion.") Beinart describes most young Jewish Americans as liberals "who were alienated by the prevailing 'group think' required around Israel. These young Jewish Americans "had imbibed some of the defining values of American Jewish political culture: a belief in open debate, a skepticism about military force, a commitment to human rights. And in their innocence, they did not realize that they were supposed to shed those values when it came to Israel." The result of this alienation has been that "for several decades, the Jewish establishment has asked American Jews to check their liberalism at Zionism's door," Beinart explains, "and now, to their horror, they are finding that many young Jews have checked their Zionism instead."

Why would this be so? According to Beinart, "Morally, American Zionism is in a downward spiral." He points out the increasingly extreme, land hungry, and racist turn in Israeli politics, describing Netanyahu's coalition government as "the product of frightening, long-term trends in Israeli society." Beinart's point is that because the mainstream American Jewish organizations "defend virtually anything any Israeli government does, they make themselves intellectual bodyguards for Israeli leaders who threaten the very liberal values they profess to admire."

Beinart ends his article by telling of "a different Zionist calling" that "has its roots in Israel's Independence Proclamation, which promised that the Jewish state 'will be based on the precepts of liberty, justice and peace taught by the Hebrew prophets.'" Using the example of solidarity work among Israeli student activists with Palestinians thrown out of their homes in Sheikh Jarrah by Israel to make room for settlers, Beinart asks, "What if American Jewish organizations brought these young people to speak at Hillel? What if this was the face of Zionism shown to America's Jewish young?"

Beinart's article is hardly alone in questioning the orthodoxy about Israel among the Jewish American mainstream organizations. Norman Finkelstein's essay in this book ("Ever Fewer Hosannas") describes other examples, including an influential essay by Tony Judt, the book by John Mearsheimer and Stephen Walt titled *The Israel Lobby*, and more. The rise of J Street, an alternative lobby group to the American Israel Public Affairs Committee (AIPAC), likewise points to the shifting sands underneath the old establishment. Without overstating the case, the significance in all of this change is that Israel's core supporters, who have enabled that country's impunity for decades, may be withering away. If ordinary people, here young Jewish Americans, raise enough of a challenge to their political leaders, they too could help bring about a change that could have major repercussions for finally and justly resolving the Israel/Palestine conflict.

The Freedom Flotilla was also organized not in the name of any Palestinian political faction but simply for the people of Gaza, and in that fact, too, one discovers a third important point about the current state of affairs: There is an ongoing crisis among the Palestinians regarding their own political leaders. In fact, all the established parties are so far away from fulfilling the needs and aspirations of their constituents that they have become a major hindrance rather than a vehicle for a just resolution of the conflict. Even after the Flotilla attack, which some pundits described as a win for Hamas, polling data revealed support in Gaza for the group to be only at 32 percent, barely different than before the attack. The Israeli siege of Gaza has indeed entrenched Hamas's rule in the Strip, but the group is not more popular than before they were elected.

Neither, however, is Fatah, the largest and most established faction in Palestinian politics. In mid-June, Fatah brazenly cancelled municipal elections to be held in the West Bank in July. Why? Because they knew they would lose, not to Hamas, but to lesser-known independents. In Nablus, the second largest city in the West Bank, Mayor Ghassan Shakaa broke with Fatah to organize his own slate of independents, knowing that a Fatah-dominated list was doomed to failure. (Fatah is often seen by Palestinians as Israel's enforcer, and, if more proof were needed, recently leaked documents illustrate how Fatah sought to undermine Turkey's push for a U.N. probe of the flotilla attack.)

Meanwhile, much of the substantive political work going on the West Bank today has little to do with the factionalism of Palestinian politics. Instead, it has a lot to do with the weekly demonstrations against the wall. Based in villages like Bil'in, Nil'in, and Ma'asara these demonstrations are organized by "popular committees" against the wall and the settlements (so called because they are committee made up of all factions where factionalism also means nothing). The Popular Committees are recovering the spirit of the first intifada of 1987, which was largely a grassroots, community-based nonviolent organizing effort on the part of the Palestinians. They also take another page from the South African struggle by echoing the strategy of the African National Congress around "ungovernability," in order to "encourage the emergence of new committees and initiatives and support them, regardless of their affiliation." Bil'in has staged weekly protests against the wall since March 2005, making them "longest continuous nonviolent popular mobilization in Palestinian history," according to noted Middle East historian Joel Beinin. Another village, Budrus, successfully forced the Israeli government to reroute the wall away from the village, and the vast majority of its land has not been confiscated. (This struggle is the subject of a new documentary by Julia Bacha called *Budrus*.) Since these actions began, the Israeli Army, which sometimes meets resistance in the form of stones being thrown at soldiers, has injured over 1,800 demonstrators and killed nineteen of them. Popular committee leaders, such as Abdallah Abu Rahmah, are usually arrested, following a long-established pattern (as Lamis Andoni explains in this book) of arresting, exiling, or killing Palestinian leaders who advocate nonviolent resistance.

The era of armed struggle has not come to an end. This conflict has been bloody for a long time, and there is every reason to believe that violence will continue to be a part of it. The daily violence of the occupation persists, more warfare is certainly possible, and bad leadership is a given. As the Israeli government feels more threatened by growing popular resistance, it will in all likelihood respond with even greater aggression. But the contours of the struggle are shifting. It's important to understand that the West Bank demonstrations alone will not herald the end of the occupation. But taken together with the Gaza Freedom Flotilla, campus activism, international solidarity work, tireless blogging and creative myth-debunking from people like Ali Abunimah, Philip Weiss and Adam Horowitz (who blog as Mondoweiss), and Max Blumenthal, and new questions around the politics of Israel, a different future now seems possible in ways it hadn't before. In short, what unites all of these examples is the resolve of ordinary people to determine the shape and destiny of the struggle for human rights for Palestinians and Israelis by inserting themselves directly into the struggle and more and more through creative paths of nonviolent resistance.

* * *

There are so many good reasons to end the Israeli/Palestinian conflict and not a single good reason to keep it going. The conflict, for example, continues to feed both a pernicious anti-Semitism and a frightening Islamophobia globally where there is far too much noxious hatred already. Resolving the conflict between these two peoples with justice and equity will advance more than the interests of Israelis and Palestinians. It will have substantial and positive repercussions around the world in a way that solving no other conflict in today would. The question is how that solution is to be found and implemented.

While difficult, it is not impossible. What is clear now, just as it was clear a generation ago, is that, from either the Palestinian or the Israeli side, there can be no military solution to this problem. The solution must instead be one that is forged through dialogue, mutual recognition, and holding true to the principles of coexistence.

What is equally clear is the future will not be made by endless negotiations. The so-called peace process initiated by the 1993 Oslo agreements, which never guaranteed the Palestinians recognition of their rights to self-determination, are merely exercises in dissimulation, obfuscation, and futility. They cannot bring about an end to the conflict.

Instead, the actions of ordinary people from around the world are forcing the parameters of coexistence to emerge with ever more clarity. They involve an end to military occupation, an abandonment of terrorism, an embrace of full equality for Arabs and Jews alike, protection of minority and communal rights, and a just resolution to the question of refugees. There is nothing extraordinary in this list, just as there is nothing out of the ordinary in desiring peace with justice or working toward the end of oppression. What the Gaza Freedom Flotilla and actions like it show is that ordinary people may be the ones who are finally going to push the conflict to a resolution, one that guarantees justice for everyone. And the extraordinary power of ordinary individuals working together may very well be the lasting legacy of the attack on the *Mavi Marmara*.

that I made my first note, there in the taxi. I don't remember the exact words, but I'm suddenly disconcerted by a sense of not quite having managed to register that this is a project so hated by the Israelis that they might try to stop the convoy by violent means.

By the time I get to the airport, the thought has gone. On this point, too, the project is very clearly defined. We are to use nonviolent tactics; there are no weapons, no intention of physical confrontation. If we're stopped, it ought to happen in a way that doesn't put our lives at risk.

WEDNESDAY 26 MAY, NICOSIA

It's warmer than in Nice. Those who are to board the ships somewhere off the coast of Cyprus are gathering at Hotel Centrum in Nicosia. It's like being in an old Graham Greene novel. A collection of odd people assembling in some godforsaken place to set off on a journey together. We're going to break an illegal blockade. The words are repeated in a variety of languages. But suddenly there's a great sense of uncertainty.

The ships are late, various problems have arisen, the coordinates still haven't been set for the actual rendezvous. The only thing that's certain is that it will be out at sea. Cyprus doesn't want our six ships putting in here. Presumably Israel has applied pressure.

Now and then I also note tensions between the various groups that make up the leadership of this unwieldy project. The breakfast room has been pressed into service as a secretive meeting room. We are called in to write details of our next of kin, in case of the worst. Everyone writes away busily. Then we are told to wait. Watch and wait. Those are the words that will be used most often, like a mantra, in the coming days. Wait. Watch and wait.

THURSDAY 27 MAY, NICOSIA

Wait. Watch and wait. Oppressive heat.

FLOTILLA RAID DIARY:
"A MAN IS SHOT. I AM SEEING IT HAPPEN."

Henning Mankell

It is five o'clock in the morning and I'm standing in the street waiting for the taxi that will take me to the airport in Nice. It's the first time in ages E. and I have had some time off together. Initially we thought we'd be able to stretch it to two weeks. It turned out to be five days. Ship to Gaza finally seems to be ready to set off and I'm to travel to Cyprus to join it, as arranged.

As instructed, I've limited my luggage to a rucksack weighing no more than 10 kilos. Ship to Gaza has a clearly defined goal: to break Israel's illegal blockade. After the war a year ago, life has become more and more unbearable for the Palestinians who live in Gaza. There is a huge shortage of the bare necessities for living any sort of decent life.

But the aim of the voyage is of course more explicit. Deeds, not words, I think. It's easy to say you support or defend or oppose this, that, and the other. But only action can provide proof of your words.

The Palestinians who have been forced by the Israelis to live in this misery need to know that they are not alone, not forgotten. The world has to be reminded of their existence. And we can do that by loading some ships with what they need most of all: medicines, desalination plants for drinking water, cement.

The taxi arrives, we agree on a price—extortionate!—and drive to the airport through empty, early morning streets. It comes to me now

1. ON BOARD THE SHIPS

FRIDAY 28 MAY, NICOSIA

I suddenly start to wonder whether I may have to leave the island without getting onto a ship. There seems to be a shortage of places. There are apparently waiting lists for this project of solidarity. But K., the friendly Swedish MP, and S., the Swedish female doctor, who are traveling with me, help keep my spirits up. Travel by ship always involves some kind of bother, I think. We carry on with our task. Of waiting. Watching and waiting.

SATURDAY 29 MAY, NICOSIA

Suddenly everything happens very quickly. We are now, but of course still only maybe, to travel sometime today on a different, faster ship to the point out at sea where the coordinates meet, and there we will join the convoy of five other vessels that will then head as a single flotilla for the Gaza Strip.

We carry on waiting. But at about 5:00 p.m. the port authorities finally give us permission to board a ship called the *Challenge*, which will take us at a speed of fifteen knots to the rendezvous point, where we will transfer to the cargo ship *Sophia*. There are already lots of people aboard the *Challenge*.

They seem a bit disappointed to see the three of us turn up. They had been hoping for some Irish campaigners who have, however, suddenly given up the idea and gone home. We climb aboard, say hello, quickly learn the rules. It's very cramped, plastic bags full of shoes everywhere, but the mood is good, calm. All the question marks seem to have been ironed out now. Soon after, the two diesel engines rumble into life. We're finally underway.

23:00

I've found a chair on the rear deck. The wind is not blowing hard, but enough to make a lot of the passengers seasick. I have wrapped myself up in blankets, and watch the moon cast an illuminated trail across the sea. I think to myself that solidarity actions can take many forms. The rumbling means there is not a lot of conversation. Just now, the journey feels very peaceful. But deceptively so.

SUNDAY 30 MAY, AT SEA, SOUTHEAST OF CYPRUS, 01:00

I can see the glimmer of lights in various directions. The captain, whose name I never manage to learn, has slowed his speed. The lights flickering in the distance are the navigation lights of two of the other ships in the convoy. We are going to lie here until daylight, when people can be transferred to other vessels. But I still can't find anywhere to sleep. I stay in my wet chair and doze.

Solidarity is born in dampness and waiting; but we are helping others to get roofs over their heads.

08:00

The sea is calmer. We are approaching the largest vessel in the flotilla. It's a passenger ferry, the "queen" of the ships in the convoy. There are hundreds of people on board. There has been much discussion of the likelihood of the Israelis focusing their efforts on this particular ship.

What efforts? We've naturally been chewing that over ever since the start of the project. Nothing can be known with any certainty. Will the Israeli Navy sink the ships? Or repel them by some other means? Is there any chance the Israelis will let us through, and repair their tarnished reputation? Nobody knows. But it seems most likely that we'll be challenged at the border with Israeli territorial waters by threatening voices from loudspeakers on naval vessels. If we fail to stop, they will probably knock out our propellers or rudders, then tow us somewhere for repair.

13:00

The three of us transfer to the *Sophia* by rope ladder. She is a limping old cargo ship, with plenty of rust and an affectionate crew. I calculate that we are about twenty-five people in all. The cargo includes cement, reinforcement bars, and prefabricated wooden houses. I am given a cabin to share with the MP, whom I view after the long days in Nicosia more and more as a very old friend. We find it has no electric light. We'll have to catch up on our reading some other time.

16:00

The convoy has assembled. We head for Gaza.

18:00

We gather in the improvised dining area between the cargo hatches and the ship's superstructure. The gray-haired Greek who is responsible for security and organization on board, apart from the nautical aspects, speaks softly and immediately inspires confidence. Words like "wait" and "watch" no longer exist. Now we are getting close. The only question is: What are we getting close to?

Nobody knows what the Israelis will come up with. We only know that their statements have been menacing, announcing that the convoy will be repelled with all the means at their disposal. But what does that mean? Torpedoes? Hawsers? Soldiers let down from helicopters? We can't know. But violence will not be met with violence from our side.

Only elementary self-defense. We can, on the other hand, make things harder for our attackers. Barbed wire is to be strung all round the ship's rail. In addition, we are all to get used to wearing life jackets, lookouts are to be posted, and we will be told where to assemble if foreign soldiers come aboard. Our last bastion will be the bridge.

Then we eat. The cook is from Egypt, and suffers with a bad leg. But he cooks great food.

MONDAY 31 MAY, MIDNIGHT

I share the watch on the port side from midnight to 3:00 a.m. The moon is still big, though occasionally obscured by cloud. The sea is calm. The navigation lights gleam. The three hours pass quickly. I notice I am tired when someone else takes over. It's still a long way to anything like a territorial boundary the Israelis could legitimately defend. I should try to snatch a few hours' sleep.

I drink tea, chat to a Greek crewman whose English is very poor but who insists he wants to know what my books are about. It's almost four before I get to lie down.

04:30

I've just dropped off when I am woken again. Out on deck I see that the big passenger ferry is floodlit. Suddenly there is the sound of gunfire. So now I know that Israel has chosen the route of brutal confrontation. In international waters.

It takes exactly an hour for the speeding black rubber dinghies with the masked soldiers to reach us and start to board. We gather, up on the bridge. The soldiers are impatient and want us down on deck. Someone who is going too slowly immediately gets a stun device fired into his arm. He falls. Another man who is not moving fast enough is shot with a rubber bullet. I think: I am seeing this happen right beside me. It is an absolute reality. People who have done nothing being driven like animals, being punished for their slowness.

We are put in a group down on the deck. Where we will then stay for eleven hours, until the ship docks in Israel. Every so often we are filmed. When I jot down a few notes, a soldier comes over at once and asks what I am writing. That's the only time I lose my temper, and tell him it's none of his business. I can only see his eyes; don't know what he is thinking. But he turns and goes.

Eleven hours, unable to move, packed together in the heat. If we want to go for a pee, we have to ask permission. The food they give us is biscuits, rusks, and apples. We're not allowed to make coffee, even though we could do it where we are sitting. We take a collective decision: not to ask if we can cook food.

Then they would film us. It would be presented as showing how generously the soldiers had treated us. We stick to the biscuits and rusks. It is degradation beyond compare. (Meanwhile, the soldiers who are off-duty have dragged mattresses out of the cabins and are sleeping at the back of the deck.)

So in those eleven hours, I have time to take stock. We have been attacked while in international waters. That means the Israelis have behaved like pirates, no better than those who operate off the coast of Somalia. The moment they start to steer this ship toward Israel, we have also been kidnapped. The whole action is illegal. We try to talk among ourselves, work out what might happen, and not least how the Israelis could opt for a course of action that means painting themselves into a corner.

The soldiers watch us. Some pretend not to understand English. But they all do. There are a couple of girls among the soldiers. They look the most embarrassed. Maybe they are the sort who will escape to Goa and fall into drug addiction when their military service is over? It happens all the time.

18:00

Quayside somewhere in Israel. I don't know where. We are taken ashore and forced to run the gauntlet of rows of soldiers while military TV films us. It suddenly hits me that this is something I shall never forgive them. At that moment they are nothing more to my mind than pigs and bastards.

We are split up, no one is allowed to talk to anyone else. Suddenly a man from the Israeli ministry for foreign affairs appears at my side. I realize he is there to make sure I am not treated too harshly. I am, after all, known as a writer in Israel. I've been translated into Hebrew. He asks if I need anything.

"My freedom and everybody else's," I say. He doesn't answer. I ask him to go. He takes one step back. But he stays.

I admit to nothing, of course, and am told I am to be deported. The man who says this also says he rates my books highly. That makes me consider ensuring nothing I write is ever translated into Hebrew again.

Agitation and chaos reign in this "asylum-seekers' reception center." Every so often, someone is knocked to the ground, tied up, and handcuffed. I think several times that no one will believe me when I tell them about this. But there are many eyes to see it. Many people will be obliged to admit that I am telling the truth. There are a lot of us who can bear witness.

A single example will do. Right beside me, a man suddenly refuses to have his fingerprints taken. He accepts being photographed. But fingerprints? He doesn't consider he has done anything wrong. He resists. And is beaten to the ground. They drag him off. I don't know where. What word can I use? Loathsome? Inhuman? There are plenty to choose from.

23:00

We, the MP, the doctor, and I, are taken to a prison for those refused right of entry. There we are split up. We are thrown a few sandwiches that taste like old dishcloths. It's a long night. I use my trainers as a pillow.

TUESDAY 1 JUNE, AFTERNOON

Without any warning, the MP and I are taken to a Lufthansa plane. We are to be deported. We refuse to go until we know what is happening to S. Once we have assured ourselves that she, too, is on her way, we leave our cell.

On board the plane, the air hostess gives me a pair of socks. Because mine were stolen by one of the commandos who attacked the boat I was on.

The myth of the brave and utterly infallible Israeli soldier is shattered. Now we can add: they are common thieves. For I was not the only one to be robbed of my money, credit card, clothes, MP3 player, laptop; the same happened to many others on the same ship as me, which was attacked early one morning by masked Israeli soldiers, who were thus in fact nothing other than lying pirates.

By late evening we are back in Sweden. I talk to some journalists. Then I sit for a while in the darkness outside the house where I live. E. doesn't say much.

WEDNESDAY 2 JUNE, AFTERNOON

I listen to the blackbird. A song for those who died.

Now it is still all left to do. So as not to lose sight of the goal, which is to lift the brutal blockade of Gaza. That will happen.

Beyond that goal, others are waiting. Demolishing a system of apartheid takes time. But not an eternity.

WHAT HAPPENED TO US IS HAPPENING IN GAZA

Iara Lee

In the pre-dawn hours of May 31, I was aboard the Turkish ship *Mavi Marmara*, part of a convoy of humanitarian vessels aiming to deliver aid to besieged civilians in Gaza, when we were attacked in international waters by a unit of Israeli commandos. Our ship had been inspected by customs agents in Turkey, a NATO member, who confirmed that there were no guns or any such weapons aboard. Indeed, the Israeli government has produced no such arms. What was aboard the ship were hundreds of civilian passengers, representatives of dozens of countries, who had planned to deliver the flotilla's much-needed materials for the Gazan people. These Palestinians have suffered under an illegal siege first imposed by Israel in 2006 and strictly enforced since early 2009—which Amnesty International has called "a flagrant violation of international law."

I am a dual U.S.-Brazilian citizen of Korean descent. I am a filmmaker and a human rights activist. The passengers on our ship—including elected officials, diplomats, media professionals, and other human rights workers—joined the flotilla as an act of civil disobedience. I decided to join the Freedom Flotilla after going to Gaza a few months before and seeing firsthand the devastation there. After hearing the pleas of the people living in Gaza to have the blockade lifted, I felt I must do something.

In the past, some boats attempting to bring much-needed supplies to Gazans had been violently harassed by Israeli forces. On December

30, 2008, the vessel *Dignity* was carrying volunteer surgeons and three tons of medical supplies when it was attacked without warning by an Israeli naval ship, which rammed the boat three times in international waters roughly ninety miles from Gaza's coast. Passengers and crew feared for their lives as their boat quickly took on water and Israeli troops threatened to open fire.

I joined the flotilla effort nonetheless because I believed that resolutely nonviolent actions which call attention to the blockade are vital in educating the public about what is taking place. Simply put, there is no decent justification for preventing shipments of humanitarian aid from reaching a people in crisis.

* * *

I expected our ships to be deterred from delivering aid to Gazans, but I did not expect murder. Israel's powerful navy could have easily approached our boat and boarded it in broad daylight or pursued nonviolent options for disabling our vessel. Instead, the Israeli military launched a nighttime assault with heavily armed soldiers. Under attack, some passengers skirmished with the boarding soldiers using broomsticks and other items at hand. The commandos and navy soldiers shot and killed nine civilians and seriously injured dozens more.

When the Zodiacs came and surrounded us, and the helicopters began sending commandos down, it was chaos. The women were told to go downstairs and to stay quiet and calm. I feared for the lives of my fellow passengers as I heard shots being fired on deck. In particular, I was very concerned about my cameraman and friends, so I went up to see what was happening. By the time I went up, I saw that many people had already been injured and that there were many dead bodies. I had expected soldiers to shoot in the air or aim at people's legs, but instead I saw the bodies of people who appeared to have been shot multiple times in the head or chest.

When it was over, the Israeli soldiers commandeered our ships, illegally kidnapped us from international waters, towed us to the port of Ashdod, and arrested all of us on board. Once in the port, they started interrogating us. They kept saying, "You're going to be deported because you are illegally in Israel." We said, "We didn't want to be here in Israel. We wanted to go to Gaza. You kidnapped us and brought us here." Only days later were we evacuated to Istanbul on Turkish Airlines planes sent by Turkey's prime minister, Recep Tayyip Erdoğan.

* * *

As surprised as I was by the brutality of the Israeli assault, I have been perhaps even more astonished by the aggressively dishonest campaign in the media that the Israeli government waged in the weeks since their initial attack on our ships. As a documentary filmmaker I am attuned to how words and images can be shaped into a narrative to convey the central truth of an event. However, watching the Israeli Defense Forces (IDF) spokespeople spread innuendo about our flotilla and create confusion about the siege of Gaza itself was a lesson for me in how media can be used in the service of disinformation.

Control of information was part of the Israeli attack on our flotilla from the start. The IDF commenced by jamming satellite communication to prevent any contact between journalists on the ships and the outside world. Only because organizers came prepared with a backup satellite link were international viewers able to see even limited footage from the passengers' perspective. But this transmission was also jammed soon after, precluding broadcast of eyewitness testimony about how commandos opened fire on civilians. The Israeli military proceeded to "confiscate" any cameras, phones, and hard drives that contained footage of the raid. All individuals aboard the flotilla, including journalists, were thrown in jail, kept in isolation as the IDF trumpeted its version of the attack nonstop.

Early on, IDF spokespeople made the inflammatory assertion that passengers had been armed with guns and opened fire on the commandos. While these falsehoods disappeared from subsequent IDF statements, the damage was done; furthermore, the statements were never properly disavowed or retracted. The impact of such accusations was compounded by the sensationalistic claim that activists tried to "lynch" boarding soldiers and by the suggestion of police sources close to the IDF that military personnel had responded with an "unbelievable demonstration of restraint."

The notion of "restraint" was starkly called into question by later autopsies showing that the nine killed passengers had received thirty bullet wounds among them—many shot multiple times in the head and back and at close range. Yet the Israeli government's refusal to release the bodies in the crucial early days, and its move to detain journalists who had witnessed wanton violence, allowed their dubious narrative to circulate unchecked in the press.

Journalist Max Blumenthal and others have documented numerous instances in which the IDF has made press releases that they have later been forced to "clarify" or remove from their website after reporters questioned their baseless accusations. One of these, published on June 2, stated in its headline that many passengers on board the *Mavi Marmara* were "Al Qaeda mercenaries." Unable to defend the charge after journalists requested proof, the IDF later changed its headline and stated that the passengers merely were "found without identification papers." The level of defamation and irresponsibility inherent in such an error is difficult to overstate, and it alone should call into question the credibility of any further Israeli government claims about the flotilla attack.

Perhaps the greatest public relations coup of government spokespeople came with their grainy, highly selective footage of passengers skirmishing with boarding commandos and their other YouTube videos. While some of the video came from their own cameras, other releases have been selectively edited from "confiscated" materials. Joining others such as the Committee to Protect Journalists, the Foreign Press Association has protested the use of stolen footage for propagandistic purposes, calling it "a clear violation of journalistic ethics and unacceptable."

None of the videos the IDF has released answer the crucial question of whether passengers trying to defend themselves against the assault had already been fired upon. While the exact timeline of events is still being reconstructed, numerous eyewitness accounts such as that of British national Jamal Elshayyal have suggested that Israeli troops fired shots without warning and may have used live ammunition before descending onto the *Mavi Marmara*. My own footage shows that they had begun firing on the ship well before boarding, creating fear among passengers that we were under possibly fatal attack; soldiers obviously did not inform passengers what type of ammunition, lethal or "non-lethal," they were using—nor when they would decide to switch between the two. As more and more survivors of the attack were released from Israeli custody and began granting interviews, an ever greater number of testimonials contradicted the IDF's self-sanitizing version of what took place.

Despite the fact that most of our footage from my days on the flotilla was stolen, my crew was able to retain much of the crucial footage of how passengers responded to the Israeli raid. When I arranged for a screening at the U.N. of the raw footage showing the scene leading up to the attack and the demeanor of passengers on board the ship, Israeli officials protested and harassed the United Nations Correspondents Association (UNCA) organizers. They later claimed that they were not permitted to show their version of events in the same news conference in which I released my footage. In fact, despite the propagandistic nature of their highly selective video, the UNCA and I had both agreed to let them show it alongside my raw footage. The Israelis themselves withdrew at the last minute.

Under these circumstances there is a clear need for a full, impartial, international inquiry into the attack on our flotilla. On Sunday, June 6, U.N. Secretary General Ban Ki-moon proposed such an inquiry. But that same day the Israeli ambassador to the United States

Michael Oren rejected the proposition, saying instead that "Israel has the right, the duty, as a democracy" to hold its own investigation. On June 13, the Israeli government announced that it is forming an internal committee to conduct a probe; it includes only token international representation, two committee members with no voting rights. While the White House has blessed this formulation, it hardly meets the demand of the rest of the world for a complete, unbiased, and truly independent investigation.

All of this suggests a clear pattern: When Israeli officials are not actively obscuring the truth about the Gaza Freedom Flotilla, they are hiding from it. The world deserves an inquiry that is not compromised by their criminality.

* * *

The Israeli government's efforts at misinformation extended to the siege itself. Its spokespeople deny that its punitive blockade of Gaza was the source of hardship for civilians there. While they actively work to create confusion in the media, the truth is clear for all who would care to see it. The overwhelming conclusion of highly respected human rights authorities is that the Israeli government, because it does not accept the legitimacy of the elected Hamas government, is pursuing a policy of what Human Rights Watch calls "collective punishment against the civilian population," illegal under international law.

The victims include children whose schools were damaged or destroyed by the Israeli military in 2009 and still lie in ruins, as well as the nearly two-thirds of the population that, according to the U.N. Food and Agriculture Organization, is unable to access adequate supplies of food.

With regard to the flotilla I was on, the Israeli government says it would have permitted our humanitarian aid to enter Gaza by land had we submitted it through "proper channels." But Israel's "proper channels"—restrictive checkpoints that have repeatedly turned away World Health Organization medical supplies and rejected or delayed the delivery of U.N. food aid—are the very source of the humanitarian crisis to begin with, a tragedy the Israeli government will not even admit exists.

Israeli spokespeople insist that the Gaza Freedom Flotilla was a provocation. It was, in the sense that civil rights protesters in the American South who sat at segregated lunch counters represented a provocation to segregationists, or in the sense that all nonviolent protests against the illegitimate acts of a government are by definition provocations. Under an illegal siege, the delivery of aid to civilians is a prohibited act; the intent of our humanitarian convoy was to violate this unjust prohibition.

Nine of my fellow passengers were killed by the Israeli military for attempting to defy the ban on delivering aid. Far more Palestinian civilians have died as a result of the siege itself. What happened to our flotilla is happening to the people of Gaza on a daily basis. It will not stop until international law is applied to all countries, Israel included.

DEFENDERS OF THE *MAVI MARMARA*

Ken O'Keefe

I have for many years understood that we, people of conscience, are the true holders of power in this world. Frustratingly, however, we have largely relinquished that power and failed to reach our full potential to create a better world, a just world. Nonetheless I have conspired with others of like mind to reveal and exercise our true power. In 2002 I initiated the TJP Human Shield Action to Iraq because I knew that the invasion of Iraq had been planned well in advance, that it was part of a "Global Spectrum Dominance" agenda as laid out by the Project for a New American Century.

I knew that protests had no chance of stopping the invasion, and that largely these protests were just a way of making us feel better about the coming mass murder by being able to say, "I protested against it." With that understanding I argued that the only viable way to stop the invasion was to conduct a mass migration to Iraq. It would be a migration in which people from around the world, especially Western citizens, would position themselves at sites in Iraq that are supposed to be protected by international law but that are routinely bombed when it is only Iraqi, Palestinian, generally nonwhite non-Westerners who will be killed. I felt 10,000 such people could stop the invasion, or at the very least expose the invasion for what it was from the start, an act of international aggression, a war crime and a crime against humanity.

When our two double-decker buses traveled from London to

Baghdad through Turkey, it was ever clear that the people of Turkey also could sense the power of this act, and they were the biggest participants in it. In the end we did not get the numbers required to stop the war, with at least one million Iraqis dead as a result, but I remain convinced that it was within our power to prevent the invasion. A massive opportunity lost, as far as I am concerned.

In 2007 I joined the Free Gaza Movement with its plan to challenge the blockade of Gaza by traveling to Gaza by sea. From the moment I heard of the plan I knew it could succeed, and ultimately I served as a captain on the first attempt. The Israeli government said throughout our preparation that we were no better than pirates and they would treat us as such. They made clear we would not reach Gaza. And still I knew we could succeed. And we did. Two boats with forty-six passengers from various countries managed to sail into Gaza on August 23, 2008; this was the first time this had been done in forty-one years. The truth is the blockade of Gaza is far more than three years old, and yet we, a small group of conscientious people, defied the Israeli machine and celebrated with tens of thousands of Gazans when we arrived that day. We proved that it could be done. We proved that an intelligent plan, with skilled manipulation of the media, could render the full might of the Israeli Navy useless. And I knew then that this was only the tip of the iceberg.

So participating in the Freedom Flotilla is like a family reunion to me. It is my long lost family whose conscience is their guide, who have shed the fear, who act with humanity. But I was especially proud to join IHH and the Turkish elements of the flotilla. I deeply admire the strength and character of the Turkish people. To them, I say, "despite your history having stains of injustice, like every nation, you are today from citizen to prime minister among the leaders in the cause of humanity and justice."

I remember being asked during the TJP Human Shield Action to Iraq if I was a pacifist. I responded with a quote from Gandhi by saying I am not a passive anything. To the contrary I believe in action, and I also believe in self-defense, 100 percent, without reservation. I would be incapable of standing by while a tyrant murders my family, and the attack on the *Mavi Marmara* was like an attack on my Palestinian family. I am proud to have stood shoulder to shoulder with those who refused to let a rogue Israeli military exert their will without a fight. And yes, we fought.

When I was asked, in the event of an Israeli attack on the *Mavi Marmara*, would I use the camera, or would I defend the ship? I enthusiastically committed to defense of the ship. I am a huge supporter of nonviolence. In fact I believe nonviolence must always be the first option. Nonetheless I joined the defense of the *Mavi Marmara* understanding that violence could be used against us and that we may very well be compelled to use violence in self-defense.

I said this straight to Israeli agents, probably of Mossad or Shin Bet, and I say it again now: On the morning of the attack I was directly involved in the disarming of two Israeli commandos. This was a forcible, non-negotiable, separation of weapons from commandos who had already murdered two brothers that I had seen that day, including one brother with a bullet entering dead center in his forehead, in what appeared to be an execution. I knew the commandos were murdering people when I removed a 9 mm pistol from one of them. I had that gun in my hands, and as an ex–U.S. Marine with training in the use of guns, it was completely within my power to use that gun on the commando who may have been the murderer of one of my brothers. But that is not what I, nor any other defender of the ship, did. I took that weapon away, removed the bullets, proper lead bullets, separated them from the weapon, and hid the gun. I did this in the hopes that we would repel the attack and submit this weapon as evidence in a criminal trial against Israeli authorities for murder.

I also helped to physically separate one commando from his assault rifle, which another brother apparently threw into the sea. I and hundreds of others know the truth that makes a mockery of the brave and moral Israeli military. We had in our full possession three completely disarmed and helpless commandos. These boys were at our mercy, they were out of reach of their fellow murderers, inside the ship and surrounded by 100 or more men. I looked into the eyes of all three of these boys and I can tell you they had the fear of God in them. They looked at us as if we were them, and I have no doubt they did not believe there was any way they would survive that day. They looked like frightened children in the face of an abusive father.

But they did not face an enemy as ruthless as they. Instead, the woman provided basic first aid, and ultimately they were released, battered and bruised for sure, but alive. Able to live another day. Able to feel the sun overhead and the embrace of loved ones. Unlike those they murdered. Despite mourning the loss of our brothers, feeling rage toward these boys, we let them go. The Israeli prostitutes of propaganda can spew all of the disgusting bile all they wish. The commandos are the murderers. We are the defenders. And yes we fought. We fought not just for our lives, not just for our cargo, not just for the people of Palestine. We fought in the name of justice and humanity. We were right to do so, in every way.

While in Israeli custody I, along with everyone else, was subjected to endless abuse and flagrant acts of disrespect. Women and the elderly were physically and mentally assaulted. Access to food and water and toilets was denied. Dogs were used against us, and we ourselves were treated like dogs. We were exposed to direct sun in stress positions while handcuffed to the point of losing circulation of blood in our hands. We were lied to incessantly; in fact, I am awed at the routineness and comfort in their ability to lie—it is remarkable, really. We were abused in just about every way imaginable, and I myself was beaten and choked to the point of blacking out… and I was beaten again while in my cell.

In all this what I saw more than anything else were cowards… and yet I also see my brothers. Because no matter how vile and wrong the Israeli agents and government are, they are still my brothers and sisters and for now I only have pity for them. Because they are relinquishing the most precious thing a human being has, their humanity.

In conclusion; I would like to challenge every endorser of Gandhi, every person who thinks they understand him, who acknowledges him as one of the great souls of our time (which is just about every Western leader)—I challenge you in the form of a question. Please explain how we, the defenders of the *Mavi Marmara*, are not the modern example of Gandhi's essence? But first read the words of Gandhi himself:

I do believe that, where there is only a choice between cowardice and violence, I would advise violence.... I would rather have India resort to arms in order to defend her honour than that she should, in a cowardly manner, become or remain a helpless witness to her own dishonour.

And lastly I have one more challenge. I challenge any critic of merit, to debate me publicly on a large stage over our actions that day. I would especially love to debate any Israeli leader who accuses us of wrongdoing; it would be my tremendous pleasure to face off with you. All I saw in Israel were cowards with guns, so I am ripe to see you in a new context. I want to debate you on the largest stage possible. Take that as an open challenge and let us see just how brave Israeli leaders are.

FROM '48 TO GAZA

Lubna Masarwa

Morning in Jerusalem. I am on my way to Silwan, where I am organizing with the residents against Israel's plan to demolish eighty-eight Palestinian homes and besiege the village. The car in front of me has a big banner on the back window that says, in Hebrew, "We are all unit 13," and another one under it saying, "Unit 13, you should have killed more of them."

Unit 13 was the military unit that killed the civilians on the *Mavi Marmara*.

Part of me wants to stop these cars and tell them: "I was there."

None of us expected what happened that night.

Hundreds of us had gathered to send a message, to Israel and to the world, that we will not accept the injustice done to our people in Gaza, that we can no longer wait for governments to take action, that we, ordinary women and men of all the ages, left our lives, our children, our families, and that we are coming to break the siege.

The environment was full of good energy and will.

When the ship set sail, tens of thousands people stood at the Istanbul port in the rain and called in one voice, "Free Palestine. Free Gaza."

On the ship, I was running meetings with the passengers about the different scenarios we may face. We had envisioned different possibilities, like a blockade on the sea, or the military boarding and arresting us. But we didn't imagine a scenario of soldiers killing civilians on the ship.

We did legal training.

We all were happy and believed that we would enter Gaza, that the international pressure would force Israel to let the ships through.

One of the passengers from Jordan was dressed in traditional Bedouin attire that includes a ceremonial sword called a Hanjar worn on the belt. One of my colleagues asked him to remove it and put it in his luggage, as we didn't want to give Israel any reason to accuse us of anything, as they usually do when Palestinians struggle for their rights.

Later I saw his knife, together with cooking knives placed on a green flag featuring words from the Quran, in a photograph taken by the Israeli Army in its attempts to discredit us and claim that we were violent.

On the morning of May 30, the organizers met with the captain to assess the timing and direction of the ships. It was important to us that we approach the territorial water of Gaza in daylight. We stayed at sea for another day for this reason. But Israel decided to attack at night, no matter how far away we were from Gaza.

When the Israeli military attacked the *Mavi Marmara*, we were deep in international water. That night, at 11:00 p.m., we saw two Israeli warships coming toward us. At about midnight we told the passengers to go to sleep. We thought the Israelis were only trying to scare us. We didn't believe they would dare do anything in international waters.

Later we saw a drone plane take off from one of the warships.

At 4:00 a.m. we lost our Internet connection and I understood that the Israelis were trying to cut us off from the outside world. I went immediately to call some journalists from the ship. This happened during morning prayers. As the passengers finished their prayers, the soldiers began to attack us.

Small Israeli vessels with tens of soldiers came close to the ship, a helicopter appeared above us, gas bombs were thrown on the ship from all directions. Within minutes, people began carrying injured people off the deck and bringing them to where I was, on the second level of the ship. Later, people started bringing in bodies, first two bodies, then another two. We put them on the floor and covered them with flags or whatever we could find.

Blood was pouring out of the bodies, from their heads. One of the women found out that her husband was one of the people killed. She sat in front of him and cried until another woman came and took her.

Another young man was sitting in front of the bodies and reading the Quran.

An old man was brought in who been shot in the head. He was laying on the floor, dying. There was nothing we could do for him except hold his hand.

It was 5:00 a.m. when I took the speaker at the *Marmara* reception and started calling the Israelis to allow medical help.

"Israeli Navy, we are civilians. Don't use violence against us. We need help. People are dying. We need you to allow medical access."

I kept asking for help, in English and Hebrew, hoping to save the old man's life.

None of my calls for help was responded to, but I didn't stop and kept repeating that we needed medical help.

The soldiers surrounded the floor where we were sitting. I could see them.

"The military has taken control of the ship," one of my Turkish colleagues declared over the speaker. "The captain's room has been taken over. Go to your seats and remain seated."

Despite the fact that they had taken control of the ship, the Israeli Navy didn't allow medical access to the wounded.

People died because of this.

At about 7:00 a.m. we were ordered to go one by one to the exit floor, which was controlled by many soldiers who came with dogs.

Their faces were camouflaged or masked, and we could see only their eyes.

I went to the soldiers and asked them if we could keep the doctors with the injured people. They said, "Shut your mouth." Later they called me and said, "Tell the injured people that if they want to stay alive they should come one by one."

One of the bodies I saw was Cevdet, who was the web director in the press room. Cevdet had left the press room with his camera to take some pictures. He was shot in his head and died immediately.

We were ordered to leave the room and go out one by one, be searched, and sit on the deck.

The ship was devastated. There was a small mountain of passengers' bags, open, and flags stained with blood. Letters written by hundreds of children to children in Gaza were on the floor, under the soldiers' boots.

We were under the control of the Israeli soldiers. Dozens of them stood in front of us, in every corner, with their guns pointed toward us. Their faces were covered with black; you could see only their eyes.

I realized that we must not be human in the eyes of the Israeli soldiers when I saw them joking with each other—one of them was petting his dog—after they had just killed innocent people in cold blood.

It took us at least seven hours to arrive at Ashdod port. During this time we were held by the military, sitting on the bloody floor with the noise from the helicopters, the dogs, the military ships around, the many soldiers with faces covered in black, and silence in the air.

The woman who had lost her husband a few hours before was there as well. So was Maha, a Palestinian woman from Gaza; the only thing she wanted was to go back home and be with her husband. Maha has cancer and had left Gaza to seek treatment. For six months she had been trying to reunite with her nine children in Gaza.

We arrived at Ashdod at 5:00 p.m. on May 31. The army told us,

"We finished with our mission. Now you will be in the hands of the immigration police."

The army killed the civilians; the police would take care of the rest.

I was allowed to leave the ship on June 1 at 1:40 a.m. I didn't have anything on me—my passport, my laptop, my wallet, everything was on the ship. I was with a group of women who were made to stand in line to get off the ship. The soldiers made lewd sexual jokes about us to each other. We were handed over to the immigration police. When they learned that I have Israeli citizenship they treated me much more roughly and separated me from the others.

For more than thirty-six hours, my three Palestinian colleagues from the '48 delegation and I were not allowed to see a lawyer, despite the fact that this is against Israeli law.

We were interrogated and taken to prison, where we were held for four days. Later, we were put under house arrest; we are not allowed to leave the state for forty-five days.

It was clear that the decision to arrest us was a political one. It was a message to all Palestinians in Israel: Do not take this kind of action. Do not resist. And, of course, do not stand with your people in Gaza.

As a Palestinian in Israel, my home is but one hour away from Gaza. I can see the houses in Gaza, but I am not allowed to go there, just as Palestinians in the West Bank are not allowed to go to Jerusalem, and Palestinians from East Jerusalem are not allowed to live in the West Bank.

I want to be connected to my people, to break Israel's siege against the Palestinians since 1948, to fight against their forceful separation of our people who live on one land.

The siege of Gaza is part of the siege of Palestine, which includes the walls, the checkpoints, the settlements and all the rest of the borders that Israel creates so they can control Palestinians' lives and divide us from each other.

Israel feels entitled to besiege, to kill, and to attack civilians in international water. It does this with the silence of the world that makes Israel believe it has the right to do these things.

Today is the time to break the silence and to take action. Together, we must say "enough is enough" to Israel.

THE PRICE OF DEFYING ISRAEL

Paul Larudee

I was one of those who chose to defy Israeli forces when they attacked and took our Freedom Flotilla ships that were trying to deliver desperately needed humanitarian aid to civilian organizations in the Israeli-blockaded Gaza Strip. Most of us resisted, to varying degrees, for which we paid a price—in my case multiple beatings in two days of captivity in Israel. At least nine paid with their lives. My multicolored skin and twisted joints are healing, even at age sixty-four, but my colleagues are gone forever, and some of the dozens of wounded may never fully recover.

All of us were unarmed. I chose to resist by jumping overboard from the *Sfendoni* soon after we were captured, far out at sea. I took the calculated risk that Israel would find it hard to explain its failure to rescue me, and that the act might disrupt their operations to at least some extent. Later, I continued to protest by refusing to speak or walk, forcing my captors to carry me. Pain was used to force me to comply, and of course when pain didn't work, they applied more pain, with the same result.

I practice nonviolence, so that is the way I resist, but it's not necessarily for everyone. A number of passengers aboard the *Mavi Marmara*, who were from thirty-two different nations, responded with their hands, feet, and whatever objects were at hand. I admire them for doing so; they knew that Israel has a reputation for disproportionate response. It also seems increasingly probable that the Israeli soldiers killed some of the victims at close range before any resistance had begun.

Let us please not try to justify Israeli actions by appealing to security arguments or "self defense." Self-defense is for those who are being attacked, not those who are attacking. Furthermore, there were no arms of any kind aboard our humanitarian aid ships. Most if not all of us would have refused to participate in the voyage otherwise. Let's not be duped into buying the snake oil that Israel is trying to peddle. If the attackers of our ships had been Iranian, would anyone be making the absurd excuses we are now hearing for Israeli actions?

Centcom Commander General David Petraeus has said that our unhealthy relationship with Israel is undermining U.S. interests in the region and the rest of the world. Our unreasonable defense of Israel's unreasonable and disproportionate actions is making us a target and destroying our credibility as a defender of democracy and human rights.

The wrath of other nations might be a reasonable price for us to bear if Israel were pursuing a policy of peace with justice. It is not. Israeli policy is and always has been to apply pain and suffering to get what it wants, whether by torturing and killing humanitarian aid volunteers, by maintaining its cruel blockade against 1.5 million Palestinian civilians in the Gaza Strip, or by making millions of Palestinians homeless, confiscating their lands, and destroying lives.

Neither Americans nor Israelis would stand still for such treatment, so why should Turks, Greeks, Palestinians or anyone else? Why should Israeli thugs be allowed to push around and abuse ordinary citizens anywhere?

It is not wise for Americans to be accomplices to Israeli crimes through our veto in the U.N. or our massive foreign aid, for which we have greater need at home. It is time to take off the rose-colored glasses and recognize Israel for what it is: a rogue nation that we need to stop coddling.

KIDNAPPED BY ISRAEL, FORSAKEN BY BRITAIN

Jamal Elshayyal

Firstly I must apologize for taking so long to update my blog. The events of the past few days have been hectic to say the least, and I am still trying to come to grips with many of the things that have happened.

It was this time last week that I was on the top deck of the *Mavi Marmara*, and first spotted Israeli warships at a distance, as they approached the humanitarian flotilla. Little did I know how deadly and bloody the events that soon unfolded would be.

What I will write in this entry is fact, every letter of it, none of it is opinion, none of it is analysis, I will leave that to you, the reader.

After spotting the warships at a distance, (at roughly 11:00 p.m.) the organizers called for passengers to wear their life vests and remain indoors as they monitored the situation. The naval warships together with helicopters remained at a distance for several hours.

At 2:00 a.m. local time the organizers informed me that they had rerouted the ship, as far away from Israel as possible, as deep into international waters as they could. They did not want a confrontation with the Israeli military, at least not by night.

Just after 4:00 a.m. local time, the Israeli military attacked the ship, in international waters. It was an unprovoked attack. Tear gas was used, sound grenades were launched, and rubber-coated steel bullets were fired from almost every direction.

Dozens of speed boats carrying about fifteen to twenty masked Israeli soldiers, armed to the teeth, surrounded the *Mavi Marmara* which was carrying 600 or so unarmed civilians. Two helicopters at a time hovered above the vessel. Commandos on board the choppers joined the firing, using live ammunition, before any of the soldiers had descended onto the ship.

Two unarmed civilians were killed just meters away from me. Dozens of unarmed civilians were injured right before my eyes.

One Israeli soldier, armed with a large automatic gun and a side pistol, was overpowered by several passengers. They disarmed him. They did not use his weapons or fire them; instead they threw his weapons overboard and into the sea.

After what seemed at the time as roughly thirty minutes, passengers on board the ship raised a white flag. The Israeli Army continued to fire live ammunition. The ship's organizers made a loudspeaker announcement saying they had surrendered the ship. The Israeli Army continued to fire live ammunition.

I was the last person to leave the top deck.

Below, inside the sleeping quarters, all the passengers had gathered. There was shock, anger, fear, hurt, chaos.

Doctors ran in all directions trying to treat the wounded, blood was on the floor, tears ran down people's faces, cries of pain and mourning could be heard everywhere. Death was in the air.

Three critically injured civilians were being treated on the ground in the reception area of the ship. Their clothes were soaked in blood. Passengers stood by watching in shock, some read out verses of the Quran to calm them, doctors worked desperately to save them.

Several announcements were made on the load speakers in Hebrew, Arabic, and English: "This is a message to the Israeli Army, we have surrendered. We are unarmed. We have critically injured people. Please come and take them. We will not attack."

There was no response.

One of the passengers, a member of the Israeli Parliament, wrote a sign in Hebrew, reading the exact same thing; she held it together with a white flag and approached the windows where the Israeli soldiers were standing outside. They pointed their laser guided guns to her head, ordering her to go away.

A British citizen tried the same sign, this time holding a British flag and taking the sign to a different set of windows and different set of soldiers. They responded in the same manner.

Three hours later, all three of the injured were pronounced dead. The Israeli soldiers who refused to allow them treatment succeeded where their colleagues had earlier failed when they targeted these three men with bullets.

At around 8:00 a.m. the Israeli Army entered the sleeping quarters. They handcuffed the passengers. I was thrown onto the ground, my hands tied behind my back, I couldn't move an inch.

I was taken to the top deck where the other passengers were, forced to sit on my knees under the burning sun.

One passenger had his hands tied so tight his wrists were all sorts of colors. When he requested that the cuffs be loosened, an Israeli soldier tightened them even more. He let out a scream that sent chills down my body.

I requested to go to the bathroom, I was prevented. Instead the Israeli soldier told me to urinate where I was and in my own clothes. Three or four hours later I was allowed to go.

I was then marched, together with the other passengers, back to the sleeping quarters. The place was ransacked, its image like that of the aftermath of an earthquake.

I remained on the ship, seated, without any food or drink, barring three sips of water, for more than twenty-four hours. Throughout this time, Israeli soldiers had their guns pointed at us. Their hands on the trigger. For more than twenty-four hours.

I was then taken off the ship at Ashdod, where I was asked to sign a deportation order. It claimed that I had entered Israel illegally and agreed to be deported. I told the officer that I, in fact, had not entered

Israel but that the Israeli Army had kidnapped me from international waters and brought me to Israel against my will; therefore I could not sign this document.

My passport was taken from me. I was told that I would go to jail.

Only then were my hands freed. I spent more than twenty-four hours with my hands cuffed behind my back.

Upon arrival at the prison I was put in a cell with three other passengers. The cell was roughly twelve feet by nine feet.

I spent more than twenty-four hours in jail. I was not allowed to make a single phone call.

The British consulate did not come and see me. I did not see a lawyer.

There was no hot water for a shower.

The only meal was frozen bread and some potatoes.

The only reason I believe I was released was because the Turkish prisoners refused to leave until and unless the other nationalities (those whose consulates had not come and released them) were set free.

I was taken to Ben-Gurion airport. When I asked for my passport, the Israeli official presented me with a piece of paper and said, "Congratulations, this is your new passport." I replied, "You must be joking; you have my passport." The Israeli official's response: "Sue me."

There I was asked again to sign a deportation order. Again I refused.

I was put on a plane headed to Istanbul.

Masked Israeli soldiers and commandos took me from international waters.

Uniformed Israeli officials locked me behind bars.

The British government did not lift a finger to help me—till this day I have not seen or heard from a British official.

The Israeli government stole my passport.

The Israeli government stole my laptop, two cameras, three phones, $1,500, and all my possessions.

My government, the British government, has not even acknowledged my existence.

I was kidnapped by Israel. I was forsaken by my country.

FIRST, THEY APPEARED AS SHADOWS

Sümeyye Ertekin

I participated in the *Mavi Marmara* flotilla as a journalist; my aim was to make a documentary about the journey. Breaking the siege was also important to me; I had traveled to Gaza twice before—but this time, it was by sea.

The first days on board were beautiful and quite a lot of fun. All the people on the *Mavi Marmara*—570 volunteers were on board from all over the world—were all focused on reaching Gaza. In our broadcasts throughout the trip, we also reported the statements made by Israel, but none of the volunteers on board was concerned in any way. They thought Israel could not do anything to such a large fleet, composed of people from fifty different countries. According to them, Israel would eventually let us through to Gaza.

The ship was not a very comfortable place. People were lying on the floor. Some were seasick. But despite these issues, people did not show any signs of stress or aggressive behavior. To the contrary, everyone was trying to help each other.

After about a day and a half at sea, we arrived at the point where we were going to wait for other ships. There, we waited for two days. In the meantime, we received around fifteen passengers from a Greek cruise ship on our same mission that had broken down. On Sunday, June 30, we met the other ships and sailed again. We were a flotilla now. The *Mavi Marmara* sailed in front, as the flagship, and at the back, a total of five ships, two of them cruise ships and three merchant ships, were following us.

That day, in the late afternoon, an announcement was made that we would reach Israel the next morning and everybody should get up at 7:00. IHH head Bülent Yıldırım was to make a statement at 10:45 that night. I was going to connect to my news channel at 11:00 and report what was happening on board. But nothing happened as planned. At around 10:00 p.m., some seventy-three miles away, in international waters, a state of emergency was announced. Israel had called the ship and asked about our route; when the captain said "Gaza," Israel asked us to change course. At first, this request was not taken into consideration. But at 11:00 p.m., a decision was made to change the route away from Israel and the captain began directing the ship west.

I was on live TV all night long. In the breaks between broadcasts, we were counting the Israeli ships. First, they appeared as shadows, then, although we sailed away from Israel, they followed us and approached us gradually. The number of warships was two at first and then increased to four. In the meantime, there were helicopters flying over us. At 4:00 a.m., when we were getting ready for a live broadcast again with Bülent Yıldırım, we learned that the number of Israeli ships around us was fourteen. We immediately started the live broadcast and reported that. Around a half-hour later, the morning call to prayer was heard on board. (The call to prayer was made five times a day on board and the prayers were performed by the religious members of our community.)

A few minutes after the call to prayer, the Israeli assault boats surrounded us. First, the soldiers attempted to board and bottles were thrown from the ship to the assault boats. When they could not enter the ship by the assault boats, they started shooting while retreating. Then a helicopter appeared over the ship and started to descend. It stopped over the deckhouse. In the meantime, there was a constant sound of shots. I was on the upper deck and went to the side, where there was a common broadcast area. I waited there and then went downstairs. I opened one of the doors to enter the ship and saw a person lying on the floor, in a pool of blood. At that moment, I started to comprehend the gravity of the situation. I told myself, "I hope no one will die."

I went down one more flight. As I descended, I saw injured people being brought in.

It was a bloodbath. The floors were like a slaughterhouse. I saw people whose internal organs were out.

At one point, an Israeli soldier came down the stairs. Everybody was so angry and wanted to hit him, but a few tried to calm people down.

In the meantime, gas and sound bombs were thrown. I started to have difficulty breathing. There were so many shots aimed at the ship, I started to think that they were aiming to sink the boat. People were running around to help each other. I saw a woman with tears in her eyes trying to give first aid to the injured ones. She was quite calm and trying to help the people around. Later, I learned her husband had been shot in the head and fell martyred in her arms.

While the clashes were ongoing, I went to the section where women were staying. I was wearing a life jacket. I started to wait on that floor. A while later, we heard an announcement in English, calling on the Israeli soldiers to stop shooting, since there were three people killed and many injured. When I learned that three people had died, I started to feel a way that I cannot describe.

The officials from the IHH started to make announcements in Turkish calling on the people to stop the resistance. However, the Israeli soldiers continued shooting. These announcements were made repeatedly, saying, "There are severely injured people. We need emergency help." But the Israeli soldiers did not care. The Israeli deputy on board wrote the same things on a big sign in Hebrew but they ignored him too. Then there were long sirens. An announcement said that the ship was under the control of Israeli soldiers. A few people from IHH came to the section of the hall where the women were staying and said, "Friends, take off your life jackets, take your passports with you and go upstairs calmly." I did what they said.

The scene I encountered was horrible. There was blood everywhere. When I entered the hall, I saw four bodies. But it was said that there were people upstairs, which meant that the number of martyrs could increase more. Everyone started to ask each other about people they knew. Some approached the bodies and started to pray. Everybody was sitting silently and started waiting. There were no Israeli soldiers inside. When I looked outside through the window, I saw dozens of Israeli soldiers with masks on their faces, standing there with their guns pointed at us.

At around 7:00 a.m., they started to take us outside one by one. They asked us to put our hands over our heads and go outside. When I went outside, I was surrounded by a few Israeli soldiers. I did not know where to go. The surrounding Israeli soldiers asked me if I was a journalist. I said, "Yes." They took my camera. Then they asked where I was from. When I said, "I am from Turkey," they started to mock me: "Then you must love Israel." Then, they said, again in a mocking tone, "You should love Israel, and hate Palestinians, all right?" Then they put plastic handcuffs on me and took me upstairs. A soldier who met me upstairs took my handcuffs off and made me sit in place. All the men were handcuffed and were made to sit on the wet floor. One of the volunteers asked for my help, saying, "My hands are cuffed so tight, can you please loosen them a little bit?" I told this to the Israeli soldiers, but could not get a response. When I insisted, they loosened his handcuffs. His hands had gone black.

They kept us waiting on the deck for around six hours. In the meantime, there was a helicopter on the ship. When it left the ship, its propeller threw up water from the sea onto us. We were freezing. The noise of the helicopter was unbearable. Around 1:00 p.m., they took us downstairs. There I saw a technological garbage dump. All of our electronic equipment, cameras, and laptops had been thrown on the floor. Most of them were broken and unusable.

We sailed to Ashdod in this hall. For a long time, we were not allowed to use the toilet. When we were, we had to go two by two, accompanied by the Israeli soldiers. We arrived at the Ashdod port around 7:00 p.m. but they did not let us off the boat for an hour and a half. The parliamentarians from Europe protested and were able to leave the ship. Then they let us reporters out. Our arms were taken by two young women, and they took us directly to the search cabin. They searched us in a strict manner. Some of us were asked to take off all our clothes. In the meantime, a soldier took my cell phone. He looked at it and put it into his pocket. My phone was not great, but he liked it. I asked him, "Will you give my phone back?" He smiled and said, "We will." But I figured from their behavior that they would not give it back. None of the electronic equipment I owned was among my belongings sent to me later.

Translated from the Turkish by **Ceren Kenar**

AN ACT OF STATE TERRORISM

Kevin Ovenden

*Kevin Ovenden is an organizer of the Viva Palestina solidarity group
and veteran of two convoys to Gaza. He spoke to Lee Sustar about the
Israeli assault on the peace flotilla—and he makes the case that the
Palestinian solidarity movement must seize the moment to build wider
support for ending the siege.*

When did it become clear that the flotilla faced violence at the hands of Israeli military forces?

I became increasingly convinced that the Netanyahu government
would stop at nothing to stop the flotilla, and the reason for my thinking was that it became clear that allowing the flotilla in—given the
level of international support that was developing on Thursday and
Friday of the previous week—would have signaled the end of the em-
bargo on Gaza.

In fact, what's happened has also signaled the end of the siege. It's
changed the situation utterly.

At the time, I believed that Israel's calculation was based on two
things—one, that the force used would be brutal, but would not lead
to such a large number of casualties—though it would lead to casualties. And second, that they would get away without any backlash
in world opinion because, quite frankly, they've gotten away with far
bigger crimes. They got away with, at least in the immediate term, the
murder of over 1,400 Palestinians in Gaza with the assault in December 2008 and January 2009.

By Saturday, May 29, and certainly by Sunday, I became convinced that this was the calculation that had been made.

Ninety miles away from Israeli territory—which is well within international waters—we made the first contact with Israeli forces when we were parallel with the north of Israel, just coming south of Lebanon. When that happened, I sent out a very short but ominous e-mail alert to friends to circulate, anticipating that there would be a violent attack on the flotilla.

The Israeli government and the right-wing media claim that Israel made an attempt at a nonviolent seizure of the ships, and their soldiers only fired back when they were attacked by the residents with pipes and other weapons. What really happened?

I was on the lead ship out of six—the *Mavi Marmara*. The initial contact was made at 11:00 p.m. on Sunday night, and people came to the top of the ship—there was obviously a lot of commotion. We had satellite broadcasting on board, and we got our message out around the world.

But for two or three hours, people were milling around, and lots of people went to get some rest, on the advice of the organizers. It was pitch black—the middle of the night.

We were ninety miles away from Israel. The internationally recognized sovereignty zones extend twenty-two miles into the sea. Obviously that doesn't apply for Gaza itself, but we were well away from Gaza. The Israelis have unilaterally extended their sea border to sixty-eight miles. But we were a further twelve to twenty-two miles outside of even that unacceptable and unsupportable extension.

So people got some rest. There were lots of people on the lookout. I woke up at 4:00 a.m. along with lots of other people—it was around the time for the Fajr morning prayer for the Muslims on the vessel. At about 4:25 a.m., the assault began.

It began with percussion grenades. They are an explosive, and they can injure people badly when they go off next to them. They were designed to create panic, which itself is an extremely reckless and violent act when you consider that this was a civilian passenger ship carrying over 500 people from thirty-two different nationalities.

The youngest participant was not yet one year old. The oldest was eighty-eight years old. We were carrying, among others, parliamentarians, including two members of the German Bundestag, and the exiled Eastern Catholic archbishop of Jerusalem, Archbishop Hilarion Capucci, who is eighty-five years old and has the use of only one leg. This is an indication of the kinds of people who were aboard the ships.

To fire percussion grenades and generate panic on a boat moving at a speed of about twenty-two knots in pitch darkness in the open sea in the Eastern Mediterranean at night is itself a violent act.

Israeli attack dinghies, called Zodiacs, moved up very quickly on the side of the boat. They were carrying fully armed Special Forces— full commando attack units.

By fully armed, I mean something like five pieces of firepower or knives—rifles, sidearms, commando knives, balaclava-covered faces, Kevlar helmets, and so on. In other words, something akin to the U.S. Navy Seals people see in the movies in a glamorized way.

A helicopter moved in over the ship, and people began to file down. There was, of course, massive commotion aboard the ship. In that commotion, some people responded quite instinctively and with good cause—and with all legal and moral authority on their side. They pushed back, fought back with their hands and with whatever was to hand on the top of the ship where the first soldiers landed. Two soldiers were pushed from the top of the ship onto the next deck down.

They had already opened fire with what I thought to be rubberized bullets. These are not bullets that are made of rubber. They have a steel core, but are surrounded by rubber, and can themselves be lethal. But almost immediately, we heard the different noise of live rounds being fired—but not indiscriminately or wildly. Rather, it was carefully targeted from both sides of the ship—which was surrounded—from the helicopter, and from those Israeli attack forces who were landing on the ship itself.

I can give you some examples of what happened—one from another colleague who was also on the Viva Palestina delegation aboard the ship, Nicci Enchmarch. She was next to one of the very first people to be killed. He was a Turkish man who was holding a camera—that's all he had in his hands. He was shot directly through the center of the forehead. The exit wounds through the back of the head took away the back third of the skull. He fell to the ground and experienced his last few seconds of life. This is the nature of the attack from the Israelis.

After they commandeered the whole ship and brutally rounded people up, they gathered together whatever they could find on the ship to pile up and show what we had used as weapons. We could see that they took knives from the kitchen, where of course there were knives. They were kitchen knives, not commando knives or anything like that—and they piled those up as if they were used as weapons.

They most certainly were not used as weapons. The evidence for that is the two Israeli soldiers, who were disarmed for the safety of everybody on the ship. They were very quickly disarmed and taken down to the area we'd set up as an improvised emergency room. They were looked after—guarded—so that there would be no reprisals from anybody who was feeling outraged.

The injuries that they sustained were injuries from being manhandled, perhaps hit with sticks. They were walking wounded. They were given back to their units as soon as possible, after the murderous attacks stopped.

This is why the Israeli lie machine is stumbling to a halt on this question. Whatever they claim, whatever selective footage they try to put forward, the brutal fact is that nine people—at least—were murdered, with gunshot wounds, and some Israeli soldiers ended up getting roughed up. That's the balance of the use of force—on the one hand, the use of force by some people to defend themselves; on the other, a truly murderous attack, a massacre.

Can you help answer the question about the confusion, about the numbers dead?

Yes. People were killed in various parts of the outside of the ship, on the decks. The attack lasted for about twenty-eight minutes. The captain was then able to broadcast by loudspeaker that the ship had been taken. He told everybody who had been on the outside of the ship to desist from demonstrating against the Israelis. Many of us, simply by our physical presence, were hoping to delay the attack and protect the lives of other people.

No one knew, when the live firing started, what would happen if the Israelis got inside the ship, and perhaps started firing wildly where there were even more people. So we then went inside to the large sleeping areas, and the Israelis poured onto the walkways and onto the very top of the ship—into the bridge and the engine room and so on.

Then, for more than an hour and a half, we appealed via the loud-speaker system, and via an Israeli Knesset member, an Arab who speaks fluent Hebrew. She went forward to the windows with a sign explaining who she was, and that we had many, many injured.

We had managed to get as many as we could to the makeshift emergency room—some of which became a makeshift mortuary. But many of the people who were killed or seriously injured were still on the roof and the top decks of the boat. It was chaos—we didn't know how many there were. She was told to go back or she'd be shot, as would anybody who attempted to make contact with the Israelis.

For more than an hour and a quarter, we were appealing for help in a situation where quite literally we had people who were bleeding to death. According to the medics, at least one of those people who died may well have had their life saved if more sophisticated medical assistance of the kind that's on board an Israeli vessel had been to hand.

But we were not allowed to evacuate any wounded over to the Israelis for more than an hour and a quarter, during which time one person died. So you can imagine the situation. There are seriously wounded people, and bodies lying in various parts of the ship. And then we were treated with a mixture of contempt, humiliation, and attempts to degrade us throughout the rest of the horrific, horrific ordeal. There was scant regard for the wounded.

We tried to get out one wounded person at a time to the Israelis. The Israelis were not at all sensitive in handling them. We had them on stretchers, but they were rudely bundled up upstairs. These are people with abdominal and serious leg wounds. We sent experienced medics, one with each of the wounded. The medics were taken, thoroughly body-searched, handcuffed, and not allowed to be with the wounded.

We weren't allowed to go upstairs, which was where most of the bodies were. So it's taken some time to piece things together.

When did you begin to perceive what a political storm the assault had caused?

I didn't fully know that until Wednesday the 2nd. We were held incommunicado, of course, but I did have a visit from a man from the British consulate.

I should say that the treatment was not acceptable at all. We had nothing you could really describe as food on the first night, and the first thing we had resembling a meal was on the Tuesday afternoon, when consulate officials were visiting—which, as they said, was hardly a coincidence.

The consulate officials were treated contemptuously. I'll give you one example: The British consulate official from Jerusalem tried to have a private conversation through a prison cell door—we weren't allowed to meet face to face—with two British citizens. The junior prison guard refused to move. When he was asked to move, he brought two other prison guards. When the diplomat explained that under all international treaties, protocol, and the law, he's entitled to speak to his nationals privately, the junior guard said, "Go to your international tribunals, go to your law, we don't care."

Of course, in a sense, the prison guard was right—he was simply reflecting the experience of all Israeli officials over the course of many, many decades, which is that whatever words are uttered at the international level, there's nothing to make those words reality.

But I heard from the British consulate official something of the scale of what had taken place. Even the new British foreign secretary—who at that point had not yet made a speech in the House of Commons—was condemning the attack and calling for an inquiry.

We'd managed to piece together among ourselves that there were, we thought, upwards of four dead. We knew that this would be a major story. As we were leaving the prison, with no real further information and being taken to the airport in coaches and prison vans, we could see Israeli police, military, and civilians through the windows.

I could see the looks on their faces. I had prepared myself for a journey where we would be jeered at and laughed at from beginning to end, from Be'er Shiva to Ben-Gurion Airport. In fact, there were looks of hatred and aggressive gestures. It struck me very quickly that the only explanation for this was that in the international arena—although Israel had killed many people—it had wounded itself enormously in its standing and its strategic goals.

One thing's for sure. This was an attempt to instill fear—to use terror to achieve a political objective. This is the dictionary definition of terrorism. Real terrorism—state terrorism, by Israel.

What's next for the movement to break the siege of Gaza?

These discussions are taking place right now among the leading components of the movement, so I don't want to say anything that preempts that. But I think that the following is common ground for everybody.

Firstly, there has never been such an event in the history of the solidarity movement with Palestine. This is the Sharpeville and the Soweto of the Palestine solidarity movement. Not of course, the Sharpeville and the Soweto for Palestinians themselves. They've experienced many such massacres—from Deir Yassin in 1948 all the way through to the attacks on Gaza in December–January of 2008 and 2009.

But for the Palestinian solidarity movement, this is the Sharpeville and Soweto, and it must be turned into such. Both of those events marked international turning points in the struggle against apartheid and the isolation of the apartheid regime in South Africa, and this strategically is what we need to work toward now. The momentum, which has come at an incredible, almost unbearable cost, is nevertheless against the Israelis. It's with the Palestinians and with all those who stand with them.

This development has several strands. First, various international bodies and governments have taken strong—and in some cases, unprecedentedly strong—positions, not just over the massacre and the call for an independent, international tribunal, but also saying clearly that the siege on Gaza has to come to an end.

This has absolutely been the position of the British government— a right-wing government has come out with a position that is stronger than the position of the Labour government eighteen months ago during the time of the Gaza atrocities. That's not a product of government thinking—it's a product of the groundswell in Britain, and many, many other countries.

Former British MP George Galloway, my close friend and colleague, was on a speaking tour in the U.S. designed to maximize support for the flotilla and for Palestine. He spoke in one city on Monday night as news was beginning to break in Houston, and there were 300 or 400 people there. By Tuesday night, he spoke in Dallas, and there were 1,200 people there. He describes it as the most electrifying meet-ing he'd ever been at, and this is someone who's been at many meetings and many momentous events, particularly around this question.

So the tide is definitely turning. First, we have to turn all our ener-gies into pushing every government and international body to come out with the strongest possible position, which has to include ending the siege on Gaza as an immediate step toward a wider advance for the Palestinian position.

Second, we have to appeal to the core of people who have already been active on one level or another around the Palestinian question, or those who are already convinced, to re-galvanize the movement, and go out and convince yet wider layers of people. We must argue the Palestinian case, and also push the case more generally to very wide layers of people.

In Britain, we're saying: How great is the price to be for blanket support for Israel, and for whatever its governments choose to do? The price has now become a murderous attack on nationals from thirty-two different countries, the murder of nine people, attacks and humiliation and mistreatment of British citizens in the Eastern Medi-terranean in an act of piracy on the high seas—an attack on a Turk-ish ship with Turkish crew. People talk of alliances, and Turkey is a NATO ally.

Is this the price they have to pay—that people who are supposed to be allies are to be murdered so that Israel is supported in anything it does? That's a price which people in Britain are not prepared to pay.

Through this argument, we can move people progressively to a deeper understanding of what's taking place. I genuinely believe that this is a major turning point—not just over the siege of Gaza, but over Palestine and the wider politics of the region. Everything we do needs to be carefully calibrated and strategically thought out to drive that home in the coming months.

FREEING GAZA; LIBERATING OURSELVES

Haneen Zoabi

My decision to join the Freedom Flotilla was a spontaneous one. The Free Gaza group had contacted us in the National Political Committee, which represents over one million Palestinian citizens of Israel, and our feeling was that we owe Gaza a great deal and should have been doing much more. The question for us was not whether we should join the flotilla, but why had there been such a long delay in our own actions. Gaza is suffering under this cruel siege—a siege designed to humiliate the Palestinians, to break their will, to walk over their dignity, and to punish them for the simple reason that they have expressed their political choices through their free will. The siege had turned Gaza into the largest prison in the whole world, and we felt we had to do something.

Personally, I joined the flotilla in solidarity to the people of Gaza, but I also felt that I was liberating myself from feelings of weakness and helplessness.

Our contingent (the Palestinian citizens of Israel) joined the flotilla on Monday, May 24. We traveled first to Turkey, where we were joined by other Arab delegations. We then organized several press conferences that attracted large numbers of journalists. I did not expect so much interest from the media.

I also did not expect that the National Political Committee, which has been working on the project of building Palestinian national institutions inside of Israel, would get so much attention. We were the smallest delegation—only four people—but we received a great deal of attention from journalists and observers, since we were the only Palestinian delegation (Gaza is under siege, nobody came from the West Bank, and no one was officially representing the Palestinian refugees). Suddenly, we found that we were representing all the Palestinians, not just the 1,200,000 of us living inside Israel.

In fact, the Palestinians of Israel are neglected by the Arab world and ignored by the international community. Our predicament is also part of the Palestinian problem, but it has yet to be acknowledged. On the National Political Committee, we carry the burden of representing those who stayed behind in their homeland after 1948 and after more than 530 Palestinian villages were levelled.

People may not realize, but in that period, the major Palestinian cities—including Yaffa, Lod, Ramla, and Haifa—were destroyed and emptied of many, but not all, of their Palestinian inhabitants. This is what is we refer to as the *nakba*, the catastrophe.

Since 1948, Israel has built 530 Jewish cities and zero cities for the Arabs. Israel also constricts the Arab cities and establishes cities for Jews adjacent to these Arab cities. Israel prevents the establishment of any link between any adjacent Arab cities and has confiscated about 93 percent of our land in favor of building cities and industrial parks exclusively for its Jewish population. We demand our rights to our own land.

This is all part of the discrimination against the citizens of Palestinian origin by the Israeli government. (The Israeli Ministry of Education even prevents Arab schools from using the term *nakba* when teaching Palestinian history.) But this is only part of the process of discrimination. In fact Israeli laws and institutions facilitate discrimination daily. Israeli law does not consider Arab land confiscation as illegal. Destroying Palestinian homes is condoned by Israeli law. Banning the teaching of Palestinian history is legal. There are nineteen laws in Israel that consider specific kinds of discrimination against Arabs to be lawful.

Such laws are not temporary measures. They are part of the character of the state of Israel, a natural consequence to the concept of "Israel as a Jewish State." But where are we in such a picture? This state does not see any way of building a homeland for Jewish Israelis without fighting its own Arab citizens.

The struggle in Israel to achieve rights for the Arabs goes hand in hand with the struggle towards democracy. That is also why we have as our objective not a Jewish state but a country for all its citizens, both Jews and Arabs. This is indeed the program that my party (the United National Democratic Party) is working for.

But Israel does not want our situation broadcast to the world. It has managed to keep us isolated from the Arab world and the international community. Through its laws, Israel has forced us to consider our Arab nation as our own enemy. It has prevented us from visiting our relatives who were forced to flee their country in 1948 and who now live in Syria. For more than fifty years, some Palestinian families have been separated and forbidden from seeing their next of kin.

Yet, since the second intifada, when the Israeli police killed thirteen Palestinian youths in a demonstration against Ariel Sharon and the occupation, we are making our case known to the Arab world and to the international community more vocally. Thus the Freedom Flotilla was a chance for us to break a siege that has been erected around us as well. It was an opportunity for us to put the issue of the forgotten million-plus Palestinians on the global agenda.

And this is what we spoke about at our press conferences and to the volunteers on the Freedom Flotilla. We tried to represent the whole Palestinian problem. We spoke about Gaza in terms of the siege. We described how the siege on us means transforming everything inside of Israel to ensure it becomes Jewish. For the West Bank, their siege is the continuous process of the peace negotiation.

Our delegation gained respect and attention from the organizers and the media. We were considered the sole Palestinian delegation on the flotilla.

***

On the *Mavi Marmara*, the atmosphere was lively for the first three days. We felt like we were making history. Intensive discussions took place about power and politics. Most importantly, we had left behind our feelings of impotence and apathy.

The ships were expected to arrive in Gaza on Monday May 31 at 10:00 a.m. On Sunday at 11:00 p.m. we were feeling calm. We were around ninety miles from the shore, well in international waters, and we were sure that the Israeli forces would not touch us there.

We never thought that we would be attacked, let alone so violently. Who were we? We were simply a group of political activists. We represented an international effort and we were peaceful. Our cargo had been inspected by the Turkish authorities and the whole world was following us and was also following Israel's moves.

In our press conferences, we had mentioned repeatedly that Israel carries the burden of any provocation. We stressed time and again that we would not start any provocation.

Contrary to our expectation and while we were still ninety miles from Gaza (and in international waters), the Israeli forces attacked us. They used a massive force that included fourteen warships and a helicopter, as if they were striking a strong, fortified base, not some 700 political activists. When I saw the size of their force, I was convinced that the one who sent this kind of attack must have also given the approval to kill. After about ten minutes, two people were already dead, and then quickly a third. The Israeli forces refused to offer any help to the wounded. We lost at least two more people that way.

After about twenty minutes from the beginning of the attack (at around 4:30 a.m.) the noise started to go down. Then, after seventy minutes, we heard voices on the megaphones indicating that everything was over and that the ship was under Israeli control. But what happened during these fifty minutes? Only when we returned to shore did we learn that four other men had also been shot dead by the Israelis.

***

What the flotilla did is to break the conspiracy of silence and to force the Gaza siege and the savage occupation on the agenda of the media and that of the politicians. The flotilla has also revealed the impotence of the Arab officials.

The flotilla has shown that the will of almost 700 political activists can force Israel to review its calculations. For the first time, Israeli Prime Minister Benjamin Netanyahu admitted that there is indeed a siege on Gaza and that Israel has to end the civilian siege. All the official Arab politicians have not and could not have done that. Netanyahu's government has started to modify the list of permitted goods into Gaza, but even if Israel were to allow everything into Gaza, we would still need to do more. What we need is not an end to the siege. What we need is equality. And we need to end the occupation.

Translated from the Arabic by **Mohamed Bayoumi**

2. UNDERSTANDING THE ATTACK

SHIP OF FOOLS

Gideon Levy

The Israeli propaganda machine has reached new highs its hopeless frenzy. It has distributed menus from Gaza restaurants, along with false information. It embarrassed itself by entering a futile public relations battle, which it might have been better off never starting. They want to maintain the ineffective, illegal, and unethical siege on Gaza and not let the "peace flotilla" dock off the Gaza coast? There is nothing to explain, certainly not to a world that will never buy the web of explanations, lies, and tactics.

Only in Israel do people still accept these tainted goods. Reminiscent of a pre-battle ritual from ancient times, the chorus cheered without asking questions. White uniformed soldiers got ready in our name. Spokesmen delivered their deceptive explanations in our name. The grotesque scene is at our expense. And virtually none of us have disturbed the performance.

The chorus has been singing songs of falsehood and lies. We are all in the chorus saying there is no humanitarian crisis in Gaza. We are all part of the chorus claiming the occupation of Gaza has ended, and that the flotilla is a violent attack on Israeli sovereignty—the cement is for building bunkers and the convoy is being funded by the Turkish Muslim Brotherhood. The Israeli siege of Gaza will topple Hamas and free Gilad Shalit. Foreign Ministry spokesman Yossi Levy, one of the most ridiculous of the propagandists, outdid himself when he unblinkingly proclaimed that the aid convoy headed toward Gaza was a violation of international law. Right. Exactly.

It's not the siege that is illegal, but rather the flotilla. It wasn't enough to distribute menus from Gaza restaurants through the Prime Minister's Office (including the highly recommended beef Stroganoff and cream of spinach soup) and flaunt the quantities of fuel that the Israeli Army spokesman says Israel is shipping in. The propaganda operation has tried to sell us and the world the idea that the occupation of Gaza is over, but in any case, Israel has legal authority to bar humanitarian aid. All one pack of lies.

Only one voice spoiled the illusory celebration a little: an Amnesty International report on the situation in Gaza. Four out of five Gaza residents need humanitarian assistance. Hundreds are waiting to the point of embarrassment to be allowed out for medical treatment, and twenty-eight already have died. This is despite all the Israeli Army spokesman's briefings on the absence of a siege and the presence of assistance, but who cares?

And the preparations for the operation are also reminiscent of a particularly amusing farce: the feverish debate among the septet of ministers; the deployment of the Masada unit, the prison service's commando unit that specializes in penetrating prison cells; naval commando fighters with backup from the special police anti-terror unit and the army's Oketz canine unit; a special detention facility set up at the Ashdod port; and the electronic shield that was supposed to block broadcast of the ship's capture and the detention of those on board.

And all of this in the face of what? A few hundred international activists, mostly people of conscience whose reputation Israeli propaganda has sought to besmirch. They are really mostly people who care, which is their right and obligation, even if the siege doesn't concern us at all. Yes, this flotilla is indeed a political provocation, and what is protest action if not political provocation?

And facing them on the seas has been the Israeli ship of fools, floating but not knowing where or why. Why detain people? That's how it is. Why a siege? That's how it is. It's like the Noam Chomsky affair all over again, but big time this time. Of course the peace flotilla will not bring peace, and it won't even manage to reach the Gaza shore. The action plan has included dragging the ships to Ashdod port, but it has again dragged us to the shores of stupidity and wrongdoing. Again we will be portrayed not only as the ones that have blocked assistance, but also as fools who do everything to even further undermine our own standing. If that was one of the goals of the peace flotilla's organizers, they won big yesterday.

Five years ago, the noted Peruvian writer Mario Vargas Llosa, who is a Jerusalem Prize laureate, after concluding his visit to Israel, said the Israeli occupation was approaching its grotesque phase. Over the weekend Vargas Llosa, who considers himself a friend of Israel, was present to see that that phase has since reached new heights of absurdity.

THE DAY THE WORLD BECAME GAZA

Ali Abunimah

Since Israel's invasion and massacre of over 1,400 people in Gaza eighteen months ago, dubbed Operation Cast Lead, global civil society movements have stepped up their campaigns for justice and solidarity with Palestinians.

Governments, by contrast, carried on with business as usual, maintaining a complicit silence.

Israel's lethal attack on the Freedom Flotilla to Gaza may change that, spurring governments to follow the lead of their people and take unprecedented action to check Israel's growing lawlessness.

LIP SERVICE

One of the bitterest images from Operation Cast Lead was that of smiling European Union heads of government visiting Jerusalem and patting Ehud Olmert, the then Israeli prime minister, on the back as white phosphorus still seared the flesh of Palestinian children a few miles away.

Western countries sometimes expressed mild dismay at Israel's "excessive" use of force, but still justified the Gaza massacre as "self-defense"—even though Israel could easily have stopped rocket fire from Gaza, if that was its goal, by returning to the negotiated June 2008 ceasefire it egregiously violated the following November.

When the U.N.–commissioned Goldstone report documented the

extensive evidence of Israeli war crimes and crimes against humanity, including the willful killings of unarmed civilians, few governments paid more than lip service to seeing justice done.

Even worse, after Cast Lead, E.U. countries and the United States sent their navies to help Israel enforce a blockade on Gaza which amounts to collective punishment of the entire population and thus violates the Fourth Geneva Convention governing Israel's ongoing occupation.

Not one country sent a hospital ship to help treat or evacuate the thousands of wounded, many with horrific injuries that overwhelmed Gaza's hospitals.

CARROT AND STICK

The blockade has never been—as Israel and its apologists claim—to stop the smuggling of weapons into Gaza.

Its goal has always been political: to cause the civilian population as much suffering as possible—while still being politically excusable—in order for the Palestinians in Gaza to reject and rise up against the Hamas leadership elected in January 2006.

The withholding of food, medicine, schoolbooks, and building supplies, among thousands of other items, as well as the right to enter and leave Gaza for any purpose became a weapon to terrorize the civilian population.

At the same time, Western aid was showered on the occupied West Bank—whose ordinary people are still only barely better off than those in Gaza—in a "carrot and stick" policy calculated to shift support away from Hamas and toward the Western-backed, unelected Palestinian Authority leadership affiliated with the rival Fatah faction, who have repeatedly demonstrated their unconditional willingness to collaborate with Israel no matter what it does to their people.

"The idea is to put the Palestinians on a diet, but not to make them die of hunger," senior Israeli government advisor Dov Weisglass

notoriously explained in 2006. By this standard the blockade—
supported by several Arab governments and the Quartet (the U.S.,
E.U., U.N. Secretary General, and Russia) has been a great success,
as numerous studies document alarming increases in child malnutrition as the vast majority of Gaza's population became dependent on
U.N. food handouts. Hundreds have died for lack of access to proper
medical care.

FILLING THE "MORAL VOID"

While inaction and complicity characterized the official response,
global civil society stepped in to fill the moral and legal void.

In the year and a half since Cast Lead, the global, Palestinian-led
campaign for boycott, divestment, and sanctions on Israel (BDS) has
been racking up impressive victories.

From the decisions by Norway's pension funds and several European banks to divest from certain Israeli companies, to university
divestment initiatives, the refusals by international artists to perform
in Israel, or the flash mobs that have brought the consumer boycott
to supermarkets around the world, Israel sees BDS as a growing "existential threat."

At this point, the effect may be more psychological than economic, but it is exactly the feeling of increasing isolation and pariah status that helped push South Africa's apartheid rulers to recognize that
their regime was untenable and to seek peaceful change with the very
people they had so long demonized, dehumanized, and oppressed.

Indeed, the BDS movement is only likely to gather pace: World-
bestselling Swedish author Henning Mankell, who was among the
passengers on the Turkish ship *Mavi Marmara* kidnapped and taken
to Israel, said on being freed: "I think we should use the experience of
South Africa, where we know that the sanctions had a great impact."

The Freedom Flotilla represented the very best, and most courageous of this civil society spirit and determination not to abandon

fellow human beings to the cruelty, indifference, and self-interest of governments.

The immediate response to Israel's attack on the flotilla may indicate that governments too are starting to come out of their slumber and shed the paralyzing fear of criticizing Israel that has assured its impunity for so long.

GROWING GAP

Indeed, the global reaction demonstrates the growing gap between the United States and Israel on one side and the rest of the world on the other.

While Israeli officials scrambled to offer justifications from the ludicrous (elite commandos armed with paintball guns) to the benign (the attack was an "inspection"), the United States has once again stood behind its ally unconditionally.

As the Obama administration forced a watered-down presidential statement in the U.N. Security Council, Israeli apologists in the mainstream U.S. media repeatedly attempted to excuse Israel's actions as lawful and legitimate.

Senior administration officials, including Joe Biden, the vice president, openly began to echo their Israeli counterparts, arguing that Israel's attack was not only legitimate but justified by its security needs.

Despite the predictable and shameless U.S. reaction, international condemnation has been unusually robust.

In his speech to the Turkish parliament following the attack, Recep Tayyip Erdoğan, the Turkish prime minister, denounced Israeli "state terrorism" and demanded that the international community exact a price.

Erdoğan vowed that "Turkey will never turn its back on Gaza" and that it would continue its campaign to lift the blockade and hold Israel accountable even if it had to do so alone.

There are hopeful signs it may not have to.

European and other countries summoned Israeli ambassadors and several recalled their envoys from Tel Aviv.

Franco Frattini, the Italian foreign minister and one of Israel's staunchest apologists in Europe, said his country "absolutely deplored the slaying of civilians" and demanded that Israel "must give an explanation to the international community" of killings he deemed "absolutely unacceptable, whatever the flotilla's aims."

Small countries showed the greatest courage and clarity. Nicaragua suspended diplomatic ties completely, citing Israel's "illegal attack." Brian Cowen, Ireland's prime minister, told parliament in Dublin that his government had "formally requested" of Israel that the vessel *Rachel Corrie*, be allowed to proceed, and warned of the "most serious consequences" should Israel use violence against it.

The boat—named after the young American peace activist killed by Israeli occupation forces in Gaza in 2003—was carrying Malaysian and Irish activists and politicians including Nobel Peace Prize winner Mairead Maguire.

CROSSED A THRESHOLD

These are still small actions, but they indicate Israel may have crossed a threshold where it can no longer take appeasement and complicity for granted.

It is a cumulative process—each successive outrage has diminished the reserve of goodwill and forbearance Israel enjoyed.

Even if most governments are not quite ready to go from words to effective actions, growing public outrage will eventually push them to impose official sanctions.

Benjamin Netanyahu, the Israeli prime minister, may have hastened that day with his fulsome pride in, and praise for, the slaughter at sea even after the outpouring of international condemnation.

Despite its intensive efforts to hide and spin what happened aboard the *Mavi Marmara* in the early hours of May 31, the world saw Israel use exactly the sort of indiscriminate brutality documented in the Goldstone report.

This time, however, it was not just "expendable" Palestinians or Lebanese who were Israel's victims, but people from thirty-two countries and every continent. It was the day the whole world became Gaza. And like the people of Gaza, the world is unlikely to take it lying down.

ISRAEL REVEALS ITS TRUE FACE

Ahdaf Soueif

This will count. A flotilla of relief boats attacked in international waters. Armed commandos boarding a vessel carrying supplies for a besieged civilian population. Nine peace activists reported killed. This
has to be made to count.

The dead have joined Rachel Corrie, Tom Hurndall, and James
Miller in giving up their lives for the Palestinians. None of these
young men and women went out to die or wanted to die or was accepting of death. Each and every one of them ultimately believed that
they were safe, that there was a boundary—call it a boundary of legal-
ity, a boundary of civilization—that Israel would not cross. They were
wrong. And in proving them wrong, Israel has revealed, once again,
its true face to the world.

This face, of course, the Palestinians know well. They see it every day in the teenage soldiers of the occupation chewing gum as
they dish out humiliations, in the settlers shooting young Palestinians with impunity, in the soldiers firing gas canisters at the heads
of demonstrators. The world saw that face in January last year when
Israel unleashed the might of its air force on Gaza—the only time
in modern warfare that a civilian population was sealed in as it was
being bombed and shelled. Now Israel is out on the high seas killing
internationals.

So never mind the multimillion-dollar public relations campaign—actions speak louder than words, and the murder of these

peace activists is Israel's message to the world. It does not matter what Mark Regev or any other Israeli spokesperson says. It does not matter what spin the Israeli government tries to put on this; the only link between Israeli words and Israeli deeds is this: Israel uses words as a decoy and an obfuscation and a cover for its deeds. It has done so for sixty-two years. These internationals, dead now, murdered, have ensured that anyone who does not see this is willfully blind.

Western governments are fond of holding up Israel as the "only democracy in the Middle East." So should we assume that the Israeli people are behind their government? That they approve these killings? Last month I was at Al-Quds University in Abu Dis. Israel's wall shaved the edge off the campus. On it, in tall blue letters, a Palestinian student had written: "My Israeli sisters: this is not the answer."

A few days ago, young Jewish Israeli activists told me they saw that the only hope for their country lies with the international community. Israel is on a path to self-destruction, they said, and it will take the region with it. It will not stop, they said, until the price it pays for its actions becomes too heavy. This price has to be a moral and economic price imposed by the world.

My anger and my sadness are so great that I have to deliberately draw a deep breath from time to time to ease the bands I feel around my chest. It doesn't matter. What does matter is that millions of people in the world are feeling the same. People everywhere see and understand what is happening. Many of us feel that Palestine is nearing its South Africa moment. This latest outrage must push it closer. And it will.

Donations will, I'm sure, flood in to the other relief boats waiting in harbor. More and more people will take the boycott to heart. More civil bodies will insist on divestment from companies that do business with Israel. The time has come for the governments that represent us to stop engaging with Israeli lies and excuses. The price of Israel's action today has to be to put the issue of sanctions squarely on the table.

ISRAEL'S SECURITY CANNOT COME AT ANY PRICE

Ben Saul

Israel's response to the Gaza flotilla is another unfortunate example of Israel clothing its conduct in the language of international law while flouting it in practice. If you believe Israeli government spokesmen, Israel is metabolically incapable of violating international law, placing it alongside Saddam Hussein's information minister in self-awareness.

Israel claims that paragraph 67(a) of the San Remo Manual on Armed Conflicts at Sea justified the Israeli operation against the flotilla. (The San Remo Manual is an authoritative statement of international law applicable to armed conflicts at sea.)

Paragraph 67(a) only permits attacks on the merchant vessels of neutral countries where they "are believed on reasonable grounds to be carrying contraband or breaching a blockade, and after prior warning they intentionally and clearly refuse to stop, or intentionally and clearly resist visit, search or capture."

Israel argues that it gave due warnings, which were not heeded.

What Israel conveniently omits to mention is that the San Remo Manual also contains rules governing the lawfulness of the blockade itself, and there can be no authority under international law to enforce a blockade which is unlawful. Paragraph 102 of the manual prohibits a blockade if "the damage to the civilian population is, or may be expected to be, excessive in relation to the concrete and direct military advantage anticipated from the blockade."

The background to that "proportionality" rule is the experience of past world wars where naval blockades had devastating effects on civilian populations.

There is little question that Israel's blockade of Gaza is disproportionate in legal terms. The proportionality rule requires an assessment of the military advantage against the harmful effects on civilians. Israel claims that the blockade is necessary to prevent Hamas from mounting indiscriminate rocket attacks on Israeli civilians.

Such attacks were well documented by the U.N.'s Goldstone report and are a serious security threat to Israel. Israel has every right to protect its civilians from indiscriminate terrorist attacks by Hamas.

The proportionality principle requires, however, that Israel's security cannot come at any price. A balancing of interests is necessary to ensure that civilians should not pay too dearly for the security needs of others.

Safeguarding the precious lives of innocents and respecting their dignity as fellow humans is the necessary burden that international law imposes on war. That is why Israel reveals its contempt for international law when, for example, in the past its leaders have pledged to "destroy 100 homes for every rocket fired."

The harmful effects of the blockade on Gazan civilians have included the denial of the basics of life, such as food, fuel, and medicine, as well as widespread economic collapse.

The U.N. agency on the ground, the U.N. Relief and Works Agency for Palestine Refugees (UNRWA), has described a "severe humanitarian crisis" in Gaza in relation to human development, health, education, "the psychological stress" on the population, high unemployment (at 45 percent) and poverty (with 300,000 people living beneath the poverty line), and the collapse of commerce, industry, and agriculture.

Such effects are manifestly excessive in relation to Israel's security objectives and cannot possibly satisfy the conditions of a lawful blockade. Disrupting wildly inaccurate rockets from being fired at relatively underpopulated areas of southern Israel cannot possibly justify the acute disruption of the daily lives and livelihoods of more than one million Gazans. Nor is it lawful to seek to pressure Hamas by instrumentally impoverishing its civilian supporters.

It seems that Israel is the only entity incapable of recognizing the effects of its blockade. The United States, European Union, and numerous independent sources have deeply criticized the disproportionate harm to Gazan civilians.

The U.N. Secretary General has condemned the "unacceptable suffering" caused by the blockade. The U.N. High Commissioner for Human Rights has criticized it for violating the law of armed conflict. The U.N. Human Rights Council, U.N. Humanitarian Affairs Coordinator, Oxfam, and Amnesty International have all strongly condemned it.

The U.N.'s Goldstone report found that blockade may even amount to international crimes: "Israeli acts that deprive Palestinians in the Gaza Strip of their means of subsistence, employment, housing and water, that deny their freedom of movement and their right to leave and enter their own country... could lead a competent court to find that the crime of persecution, a crime against humanity, has been committed."

Israel has further argued that it offered the Gaza flotilla an opportunity to deliver aid through the proper Israeli channels.

It is very difficult to regard that offer as sincere given Israel's track record. Israel's practices concerning the transit of goods through Israeli entry points has been arbitrary at best and deliberately obstructive at worst.

The United Nations notes that everything from crayons to soccer balls to musical instruments has been denied entry into Gaza—hardly rocket components. Goods sit idle for months or are never delivered at all. In such circumstances, no one could have any confidence that the goods would ever reach Gaza.

As yet, it is still unknown exactly what happened on board the flotilla vessels boarded by Israeli forces. Even at this early stage, however, some international law matters are fairly clear.

First, absent any intention by the flotilla to attack Israel, or any suspicion of piracy, it was unlawful for Israel to forcibly board foreign merchant vessels in international waters.

Second, such action amounted to an unlawful interference in the enforcement jurisdiction of the "flag-States" (countries of registration) of those vessels, such as Turkey.

Third, it violated the fundamental principle of freedom of navigation on the high seas, codified in the U.N. Convention on the Law of the Sea of 1982.

Fourth, under international human rights law, the apprehension and detention of those on board the vessels likely amounts to arbitrary, unlawful detention, contrary to Article 9 of the International Covenant on Civil and Political Rights, since there is no lawful basis for detention.

Fifth, if Israeli forces killed people, they may not only have infringed the human right to life, but they may also have committed serious international crimes. Under Article 3 of the Rome Convention for the Suppression of Unlawful Acts Against the Safety of Maritime Navigation of 1988, it is an international crime for any person to seize or exercise control over a ship by force, and also a crime to injure or kill any person in the process.

Ironically, that treaty was adopted after Palestinian terrorists hijacked the Italian cruise ship, the Achille Lauro, in 1985, in which a Jewish American was killed.

In such cases, any claim of self-defense by Israeli forces is irrelevant. The treaty necessarily adopts a strict approach. One cannot attack a ship and then claim self-defense if the people on board resist the unlawful use of violence.

Legally speaking, government military forces rappelling onto a ship to illegally capture it are treated no differently than other criminals. The right of self-defense in such situations rests with the passengers on board: A person is legally entitled to resist one's own unlawful capture, abduction, and detention.

Whether doing so is wise, in the face of heavily armed commandos, is a different question. Whether running the gauntlet of an Israeli military blockade is sensible or foolhardy is another.

This latest sad and shocking episode is a reminder of Israel's recklessness toward the lives of others, its utter disregard for international opinion, and its incivility as an outlaw of the international community.

Israel has become its own worst enemy. It prioritizes its own interests with a callous lack of empathy for others. It is simply unable to imagine the suffering it inflicts upon others, and treats harm to Israelis as the only game in town. Its absolutism of mind and politics has crushing consequences for Palestinians.

Far from ensuring its own security, Israel is unraveling it: No one should be surprised if Israel has just succeeded in recruiting the next generation of martyrs keen to attack it.

Absolutism, violence, and the evaporation of peace in the region will continue as long as the international community continues to handle Israel with kid gloves.

THE REAL THREAT ABOARD
THE FREEDOM FLOTILLA

Noam Chomsky

Israel's violent attack on the Freedom Flotilla carrying humanitarian aid to Gaza shocked the world.

Hijacking boats in international waters and killing passengers is, of course, a serious crime.

But the crime is nothing new. For decades, Israel has been hijacking boats between Cyprus and Lebanon and killing or kidnapping passengers, sometimes holding them hostage in Israeli prisons.

Israel assumes that it can commit such crimes with impunity because the United States tolerates them and Europe generally follows the U.S.'s lead.

As the editors of the *Guardian* rightly observed on June 1, "If an armed group of Somali pirates had yesterday boarded six vessels on the high seas, killing at least ten passengers and injuring many more, a NATO task force would today be heading for the Somali coast." In this case, the NATO treaty obligates its members to come to the aid of a fellow NATO country, Turkey, attacked on the high seas.

Israel's pretext for the attack was that the Freedom Flotilla was bringing materials that Hamas could use for bunkers to fire rockets into Israel.

The pretext isn't credible. Israel can easily end the threat of rockets by peaceful means.

The background is important. Hamas was designated a major

terrorist threat when it won a free election in January 2006. The United States and Israel sharply escalated their punishment of Palestinians, now for the crime of voting the wrong way.

The siege of Gaza, including a naval blockade, was a result. The siege intensified sharply in June 2007 after a civil war left Hamas in control of the territory.

What is commonly described as a Hamas military coup was in fact incited by the United States and Israel, in a crude attempt to overturn the elections that had brought Hamas to power.

That has been public knowledge at least since April 2008, when David Rose reported in *Vanity Fair* that George W. Bush, National Security Adviser Condoleezza Rice, and her deputy, Elliott Abrams, "backed an armed force under Fatah strongman Muhammad Dahlan, touching off a bloody civil war in Gaza and leaving Hamas stronger than ever."

Hamas terror included launching rockets into nearby Israeli towns, criminal, without a doubt, though only a minute fraction of routine U.S.-Israeli crimes in Gaza.

In June 2008, Israel and Hamas reached a ceasefire agreement. The Israeli government formally acknowledges that until Israel broke the agreement on November 4 of that year, invading Gaza and killing half a dozen Hamas activists, Hamas did not fire a single rocket.

Hamas offered to renew the ceasefire. The Israeli cabinet considered the offer and rejected it, preferring to launch its murderous invasion of Gaza on December 27.

Like other states, Israel has the right of self-defense. But did Israel have the right to use force in Gaza in the name of self-defense? International law, including the U.N. Charter, is unambiguous: A nation has such a right only if it has exhausted peaceful means. In this case such means were not even tried, although, or perhaps because, there was every reason to suppose that they would succeed.

Thus the invasion was sheer criminal aggression, and the same is true of Israel's resorting to force against the flotilla. The siege is savage, designed to keep the caged animals barely alive so as to fend off international protest, but hardly more than that. It is the latest stage of longstanding Israeli plans, backed by the United States, to separate Gaza from the West Bank.

The Israeli journalist Amira Hass, a leading specialist on Gaza, outlines the history of the process of separation: "The restrictions on Palestinian movement that Israel introduced in January 1991 reversed a process that had been initiated in June 1967.

"Back then, and for the first time since 1948, a large portion of the Palestinian people again lived in the open territory of a single country—to be sure, one that was occupied, but was nevertheless whole...." Hass concludes: "The total separation of the Gaza Strip from the West Bank is one of the greatest achievements of Israeli politics, whose overarching objective is to prevent a solution based on international decisions and understandings and instead dictate an arrangement based on Israel's military superiority."

The Freedom Flotilla defied that policy and so it must be crushed. A framework for settling the Arab-Israeli conflict has existed since 1976, when the regional Arab States introduced a Security Council resolution calling for a two-state settlement on the international border, including all the security guarantees of U.N. Resolution 242, adopted after the June War in 1967.

The essential principles are supported by virtually the entire world, including the Arab League, the Organization of Islamic States (including Iran), and relevant non-state actors, including Hamas.

But the United States and Israel have led the rejection of such a settlement for three decades, with one crucial and highly informative exception. In President Bill Clinton's last month in office, January 2001, he initiated Israeli-Palestinian negotiations in Taba, Egypt, that almost reached an agreement, participants announced, before Israel terminated the negotiations.

Today, the cruel legacy of a failed peace lives on. International law cannot be enforced against powerful states, except by their own citizens. That is always a difficult task, particularly when articulate opinion declares crime to be legitimate, either explicitly or by tacit adoption of a criminal framework, which is more insidious, because it renders the crimes invisible.

THREE REFLECTIONS

Rashid Khalidi

Israel's act of state piracy on the high seas provokes a number of reflections.

First, tragic though these events were, we must not lose sight of the circumstance that engendered them. This is Israel's ongoing siege of 1.5 million Palestinians in the Gaza Strip. In spite of its much trumpeted "loosening" of its blockade—which has happened solely because of the courageous actions of those who organized and took part in this and earlier humanitarian missions to Gaza, in the face of the disgraceful inaction of the West and the Arab world—the siege of Gaza is still in force.

What happens inside the Gaza Strip is subject to a barrage of disinformation propagated by the disciplined international public relations machine which has been one of the great strengths of the Zionist movement since its inception. In effect denying the humanity of 1.5 million Palestinians, Israel describes the Gaza Strip as a "terrorist entity." It thereby justifies any manner of deprivation and abuses against the civilian population. These actions are then covered up with false reports that Gazans are thriving on the generous amounts of food that Israel magnanimously allows them to receive.

This propaganda contradicts all reports out of Gaza, which depict an entire population penned into an open-air prison camp with their economy crippled by the blockade, suffering appalling public health conditions, and prevented from leaving the Strip freely or from rebuilding from the devastation of Israel's assault in the winter of 2008–2009. Tons of sewage pour into the Mediterranean for lack of treatment because spare parts for the sewage plant cannot get through the blockade, 90 percent of Gaza's people drink polluted water because the water supply system cannot be repaired for the same reason, and the electrical system, smashed by Israeli bombing, can only supply current intermittently.

The cumulative effect of this siege amounts to collective punishment of an entire population under belligerent occupation (which Israel's high seas blockade has once again proven is still in place), constitutes a violation of the Fourth Geneva Convention, and is a potential war crime, and perhaps a crime against humanity. The latter were among the conclusions of the report of the committee headed by the respected international jurist, Judge Richard Goldstone. The saga of the flotilla has brought further welcome attention to the reality of Gaza and has further shredded the screen of lies Israel has erected to conceal its actions there.

Secondly, it is worth reflecting on discrepancies between how the attack on the *Mavi Marmara* was reported on by the mainstream American media and how it was depicted elsewhere. Utilizing what has become a favored tactic for muzzling the press, one perfected during the 2008–2009 assault on the Gaza Strip—keeping the victims forcibly under wraps and isolated from reporters—Israeli forces kidnapped the passengers on the flotilla, stole their phones and cameras, and held them incommunicado for two days. All the while, Israel's P.R. machine tirelessly propagated its fanciful depiction of the events that took place at sea. Because there was initially little access to alternate sources of information, the Israeli spinners thus had a crucial twenty-four to forty-eight hours in which to establish their false version of events. This concoction quickly became ascendant in the mainstream American media and on Capitol Hill, where politicians soon fell over one another striving to read the lines fed to them by AIPAC.

As those detained at sea were finally released from Israeli captivity, the truth of what happened on the ships finally came out. These facts, however, were slow to be picked up by the U.S. media. They never made any impact on the American political sphere, which lives in a parallel reality, a dark cave where politicians are careful only to describe the flickering shadows cast for them by the Israel lobby. The situation was quite different everywhere else in the world. There, what actually happened on the hijacked ships very quickly asserted itself over the fairy tale retailed by the Israeli government about poor defenseless Israelis being viciously assaulted by those on the humanitarian flotilla. Perhaps only Israel would have the chutzpah to portray as victims its elite naval commandos (a unit that had engaged in innumerable deadly operations in the past, and that left several passengers dead with bullets in the head fired at close range, execution-style). Beyond that, it had the sheer gall to compare the "attack" on these heavily armed commandos to the mob lynching of innocent, unarmed men of color in the American South. Such distortions were allowed to pass unchallenged by most of the U.S. media.

In contrast, in virtually every European country, including those that are generally pro-Israel, and in the rest of the world, the bulk of the media and public opinion did not swallow this ludicrous Israeli story. Even in Israel, many journalists and commentators were not taken in by the government line, and described the operation as the brutal fiasco it was. However, for the Netanyahu government and its supporters, the fact that their skewed version of reality was rejected virtually everywhere was simply taken as further evidence that Israel lives beleaguered in a world largely populated by crypto-anti-Semites. By contrast, for most people the world over, including increasing numbers of informed Americans, Israel's actions and this great discrepancy in explaining them was further proof that Israel's government has lost its bearings, is unbalanced and dangerous, and is no longer able to measure the impact of its actions.

This brings us to the third and perhaps most interesting reflection. What could Israel's leaders possibly have been thinking when they ordered an attack on a Turkish-flagged ship on the high seas, knowing that Turkey is and has been for over half a century Israel's only Middle East ally? This could also be asked of many earlier Israeli decisions. Previously, the answer was in large part a smug certainty in Jerusalem, where the political elite is located, and in the Qirya (the Israeli Pentagon) in Tel Aviv, that the United States would cover for Israel, whatever happened. In both places there also reigned the confident assumption that however much Israel actions harmed U.S. interests, a cowed executive would swallow its bile, under the pressure of the Israel lobby and its trained chorus on Capitol Hill and in the media.

In this case also, the United States continued to cover for Israel in the Security Council, accepting an Israeli-controlled investigation into the attack on the flotilla instead of an impartial international one. One can judge the surreal atmosphere in Washington from the fact that 329 representatives and eighty-seven senators signed letters demanding support for Israel's act of "self-defense." Needless to say, many other reasonable options were open to the Obama administration notwithstanding this Congressional kowtowing to Israel. These ranged from invoking NATO solidarity in the face of an unprovoked, lethal attack on the high seas on a ship belonging to an Alliance member-state, to simply abstaining on a U.N. Security Council condemning Israel's action and demanding a genuine international investigation with Turkish participation. Naturally, it was unimaginable that Washington would allow the Israeli Navy to be treated as they should have been: like those engaged in non-state piracy off the Somali coast.

However, notwithstanding this disappointing exhibition of fealty to Israel, the U.S. executive branch is beginning to express dissent from some Israeli policies. This was apparent over issues of nuclear non-proliferation, where the U.S. position of effectively putting Israel on the same level as Iran has made the Israeli government quietly furious and its partisans noisily apoplectic; over public comments by the most senior officials from the President on down implicitly questioning Israel's strategic value to the United States; and over a reiteration that the United States considers East Jerusalem to be occupied territory. On these issues of great importance to Israel, the last several administrations never dared to take such stands.

So, given its strained relations with the Obama administration, why has the Netanyahu government chosen to spurn its sole Middle Eastern ally? (Similarly, it is meanwhile alienating Jordan, one of the few states in the region friendly to it, by opposing that country's desire to use its abundant uranium deposits to develop its own nuclear energy industry.) One hesitates to believe that the fevered writings of Israel's neocon boosters like Michael Rubin, who has proclaimed Turkey "an Islamic Republic," and announced that it long ago shifted from being an ally to an enemy, could possibly reflect the thinking of Israeli leaders. But this Israeli government may have reached rock bottom: they may actually believe their own maudlin propaganda about the entire world being against them, and may therefore think that since Israel will be condemned anyway, it should do as it pleases.

Remarkably, Israel's leaders appear to have both misread how the Turkish government and people would respond to an attack on one of its ships, and to have decided it did not matter anyway. They may have arrogantly assumed that just as they could defy Washington over settlements in the hope that the Obama administration would lose strength in the November 2010 midterm elections and would be gone after those of 2012, they could also force the United States to choose Israel over Turkey. The latter is a grave misreading of the strategic value of both countries to the United States. Israel is declining in importance for many American policy-makers, and indeed is coming to be seen as a problem for the United States. Turkey is not just a NATO ally with troops in Afghanistan, and with influence in crucial regions ranging from the Aegean, the Balkans, the Caucasus, and Central Asia to the Middle East. It is also facilitating the United States' withdrawal from Iraq, and like all Middle Eastern states except

Israel, has a sane and pragmatic understanding of how to deal with regional problems created by Iran's clerical regime. Because it would not cravenly acquiesce in the face of Israel's piracy, Turkey will now face the wrath of the Israel lobby, the sniping of neocon hit men, and a deterioration of relations with Israel. However, events will show how foolish Israel's action was, and that in the long run Israel needs Turkey, while it is not at all clear that Turkey needs Israel.

Not all in the Israeli hierarchy are blind to these larger realities: "Israel is gradually turning from an asset to the United States to a burden," the Chief of the Mossad intelligence service told an Israeli Knesset committee soon after the flotilla fiasco on June 1, 2010. Two former prime ministers earlier warned that if Israel stays on its present course, it will become an apartheid state and an international pariah. But a circle-the-wagons mentality has taken hold of the Israeli political elite. When one adds their longstanding addiction to the use of force, one understands otherwise inexplicable actions, from the assaults on Lebanon in 2006, to Gaza in 2008–2009, to that on the *Mavi Marmara*. As John Mearsheimer put it recently, this elite "remains firmly committed to the belief that what cannot be solved by force can be solved with greater force."

Israel was established by using force to establish facts on the ground in Palestine, and by savvy control of the discourse about Palestine. This latest fiasco illustrates once again that Israel's present leaders are obsessed only with smashing yet another "terrorist threat" with brute force, and seizing yet another hilltop in the West Bank or East Jerusalem. They demand acceptance of the legitimacy of these crude actions and then whine about Israel being "delegitimized" when they do not get it. The once-formidable Israeli P.R. machine is no longer up to its task, for it is being asked to "sell" policies—endless occupation, rank discrimination, the siege of a civilian population, savage attacks on neighbors—that are increasingly abhorrent to people the world over. Barring a rapid, radical change in these policies, this is a recipe for the total isolation of Israel. This was a state created and sustained largely by its leaders' ability accurately to read and influence the international environment. That ability seems to have disappeared in the current leadership generation. Given current trends in American public opinion (especially among the young), Israel's last line of defense—the U.S. media and Congress—can only be kept in their cave for so long. Once they see the light, there will be no one left to justify an approach premised on the use of force and greater force, and with no grounding in law or morality.

THE GAZA OCCUPATION AND SIEGE ARE ILLEGAL

George Bisharat

Israel's deadly attack on the Gaza Freedom Flotilla was flagrantly illegal. The flotilla, carefully searched for arms before disembarkation, enjoyed the right of free navigation in international waters, and Israel had no legal justification to interrupt its peaceful mission.

Flotilla passengers were entitled to defend themselves against Israel's forcible boarding of the *Mavi Marmara*, whether or not Israeli commandos fired immediately on landing on the ship's deck, as the passengers maintain. Dropping 100 armed soldiers on a ship from the sky is not a peaceful maneuver. Nor can Israeli armed commandos claim self-defense, any more than a purse snatcher facing a victim who elects to fight back. Hence, Israel is culpable for the killings that followed.

Israel has claimed that it is in "armed conflict" with the Hamas government in the Gaza Strip and that its actions on the high seas to enforce the blockade of the Gaza Strip are therefore permissible. That claim is wrong.

In fact, under customary international law that Israel accepts as binding, Israel continues to occupy the Gaza Strip, despite the withdrawal of its ground troops and settlers from that region in 2005. A territory is "occupied" when foreign forces exercise "effective control" over it, whether accomplished through the continuous presence of ground troops or not.

Israel patrols the territorial waters and airspace of the Gaza Strip, regulates Gaza's land borders, restricts internal movements by excluding Gazans from a "buffer zone" that includes up to 40 percent of the Strip's agricultural land, and controls the Gaza Strip's supplies of electricity, heating oil, and petrol. Together these factors amount to remote but "effective control." Thus, the Gaza Strip remains occupied, as the United Nations, the U.S. government and the International Committee of the Red Cross have all recognized.

Israel has authority to halt arms imports into the Gaza Strip. But it also owes a general duty of protection to civilians under its control, and has specific duties to allow them access to adequate food and medical supplies, and to maintain public health standards—duties it has deliberately violated in imposing the siege on Gaza. Currently 77.2 percent of Gaza Palestinians either face or are vulnerable to hunger; of these, 65 percent are children younger than eighteen. According to UNICEF, 10 percent of Gaza children show signs of stunting, while the World Health Organization maintains that another 10 percent face chronic malnutrition.

Moreover, collective punishment is specifically barred under Article 33 of the Fourth Geneva Convention. Israeli officials have repeatedly stated that the objective of the blockade is to weaken the Gaza economy and undermine support for Hamas. That is a political, not a military, objective, and it is impermissible under international law to target innocent civilians to achieve nonmilitary goals.

Actions taken to enforce an illegal siege cannot themselves be legal. Israel's blockade violates the human rights of Gaza Palestinians and must be brought to an end.

Israel's attack on the Freedom Flotilla is the logical consequence of years of Israeli impunity from international law—abetted by the diplomatic cover provided it by our government. At some point, genuine friends of both Israeli Jews and Palestinian Arabs must impress on Israel that its serial lawlessness is good for no one, multiplying resentment and pain, and pushing the prospects of regional peace into a more distant future.

ISRAEL'S ANTI-1967 MOMENT

Adam Horowitz and Philip Weiss

The Freedom Flotilla was not able to deliver its 10,000 tons of humanitarian aid to the besieged Gaza Strip, but it accomplished something more important—it finally broke the blockade on the world's understanding of the Gaza crisis. The Israeli attack on the flotilla must be seen alongside the Israeli attack on Gaza in the winter of 2008–2009 as marking the period in which the world's understanding of the Israeli occupation irrevocably shifted. In this opening, the brutality of the Israeli occupation came into full view and the issue of Palestinian persecution was placed on op-ed pages and even legal briefs. In the end, these events may mark when the age of Israeli impunity came to an end.

In a generational sense, Operation Cast Lead and the flotilla attack can be understood as the anti–1967 war. It was the 1967 war that helped solidify Israel's image in the eyes of the world, and in particular of American Jewry, as the scrappy underdog beating the odds. That image has now changed forever, and the ongoing siege of Gaza has caused many to consider what Zionism has built in the Middle East.

The Goldstone report stands as the defining indictment of this era. The report, which found that both Israel and Hamas committed war crimes and possible crimes against humanity, specifically includes the persecution of Gaza, highlighting cases where Israel intentionally attacked civilian infrastructure, including water wells, chicken farms, and the last operating flour mill in the Strip. Not surprisingly, the report and Goldstone himself became the targets of unrelenting criticism and vitriol because it pulled back the curtain on Israeli actions. For those who harbored doubts about the Goldstone report's findings, those doubts were dispelled by the flotilla attack. The killings on the *Mavi Marmara* vindicated Goldstone's reading of Israeli methods. And note that the Israeli defense of its actions is exactly the same as its defense of its actions in Gaza: We had a right to cross international lines, we got severe provocation, supposed civilians were actually combatants, no country would permit this situation to endure, we defended ourselves, just look at the video. In Gaza the Israelis killed 1,200–1,400 with minimal loss of life on the Israeli side; and the numbers were imbalanced on the *Mavi Marmara* as well.

And now the efforts to smear the activists on the boats as jihadists, which the *Washington Post* and other American outlets have taken up with energy, recall the efforts to portray the Gazans as a crazed, extremist population.

The vindication for Goldstone is that anyone with eyes in her head knows that there was something terribly wrong with the flotilla action—as anyone with eyes knew that there was something wrong about the Gaza onslaught. But at that time the West was still in denial, and the Israeli-American dismissal of the Goldstone report can now be seen as a defensive effort to cover up atrocities. Who can question Goldstone's conclusions now: that Israel targeted civilian infrastructure disproportionately, and without distinction between civilians and resisters? Israel has once again shown us the playbook.

This awareness was seen in a shift in the discourse surrounding the flotilla attack, especially online as Internet journalists, led by Ali Abunimah, repeatedly exposed Israeli *hasbara*. The awareness even penetrated the establishment media; at the *New York Times* website, Robert Mackey's Lede blog cataloged the work of those discrediting Israeli spin. He highlighted Max Blumenthal's reporting on doctored IDF audio of the attack and Noam Sheizaf's work on Turkish photos of the *Mavi Marmara* attack that contradicted IDF claims. Other significant reporting includes Lia Tarachansky and Blumenthal's work disproving the IDF's claim that the flotilla was linked to Al Qaeda, Jared Malsin's work confirming the doctored audio, and Abunimah's reconstruction of the path of the *Mavi Marmara* to show that it was actually fleeing at the time of the Israeli attack.

Despite the Israeli Foreign Ministry's best efforts, these Internet journalists were able to shape the story and fill crucial voids in the narrative of the attack that persisted in large part because Israel refused to share the entirety of the video and still footage it confiscated from flotilla passengers. In the past, Israel's control of the story of the conflict, especially in the West, has been an enormous source of power. Now we see that power breaking down at an incredibly swift rate. The one "success" in their *hasbara* effort has been a racist "we are the world" knock-off video that really only confirmed how absolutely tone-deaf many Israelis were to feelings around the world.

In another age, novelist Leon Uris helped supply a narrative of the Israel/Palestine conflict that survived for generations, but today the story is being told firsthand over the Internet. Portions of the attack on the *Mavi Marmara* were broadcast nearly live over a live-stream video channel online. In addition, several filmmakers onboard were able to smuggle footage off the boat, most notably Iara Lee from the Cultures of Resistance project, whose footage helped contradict the official Israeli version of events. So far, Israel has not found an effective response to this democratization of the media. And who knows, before long, people may talk about how the Gazans ended up in Gaza in the first place, the Nakba of 1948. Who's going to believe "a land without people, for a people without a land" when there are ten You-Tube videos to prove you wrong?

We say that the age of Israeli impunity may be coming to an end because of the surge in international grassroots effort to hold Israel accountable. The global boycott, divestment, and sanctions (BDS) was catalyzed by the Israeli assault on Gaza, and the flotilla attack only added fuel to the fire. In the week following the attack a flurry of boycott activities spread the globe from dockworkers in Sweden refusing to unload Israeli ships, to Britain's largest Union, UNITE, deciding to promote an Israeli boycott, to the popular band the Pixies refusing to play Tel Aviv. In addition, Ecuador, Turkey, and South Africa recalled their ambassadors from Israel, and over fifteen other countries summoned the resident Israeli ambassadors to express their outrage. This anger seems to have coalesced at the United Nations, where Secretary General Ban Ki-moon is pressing forward with plans for an international investigation into the flotilla attack despite an Israeli attempt to derail the effort with a domestic inquiry.

Some are already referring to this new U.N. investigation as "Goldstone II." Palestinian commentator Ali Abunimah pointed out on the Al Jazeera English website that if the attack on Gaza moved the world's people, it seemed the flotilla attack moved its governments. He pointed to the international composition of the flotilla and wrote, "It was the day the whole world became Gaza. And like the people of Gaza, the world is unlikely to take it lying down." And so the Gaza flotilla raid may one day prove to be a hinge of modern history.

"YOU WILL HAVE NO PROTECTION"

Alice Walker

You will have no protection.
    – Medgar Evers to civil rights activists in Mississippi,
        shortly before he was assassinated, June 12, 1963

My heart is breaking; but I do not mind. For one thing, as soon as I wrote those words I was able to weep. Which I had not been able to do since learning of the attack by armed Israeli commandos on defenseless peace activists carrying aid to Gaza who tried to fend them off using chairs and sticks. I am thankful to know what it means to be good; I know that the people of the Freedom Flotilla are/were, in some cases, some of the best people on earth. They have not stood silently by and watched the destruction of others, brutally, sustained, without offering themselves, weaponless except for their bodies, to the situation. I am thankful to have a long history of knowing people like this from my earliest years, beginning in my student days of marches and demonstrations: for peace, for non-separation among peoples, for justice for Women, for People of Color, for Cubans, for Animals, for Indians, and for Her, the planet.

I am weeping for the truth of Medgar's statement; so brave and so true. I weep for him gunned down in his carport, not far from where I would eventually live in Mississippi, with a box of T-shirts in his arms that said: Jim Crow Must Go. Though trained in the United States military under racist treatment one cringes to imagine, he remained a peaceful soldier in the army of liberation to the end. I weep and will always weep, even through the widest smiles, for the beautiful young wife, Myrlie Evers, he left behind, herself still strong and focused on the truth of struggle; and for their children, who lost their father to a fate they could not possibly, at the time, understand. I don't think any of us could imagine during that particular phase of the struggle for justice that we risked losing not just our lives, which we were prepared to give, but also our children, who we were not.

Nothing protected Medgar, nor will anything protect any of us; nothing but our love for ourselves and for others whom we recognize unfailingly as also ourselves. Nothing can protect us but our lives. How we have lived them; what battles, with love and compassion our only shield, we have engaged. And yet, the moment of realizing we are truly alone, that in the ultimate crisis of our existence our government is not there for us, is one of shock. Especially if we have had the illusion of a system behind us to which we truly belong. Thankfully I have never had opportunity to have this illusion. And so, every peaceful witnessing, every nonviolent confrontation has been a pure offering. I do not regret this at all.

When I was in Cairo last December to support Code Pink's efforts to carry aid into Gaza I was unfortunately ill with the flu and could not offer very much. I lay in bed in the hotel room and listened to other activists report on what was happening around the city as Egypt refused entry to Gaza to the 1,400 people who had come for the accompanying Freedom March. I heard many distressing things, but only one made me feel, not exactly envy, but something close; it was that the French activists had shown up, en masse, in front of their embassy and that their ambassador had come out to talk to them and to try to make them comfortable as they set up camp outside the building. This small gesture of compassion for his country's activists in a strange land touched me profoundly, as I was touched decades ago when someone in John Kennedy's White House (maybe the cook) sent out cups of hot coffee to our line of freezing student and teacher demonstrators as we tried, with our signs and slogans and songs, to protect a vulnerable neighbor, Cuba.

Where have the Israelis put our friends? I thought about this all night. Those whom they assassinated on the ship and those they injured? Is "my" government capable of insisting on respect for their dead bodies? Can it demand that those who are injured but alive be treated with care? Not only with care, but the tenderness and honor they deserve? If it cannot do this, such a simple, decent thing, of what use is it to the protection and healing of the planet? I heard a spokesman for the United States opine at the United Nations (not an exact quote) that the Freedom Flotilla activists should have gone through other, more proper, channels, not been confrontational with their attempt to bring aid to the distressed. This is almost exactly what college administrators advised half a century ago when students were trying to bring down apartheid in the South and getting bullets, nooses, bombings, and burnings for our efforts. I felt embarrassed (to the degree one can permit embarrassment by another) to be even vaguely represented by this man: a useless voice from the far past. One had hoped.

The Israeli spin on the massacre, that the commandos were under attack by the peace activists and that the whole thing was like a "lynching" of the armed attackers, reminds me of a Redd Foxx joke. I loved Redd Foxx, for all his vulgarity. A wife caught her husband in bed with another woman, flagrant, in the act, skin to skin. The husband said, probably through pants of aroused sexual exertion: "All right, go ahead and believe your lying eyes!" It would be fun, were it not tragic, to compare the various ways the Israeli government and our media will attempt to blame the victims of this unconscionable attack for their own imprisonment, wounds, and deaths.

So what to do? Rosa Parks sat down in the front of the bus. Martin Luther King, Jr., followed her act of courage with many of his own, and using his ringing, compassionate voice he aroused the people of Montgomery, Alabama, to commit to a sustained boycott of the bus company, a company that refused to allow people of color to sit in the front of the bus, even if it was empty. It is time for us, *en masse*, to show up in front of our conscience, and sit down in the front of the only bus we have: our very lives.

What would that look like, be like, today, in this situation between Palestine and Israel? This "impasse" that has dragged on for decades. This "conflict" that would have ended in a week if humanity as a whole had acted in defense of justice everywhere on the globe. Which maybe we are learning! It would look like the granddaughter of Rosa Parks, the grandson of Martin Luther King, Jr. It would look like spending our money only where we can spend our lives in peace and happiness; freely sharing whatever we have with our friends.

It would be to support boycott, divestment, and sanctions (BDS) against Israel to end the occupation of Gaza and the West Bank and by this effort begin to soothe the pain and attend the sorrows of a people wrongly treated for generations. This action would also remind Israel that we have seen it lose its way and have called to it, often with love, and we have not been heard. In fact, we have reached out to it only to encounter slander, insult, and, too frequently, bodily harm.

Disengage, avoid, and withhold support from whatever abuses, degrades, and humiliates humanity.

This we can do. We the people, who ultimately hold all the power. We the people, who must never forget to believe we can win.

We the people.

It has always been about us; as we watch governments come and go. It always will be.

3. THE BLOCKADE OF GAZA

LIST OF ITEMS PROHIBITED/
PERMITTED INTO THE GAZA STRIP*

Gisha.org

The following list is approximate and partial, and it changes from time to time. It is based on information from Palestinian traders and businesspeople, international organizations, and the Palestinian Coordination Committee, all of whom "deduce" what is permitted and what is banned based on their experience requesting permission to bring goods into Gaza and the answers they receive from the Israeli authorities (approved or denied). It is not possible to verify this list with the Israeli authorities, because they refuse to disclose information regarding the restrictions on transferring goods into Gaza. It should be noted that Israel permits some of the "prohibited" items into Gaza (for example: paper, biscuits, and chocolate), on the condition that they are for the use of international organizations, while requests from private merchants to purchase them are denied.

THE PYRRHIC VICTORY OF JAM AND HALVAH

*On Monday, June 7, 2010, Israel permitted jam, halvah, and shaving razors to enter Gaza, and it has said that it is willing to allow additional foods such as coriander, cardamom, and cookies into Gaza, after banning them for three years.

Gisha is pleased to learn that coriander no longer presents a threat to Israeli security.

However, Israel continues to prevent the transfer of purely civilian goods, such as fabrics, fishing rods, and food wrappers, as part of what it calls "economic warfare" aimed at crippling Gaza's economy. In doing so, it denies 1.5 million human beings the right to engage in productive, dignified work.

It is not enough to permit Gaza residents to purchase Israeli-made cookies. Israel should stop banning raw materials such as industrial margarine and glucose, so that Gaza residents can produce their own cookies and restart the economy that has been paralyzed for three years.

International law requires Israel to allow the free passage of goods and people into and out of the Gaza Strip, subject only to individual security checks.

Additional details about the Israeli restrictions on goods coming into Gaza are available in a position paper by Gisha, titled: *Restrictions on the transfer of goods to Gaza: Obstruction and obfuscation and in Gisha's Frequently Asked Questions on the closure.*

Prohibited Items	Permitted Items
sage (allowed as of May 25, 2010)	flour
coriander (allowed as of June 7, 2010)	sugar
spices (allowed as of June 7, 2010)	sweetener
jam (allowed as of June 7, 2010)	rice
halva (allowed as of June 7, 2010)	salt
vinegar (allowed as of June 27, 2010)	cooking oil
nutmeg (allowed as of June 22, 2010)	semolina
chocolate (allowed as of June 22, 2010)	yeast
fruit preserves (allowed as of June 9, 2010)	pasta
seeds and nuts (allowed as of June 22, 2010)	chickpeas
biscuits (allowed as of June 9, 2010)	beans
sweets (allowed as of June 22, 2010)	kidney beans
potato chips (allowed as of June 9, 2010)	lentils
gas for soft drinks	peas
dried fruit (allowed as of June 22, 2010)	bulgur wheat
fresh meat	corn
plaster	lupini beans
tar	powdered milk
wood for construction	dairy products
cement	margarine

Prohibited Items (contd.)

iron
glucose
industrial salt
plastic/glass/metal containers
industrial margarine
tarpaulin sheets for huts
fabric (for clothing)
flavor and smell enhancers
fishing rods
various fishing nets
buoys
ropes for fishing
nylon nets for greenhouses (allowed as of June 14, 2010)
spare parts for tractors
dairies for cowsheds
irrigation pipe systems
ropes to tie greenhouses (allowed as of June 14, 2010)
planters for saplings
heaters for chicken farms
musical instruments
size A4 paper
writing implements (allowed as of June 22, 2010)
notebooks
newspapers
toys (allowed as of June 22, 2010)
razors (allowed as of June 7, 2010)
sewing machines and spare parts
heaters
horses
donkeys
goats
cattle
chicks
towels (allowed as of June 22, 2010)
buttons (allowed as of June 13, 2010)
mattresses (allowed as of June 22, 2010)
kitchenware (allowed as of June 22, 2010)
perfume (allowed as of June 28, 2010)
cosmetic products (allowed as of June 28, 2010)

Permitted Items (contd.)

hummus paste
frozen meat, fish, and vegetables
vitamins and oil for animal feed
empty bags for flour
medicine and medical equipment
diapers
feminine hygiene products
toilet paper
baby wipes
shampoo and conditioner
soap and liquid soap
toothpaste
laundry detergent
fabric softener
dish soap
glass cleaner
floor cleaning fluid
cleaning liquid for bathroom
chlorine
insecticide for household use
coffee
tea
salami meat
canned meat
canned fish
sponges for cleaning dishes
sponges for washing
mopping rags
cleaning rags
all canned food except canned fruit
za'atar spice
black pepper
sesame
powdered chicken stock
blankets
matches
candles
brooms
mops
dustpans
trash cans
aniseed
chamomile
cinnamon

Permitted Items (contd.)

wastewater purification powder
glass – 200 trucks
water coolers and heaters
mineral water
tahini (sesame paste)
hair brushes
hair combs
shoes
clothes
wood (for doors and window
    frames)
aluminum
soft plastic bags
fruit
vegetables
hay
fertilized eggs
pesticides for agriculture
soil for agriculture
particles for soil dilution
chemical fertilizer
plastic buckets
plastic crates for fruits and
    vegetables
plastic chicken cages
egg cartons

GAZA: TREADING ON SHARDS

Sara Roy

"Do you know what it's like living in Gaza?" a friend of mine asked. "It is like walking on broken glass tearing at your feet."

On January 21, fifty-four House Democrats signed a letter to President Obama asking him to dramatically ease, if not end, the siege of Gaza. They wrote:

> The people of Gaza have suffered enormously since the blockade imposed by Israel and Egypt following Hamas's coup, and particularly following Operation Cast Lead.... The unabated suffering of Gazan civilians highlights the urgency of reaching a resolution to the Israeli-Palestinian conflict, and we ask you to press for immediate relief for the citizens of Gaza as an urgent component of your broader Middle East peace efforts.... Despite ad hoc easing of the blockade, there has been no significant improvement in the quantity and scope of goods allowed into Gaza.... The crisis has devastated livelihoods, entrenched a poverty rate of over 70%, increased dependence on erratic international aid, allowed the deterioration of public infrastructure, and led to the marked decline of the accessibility of essential services.

This letter is remarkable not only because it directly challenges the policy of the Israel lobby—a challenge no doubt borne of the extreme crisis confronting Palestinians, in which the United States has played an extremely damaging role—but also because it links Israeli security to Palestinian well-being. The letter concludes, "The people of Gaza, along with all the peoples of the region, must see that the United States is dedicated to addressing the legitimate security needs of the State of Israel and to ensuring that the legitimate needs of the Palestinian population are met."

I was last in Gaza in August 2009, my first trip since Israel's war on the territory one year ago. I was overwhelmed by what I saw in a place I have known intimately for nearly a quarter of a century: a land ripped apart and scarred, the lives of its people blighted. Gaza is decaying under the weight of continued devastation, unable to function normally. The resulting void is filled with vacancy and despair that subdues even those acts of resilience and optimism that still find some expression. What struck me most was the innocence of these people, over half of them children, and the indecency and criminality of their continued punishment.

The decline and disablement of Gaza's economy and society have been deliberate, the result of state policy—consciously planned, implemented, and enforced. Although Israel bears the greatest responsibility, the United States and the European Union, among others, are also culpable, as is the Palestinian Authority (P.A.) in the West Bank. All are complicit in the ruination of this gentle place. And just as Gaza's demise has been consciously orchestrated, so have the obstacles preventing its recovery.

Gaza has a long history of subjection that assumed new dimensions after Hamas's January 2006 electoral victory. Immediately after those elections, Israel and certain donor countries suspended contacts with the P.A., which was soon followed by the suspension of direct aid and the subsequent imposition of an international financial boycott of the P.A. By this time Israel had already been withholding monthly tax revenues and custom duties collected on behalf of the

Authority, had effectively ended Gazan employment inside Israel, and had drastically reduced Gaza's external trade.

With escalating Palestinian-Israeli violence, which led to the killing of two Israeli soldiers and the kidnapping of Corporal Gilad Shalit in June 2006, Israel sealed Gaza's borders, allowing for the entry of humanitarian goods only, which marked the beginning of the siege, now in its fourth year. Shalit's abduction precipitated a massive Israeli military assault against Gaza at the end of June, known as Operation Summer Rains, which initially targeted Gaza's infrastructure and later focused on destabilizing the Hamas-led government through intensified strikes on P.A. ministries and further reductions in fuel, electricity, water delivery, and sewage treatment. This near daily ground operation did not end until October 2006.

In June 2007, after Hamas's seizure of power in the Strip (which followed months of internecine violence and an attempted coup by Fatah against Hamas) and the dissolution of the national unity government, the P.A. effectively split in two: a de facto Hamas-led government—rejected by Israel and the West—was formed in Gaza, and the officially recognized government headed by President Mahmoud Abbas was established in the West Bank. The boycott was lifted against the West Bank P.A. but was intensified against Gaza.

Adding to Gaza's misery was the decision by the Israeli security cabinet on September 19, 2007, to declare the Strip an "enemy entity" controlled by a "terrorist organization." After this decision Israel imposed further sanctions that include an almost complete ban on trade and no freedom of movement for the majority of Gazans, including the labor force. In the fall of 2008 a ban on fuel imports into Gaza was imposed. These policies have contributed to transforming Gazans from a people with political and national rights into a humanitarian problem—paupers and charity cases who are now the responsibility of the international community.

Not only have key international donors, most critically the United

States and European Union, participated in the sanctions regime against Gaza, they have privileged the West Bank in their programmatic work. Donor strategies now support and strengthen the fragmentation and isolation of the West Bank and Gaza Strip—an Israeli policy goal of the Oslo process—and divide Palestinians into two distinct entities, offering largesse to one side while criminalizing and depriving the other. This behavior among key donor countries reflects a critical shift in their approach to the Palestine/Israel conflict from one that opposes Israeli occupation to one that, in effect, recognizes it. This can be seen in their largely unchallenged acceptance of Israel's settlement policy and the deepening separation of the West Bank and Gaza and isolation of the latter. This shift in donor thinking can also be seen in their unwillingness to confront Israel's de facto annexation of Palestinian lands and Israel's reshaping of the conflict to center on Gaza alone, which is now identified solely with Hamas and therefore as alien.

Hence, within the annexation (West Bank)/alien (Gaza Strip) paradigm, any resistance by Palestinians, be they in the West Bank or Gaza, to Israel's repressive occupation, including attempts at meaningful economic empowerment, are now considered by Israel and certain donors to be illegitimate and unlawful. This is the context in which the sanctions regime against Gaza has been justified, a regime that has not mitigated since the end of the war. Normal trade (upon which Gaza's tiny economy is desperately dependent) continues to be prohibited; traditional imports and exports have almost disappeared from Gaza. In fact, with certain limited exceptions, no construction materials or raw materials have been allowed to enter the Strip since June 14, 2007. Indeed, according to Amnesty International, only forty-one truckloads of construction materials were allowed to enter Gaza between the end of the Israeli offensive in mid-January 2009 and December 2009, although Gaza's industrial sector presently requires 55,000 truckloads of raw materials for needed reconstruction. Furthermore, in the year since they were banned, imports of diesel and petrol from Israel into Gaza for private or commercial use were allowed in small amounts only four times (although the United Nations Relief and Works Agency, UNRWA, periodically receives diesel and petrol supplies). By August 2009, 90 percent of Gaza's total population was subject to scheduled electricity cuts of four to eight hours per day, while the remaining 10 percent had no access to any electricity, a reality that has remained largely unchanged.

Gaza's protracted blockade has resulted in the near total collapse of the private sector. At least 95 percent of Gaza's industrial establishments (3,750 enterprises) were either forced to close or were destroyed over the past four years, resulting in a loss of between 100,000 and 120,000 jobs. The remaining 5 percent operate at 20 to 50 percent of their capacity. The vast restrictions on trade have also contributed to the continued erosion of Gaza's agricultural sector, which was exacerbated by the destruction of 5,000 acres of agricultural land and 305 agricultural wells during the war. These losses also include the destruction of 140,965 olive trees, 136,217 citrus trees, 22,745 fruit trees, 10,365 date trees, and 8,822 other trees.

Lands previously irrigated are now dry, while effluent from sewage seeps into the groundwater and the sea, making much of the land unusable. Many attempts by Gazan farmers to replant over the past year have failed because of the depletion and contamination of the water and the high level of nitrates in the soil. Gaza's agricultural sector has been further undermined by the buffer zone imposed by Israel on Gaza's northern and eastern perimeters (and by Egypt on Gaza's southern border), which contains some of the Strip's most fertile land. The zone is officially 300 meters wide and 55 kilometers long, but according to the United Nations, farmers entering within 1,000 meters of the border have sometimes been fired upon by the IDF. Approximately 30 to 40 percent of Gaza's total agricultural land is contained in the buffer zone. This has effectively forced the collapse of Gaza's agricultural sector.

These profound distortions in Gaza's economy and society

will—even under the best of conditions—take decades to reverse. The economy is now largely dependent on public-sector employment, relief aid, and smuggling, illustrating the growing informalization of the economy. Even before the war, the World Bank had already observed a redistribution of wealth from the formal private sector toward black market operators.

There are many illustrations, but one that is particularly startling concerns changes in the banking sector. A few days after Gaza was declared an enemy entity, Israel's banks announced their intention to end all direct transactions with Gaza-based banks and deal only with their parent institutions in Ramallah, in the West Bank. Accordingly, the Ramallah-based banks became responsible for currency transfers to their branches in the Gaza Strip. However, Israeli regulations prohibit the transfer of large amounts of currency without the approval of the Defense Ministry and other Israeli security forces. Consequently, over the past two years Gaza's banking sector has had serious problems in meeting the cash demands of its customers. This in turn has given rise to an informal banking sector, which is now controlled largely by people affiliated with the Hamas-led government, making Hamas Gaza's key financial middleman. Consequently, moneychangers, who can easily generate capital, are now arguably stronger than the formal banking system in Gaza, which cannot.

Another example of Gaza's growing economic informality is the tunnel economy, which emerged long ago in response to the siege, providing a vital lifeline for an imprisoned population. According to local economists, around two-thirds of economic activity in Gaza is presently devoted just to smuggling goods into (but not out of) Gaza. Even this lifeline may soon be diminished, as Egypt, apparently assisted by U.S. government engineers, has begun building an impenetrable underground steel wall along its border with Gaza in an attempt to reduce smuggling and control the movement of people. At its completion the wall will be six to seven miles long and fifty-five feet deep.

The tunnels, which Israel tolerates in order to keep the siege intact, have also become an important source of income for the Hamas government and its affiliated enterprises, effectively weakening traditional and formal businesses and the rehabilitation of a viable business sector. In this way, the siege on Gaza has led to the slow but steady replacement of the formal business sector by a new, largely black-market sector that rejects registration, regulation, or transparency and, tragically, has a vested interest in maintaining the status quo.

At least two new economic classes have emerged in Gaza, a phenomenon with precedents in the Oslo period: One has grown extremely wealthy from the black-market tunnel economy; the other consists of certain public-sector employees who are paid *not* to work (for the Hamas government) by the Palestinian Authority in the West Bank. Hence, not only have many Gazan workers been forced to stop producing by external pressures, there is now a category of people who are being rewarded for their lack of productivity—a stark illustration of Gaza's increasingly distorted reality. This in turn has led to economic disparities between the haves and have-nots that are enormous and visible, as seen in the almost perverse consumerism in restaurants and shops that are the domain of the wealthy.

Gaza's economy is largely devoid of productive activity in favor of a desperate kind of consumption among the poor and the rich, but it is the former who are unable to meet their needs. Billions in international aid pledges have yet to materialize, so the overwhelming majority of Gazans remain impoverished. The combination of a withering private sector and stagnating economy has led to high unemployment, which ranges from 31.6 percent in Gaza City to 44.1 percent in Khan Younis. According to the Palestinian Chamber of Commerce, the de facto unemployment rate is closer to 65 percent. At least 75 percent of Gaza's 1.5 million people now require humanitarian aid to meet their basic food needs, compared with around 30 percent ten years ago. The United Nations further reports that the number of Gazans living in abject poverty—meaning those who are totally unable to feed their families—has tripled to 300,000, or approximately 20 percent of the population.

Access to adequate amounts of food continues to be a critical problem, and appears to have grown more acute after the cessation of hostilities a year ago. Internal data from September 2009 through the beginning of January 2010, for example, reveal that Israel allows Gazans no more (and at times less) than 25 percent of needed food supplies, with levels having fallen as low as 16 percent. During the last two weeks of January, these levels declined even more. Between January 16 and January 29 an average of 24.5 trucks of food and supplies per day entered Gaza, or 171.5 trucks per week. Given that Gaza requires 400 trucks of food alone *daily* to sustain the population, Israel allowed in no more than 6 percent of needed food supplies during this two-week period. Because Gaza needs approximately 240,000 truckloads of food and supplies per year to "meet the needs of the population and the reconstruction effort," according to the Palestinian Federation of Industries, current levels are, in a word, obscene. According to the Food and Agriculture Organization and World Food Program, "The evidence shows that the population is being sustained at the most basic or minimum humanitarian standard." This has likely contributed to the prevalence of stunting (low height for age), an indicator of chronic malnutrition, which has been pronounced among Gaza's children younger than five, increasing from 8.2 percent in 1996 to 13.2 percent in 2006.

Gaza's agony does not end there. According to Amnesty International, 90 to 95 percent of the water supplied by Gaza's aquifer is "unfit for drinking." The majority of Gaza's groundwater supplies are contaminated with nitrates well above the acceptable WHO standard—in some areas six times that standard—or too salinated to use. Gaza no longer has any source of regular clean water. According to one donor account, "Nowhere else in the world has such a large number of people been exposed to such high levels of nitrates for such a long period of time. There is no precedent, and no studies to help us understand what happens to people over the course of years of nitrate poisoning," which is especially threatening to children. According to Desmond Travers, a co-author of the Goldstone report, "If these issues are not addressed, Gaza may not even be habitable by World Health Organization norms."

It is possible that high nitrate levels have contributed to some shocking changes in the infant mortality rate (IMR) among Palestinians in the Gaza Strip and West Bank. IMR, widely used as an indicator of population health, has stalled among Palestinians since the 1990s and now shows signs of increasing. This is because the leading causes of infant mortality have changed from infectious and diarrheal diseases to prematurity, low birth weight, and congenital malformations. These trends are alarming (and rare in the region), because infant mortality rates have been declining in almost all developing countries, including Iraq.

The people of Gaza know they have been abandoned. Some told me the only time they felt hope was when they were being bombed, because at least then the world was paying attention. Gaza is now a place where poverty masquerades as livelihood and charity as business. Yet, despite attempts by Israel and the West to caricature Gaza as a terrorist haven, Gazans still resist. Perhaps what they resist most is surrender: not to Israel, not to Hamas, but to hate. So many people still speak of peace, of wanting to resolve the conflict and live a normal life. Yet, in Gaza today, this is not a reason for optimism but despair.

NOT BY CEMENT ALONE

Amira Hass

The achievement of the failed flotilla to Gaza—mainly, it must be conceded, by its dead—is that the demand is being heard from everywhere that Israel halt its policy of siege. The government of Israel was not willing to listen to the desperate supplications of John Ging, the head of U.N. Relief and Works Agency in Gaza. Now it must heed French President Nicolas Sarkozy and Turkish Prime Minister Recep Tayyip Erdoğan. But unknowingly, this flotilla, like its predecessors and the ones still to come, serves the Israeli goal, which is to complete the process of separating the Gaza Strip from the West Bank. The process, it will be said here for the millionth time, started in 1991 and not after the rise of Hamas rule. Its purpose was to thwart the two-state solution, which the world understood at that time as based on all of Gaza and the West Bank, and the link between them.

Since the method of sailing to Gaza started about two years ago, none of its initiators purported to meet the need for this or that product. Israel is attempting by signs and wonders to prove there is no hunger in Gaza. The initiators are actually thinking about hunger of a different kind: a very human hunger for a direct link to the world, to freedom of movement of people, not just goods. The seaborne method was later switched to overland breaches to the Strip via Rafah, to Egypt's displeasure and Israel's joy.

Israel brought the closure to grotesque and petty proportions, attracting attention with its prohibition on macaroni and permission for cinnamon, the counting of calories and delaying cement even for a sewage treatment plant. Israel expanded the closure to the extent of prohibiting Gazans from working, creating, manufacturing, and earning a living, with the declared goal of bringing down Hamas. But it achieved the opposite. That rule only grew stronger, proving its resourcefulness, its ability to suppress internal opposition and engender support by international activists who are ideologically opposed to its methods and philosophy. The siege strengthened Hamas to such an extent that Palestinian conspiracy theorists are convinced this was Israel's intention from the outset.

Most Israelis, who have given up on real information, find it difficult to absorb that some people in the world are shocked at the existence of a huge prison whose warden is the Jewish state. But those who are shocked have become partners in the pressure campaign—supported, if not instigated by Hamas—against Egypt to unilaterally open the Rafah crossing, as if it is the occupier and not Israel.

And what serves the goal of separating Gaza from the West Bank better than forgetting the sealed Erez crossing between Gaza and Israel, and focusing on Rafah and cement? Unintentionally, the runners of the maritime and media blockade focused attention on aspects that do not undermine the essence of Israel's closure of Gaza. And that essence is denying the right and thwarting the will of Gazans to be an active, permanent, and natural part of Palestinian society.

Long before Israel prohibited the entry of cement into the Strip, it prohibited Gazans from studying in the West Bank. While it still permitted guavas to be exported from Khan Yunis to Jordan, it forbade Gazans to enter the West Bank even via the Allenby Bridge or to meet relatives and friends. Step by step, Israel developed draconian restrictions on Palestinians' freedom of movement, until it declared every Gazan in the West Bank, now and especially in the future, an illegal alien and an infiltrator. These are the essential prohibitions that must be breached. These are the prohibitions about whose existence Erdoğan and U.S. President Barack Obama must be taught, and their abolition demanded.

DIGGING BEHIND THE GAZA BLOCKADE

Nadia Hijab

Fact: Israel's policy of sealing Gaza from the rest of the world predates the Hamas takeover of the Strip in June 2007 and its victory in the 2006 Palestinian parliamentary elections. It started in the early 1990s, long before Hamas became the movement it is today. A quick dip in the history of the conflict helps understand what is going on in Gaza and the extent of the horror that human rights advocates have sought to challenge by sea.

A SNAPSHOT OF THE OCCUPATION

Soon after Israel occupied the West Bank, Gaza, and East Jerusalem in 1967, it began to integrate the economy and basic services of the territories into its own and to curtail their socioeconomic development, as Harvard scholar Sara Roy has carefully documented. Israel also attempted to crush resistance to occupation with an iron fist. For example, former Prime Minister Ariel "Bulldozer" Sharon ordered hundreds of homes bulldozed in 1970 to carve a street straight and wide enough for Israeli troops and armored vehicles to move through a refugee camp to chase resistance fighters. Demolishing homes en masse became one of the ongoing features of Israel's crush-and-control policies and the subject of in depth reports by Human Rights Watch and other organizations.

The first Palestinian intifada of 1987–1991 brought about a shift in

Israel's occupation policies. No longer able to control the population through the measures of the previous twenty years, Israel gradually began separating the Palestinian and Israeli populations. The "permit system" was introduced in Gaza in 1988, and the closure policy was first imposed in 1991. Closures were institutionalized after March 1993, Gaza was sealed off by an electronic wall in 1994, and a "pass system" was introduced in 1994, with passes given to less than 3 percent of the population in 1995. And these were the best years of the Palestinian-Israeli peace process launched in September 1993.

Up until Israel's redeployment from Gaza in the summer 2005, three blocs of Israeli settlements of some 6,000 Israeli settlers together with bypass roads and military bases directly controlled a third of the tiny Strip—twice the size of Washington, D.C.—leaving 1.1 million Palestinians in cantons in the remainder. After its withdrawal, Israel continued to besiege Gaza from land, sea, and air. Thus it remains, under international law, accountable for the welfare of the civilian population.

Israel maintains that its policies are intended to ensure security for its population. Yet Israel can never hope to feel secure so long as it is besieging Gaza and settling its people in the West Bank and East Jerusalem, in violation of international law, while avoiding the root causes of the conflict that began in 1948. Palestinians have resisted Israel's violations of their human rights, both violently and nonviolently. In effect, the violence of Israel's occupation has bred counterviolence. For example, it was on March 5, 2002, after thirty-five years of occupation, that the first Qassam rocket was launched into Israeli territory.

There is a much easier, more effective, way to achieve security until a just peace can be reached: a ceasefire. Ceasefires between Israel and Hamas have worked for months on end. Indeed, a formal ceasefire was in place before Israel launched its fierce attacks on Gaza in December 2008. Under the agreement, Hamas was to end the rocket attacks and Israel to lift the blockade. Hamas ended the attacks and prevented smaller groups from firing rockets. But Israel actually *tightened* its blockade although the ceasefire held for five months, as even the powerful pro-Israel lobby in the United States acknowledged. U.N. supplies were restricted to such an extent that the U.N. was unable to maintain its usual reserves and in November 2008 ran out of food for the first time since it had set up operations.

THE BLOCKADE'S IMPACT

The blockade in its present form began after Hamas won parliamentary elections in 2006, and was tightened after Hamas-Fatah clashes in June 2007 left Hamas in control of the Strip. Israel's measures were superimposed on an economy that was crumbling after forty years of occupation and siege. Humanitarian workers and human rights advocates have been warning since that the situation could tip from crisis to catastrophe at any time. For example, the *New York Times* reported on November 6, 2007, that Gazans faced a sewage disaster far greater than the overflow that killed five people in March that year, one that could affect as many as 250,000 Gazans. Without construction materials and electricity, it has not been possible to manage Gaza's sewage.

The blockade remained in place after Israel's massive attack on Gaza in December 2008 and January 2009, making it impossible to reconstruct thousands of homes and schools destroyed during the fighting. Some human rights activists began to refer to it as a "slow genocide." This may sound like an exaggeration, but the Palestinians in Gaza were already very vulnerable to disease, ill health, and malnutrition after years of siege, and were experiencing increases in cancers, deformed births, and preventable deaths. The infrastructure was rotten and water and food were contaminated. Any epidemic could have pushed them over the brink. In other words, Israel's blockade would not directly kill tens of thousands of Palestinians, but it would create the conditions for tens of thousands to die.

Does the siege, coming after years of occupation and de-development, constitute genocide? The Convention on the Prevention and Punishment of the Crime of Genocide—a clear, concise document adopted by the United Nations in December 1948—states that genocide is any of five acts committed "with intent to destroy, in whole or in part, a national, ethnical, racial or religious group."

Three acts appear to apply to the situation in Gaza: "(a) Killing members of the group; (b) Causing serious bodily or mental harm to members of the group; (c) Deliberately inflicting on the group conditions of life calculated to bring about its physical destruction in whole or in part."

Legal scholars disagree about how to interpret the Convention's articles and it has proven difficult, over the years, to define crimes as genocide, let alone to prevent or end them. In line with the Bosnia precedent—the only authoritative legal treatment of genocide to date—it would be necessary to establish *deliberate intent* for an accusation of genocide against Israel to stand up in court.

Israel's leadership has not, of course, issued a declaration of intent. However, many leading Israeli officials can be said to have done so. For example:

- Putting the Palestinians of Gaza "on a diet"—Dov Weisglass, chief aide to Ariel Sharon, in 2006.
- Exposing them to "a bigger shoah (Holocaust)"—Matan Vilnai, former deputy defense minister, in 2008.
- Issuing religious edits exhorting soldiers to show no mercy—the Israeli Army rabbinate during the December 2008–January 2009 conflict.

Whether the siege constitutes genocide or not is still under discussion, but what is clear is that the blockade is collective punishment and as such a violation of international law so grave that it could constitute a crime against humanity. The September 2009 report by

Justice Richard Goldstone and his team to the U.N. Human Rights Council said that depriving the Gaza Palestinians of their means of sustenance, employment, housing and water, freedom of movement, and access to a court of law, could amount to persecution and a competent court could find "that crimes against humanity have been committed."

By the spring of 2010, U.N. organizations had lined up to counter Israeli claims that there was no "humanitarian crisis." The World Health Organization warned that the health system was on the verge of collapse. The United Nations' humanitarian coordinator in the Occupied Palestinian Territories said that Gaza's agricultural sector was suffocating and noted that the "absurdity" of a situation in which Gaza's coastal population was forced to import fish through tunnels.

The most damning report of the time was that of the International Committee of the Red Cross. The ICRC rarely speaks out, but it clearly stated that the closure constituted collective punishment in clear violation of Israel's obligations under international humanitarian law. And, should anyone need affirmation that there is no such thing as a "better blockade," the ICRC said the hardship facing Gaza's Palestinians could not be addressed by providing more humanitarian aid: "The only sustainable solution is to lift the closure."

ACTING TO END INJUSTICE

Nevertheless, and despite the ICRC report, America and Israel began trying to devise a kinder, gentler blockade of Gaza to offset world outrage about Israel's May 31, 2010, attacks on the Freedom Flotilla of unarmed humanitarians challenging the illegality and immorality of the siege. As they tinkered with the edges, they ignored the much more fundamental way in which the unarmed humanitarians of the Freedom Flotilla challenged Israel's policies.

For decades, Israel has used the same strategy to achieve its objectives and to rout all challengers: overwhelming force. When the world

sees violence and counter-violence—even when Israel uses disproportionate force as in Beirut in 1982 and 2006 and Gaza in 2008—Israel claims self-defense and usually manages to spin the facts its way.
And, as it has not yet been held to account in any meaningful way, it
has seen no reason to change its strategy.

However, when Israel meets nonviolence with violence, the strategy backfires. Israel is pitching the self-defense line to try to shield
itself from criticism of its attack on the Freedom Flotilla—but it's not
working.

Things will continue to unravel because Israel only knows how to
use force to try to get its way. Ironically, its overkill has made the use
of force so costly for those who favor armed resistance that the stage
has been left clear for those who believe it is more effective to use civil
resistance against a vastly superior armed force. It should be noted
that Palestinian civil resistance is not new, although it has recently
been "discovered" by the mainstream media.

The first Palestinian intifada was almost completely nonviolent
and imposed itself on the world consciousness, making a powerful
case for Palestinian rights. Unfortunately, the then Palestinian leadership did not know how to translate the power it generated into diplomatic gains. That uprising was just one of a series of major acts of
civil resistance stretching back a century. In recent years, Palestinian
villagers' civil resistance against Israel's illegal wall in the West Bank
has also had an impact.

Since the December 2008 attack on Gaza, the boycott, divestment, and sanctions movement launched by Palestinian civil society
in 2005 has gained momentum, imposing both a financial and moral
cost on Israel's occupation and other violations of Palestinian human
rights. Richard Falk, the U.N. Special Rapporteur on the situation
of human rights in the Palestinian territories occupied since 1967,
speaks of a battle of legitimacy that Israel is losing in spite of its military prowess.

The real dilemma for Israel is that all of the force it brings to bear

is aimed at achieving the unachievable: keeping the territories it occupied in 1967, illegal under international law; privileging Jews over
non-Jews within Israel, in violation of the United Nations Charter
and international conventions; and denying Palestinian refugees their
right of return. Imaginations are fired and energies rekindled by the
power of nonviolence to limit the violence of power. There are only
two alternatives for Israel: to make its peace with justice and equality,
or to experience growing and costly isolation.

ISRAEL ITSELF MAY BE AMONG
THE VICTIMS OF ITS OWN PATHOLOGY

Eyad Al Sarraj

Resorting to brute force is an expression of fear. Its deployment yesterday by the Israeli soldiers who raided and opened fire on the Freedom Flotilla en route to Gaza, killing nine civilians and injuring dozens more, will not serve Israel or treat its existential anxiety.

As a psychiatrist and a resident of Gaza, I understand Israel's reflexive use of force against civilians as a symptom of a structural pathology. Israel resorts to the use of maximum force as a form of intimidation. But this is the choice of the weak. It is quite possible that through Israel's actions, it is tightening its own noose.

More than a decade ago Prime Minister Benjamin Netanyahu published a book defending Israel's right to "a place under the sun." But it is the racist desire to create "a nation above nations" that is the desire of Zionist extremists. In this context, peace is anathema; the siege and war on Gaza are legitimate and justified; Israel will use every possible means to avoid reaching a peace agreement with the Palestinians. Indeed, Israel is marching rapidly toward becoming an apartheid state.

Due to the Israeli blockade of Gaza, the unemployment rate in the Strip is near 50 percent. The World Bank has stated that 90 percent of water in Gaza is not suitable for human consumption, 80 percent of the population lives on less than a dollar a day, and 70 percent depend on charity for food supplies. Chronic malnutrition affects 15 percent of Gaza's children, and its serious consequences for their cognition and growth will be felt for years to come. The boats that the Israeli soldiers attacked were carrying food, medicines, and materials to build prefabricated homes for the people of Gaza. The Freedom Flotilla was a new attempt to break this Israeli blockade, condemned by the human rights community the world over.

Former U.S. President Jimmy Carter has called the blockade an assault on civilization. Justice Richard Goldstone has rightly called Israeli actions crimes against humanity. So many voices, including those of many Jews, have called upon Israel to end this draconian siege.

One and a half million Palestinians remain prisoners of the largest open-air jail on earth since Israel's siege on Gaza began in December of 2008. Then, Israel's army demolished 15,000 homes, destroyed factories and ministries, and chopped off the minarets from mosques. Even the American School in Gaza, a sprawling establishment, was completely destroyed and Israel bombed schools run by the United Nations. Israel used illegal weapons against the people of Gaza during this war, killing hundreds and wounding thousands of civilians including children.

The attack on the Freedom Flotilla is just the latest act of Israel's violence. Now there is defiance in the streets of Gaza from people who demand that the world force Israel to respect them as human beings.

For the Palestinians, this is the time for us to be reunited. It is doubtful if Palestinian factions will rise to the occasion and end their internal strife as their political alliances dictate otherwise. It is also doubtful that many Arab regimes will heed the calls from the people of Gaza, as they are not independent from external political and economic pressure.

Yet the mass killing of those on board the freedom boats has drawn condemnation around the globe with critical statements from the United Nations and from European capitals. Israel's action may reinforce calls to boycott its products. This could be a turning point in the struggle to end the siege and the Israeli occupation.

1,000 DAYS

Raji Sourani

The Israeli attacks on the Gaza Freedom Flotilla, and the killing of nine passengers on board the *Mavi Marmara*, focused international attention on the closure of the Gaza Strip, forcing the issue onto the front pages of the world's media outlets. Israel has subjected Gaza to varying forms of illegal closure since 1991. In its current form, the closure of Gaza has been enforced by Israel for three years—over 1,000 consecutive days during which the Gaza Strip has been closed off from the rest of the world. Prior to the naval attack, most politicians and media outlets had chosen to ignore this reality; the killing of nine civilians in international waters meant that this was no longer possible.

However, as talks progress regarding the "easing" of the closure, it is important to highlight two issues: First, there are no partial violations of international law, the closure is an illegal form of collective punishment that must be ended entirely; second, the closure is only one manifestation of Israel's illegal policies and must be viewed in the broader context of other violations of international law perpetrated by Israeli forces.

For fifteen years, the Palestinian Center for Human Rights (PCHR) has been Palestine's foremost human rights organization. Our experience has taught us that in order to end these violations of international law—and to alleviate the suffering of civilians—there must be legal accountability. Those responsible for the commission of war crimes—for the death, injury, and suffering of innocent civilians—must be held to account. The only consequence of continued impunity is the ongoing and escalating violation of international law, as evidenced by the current reality of life in the Occupied Palestinian Territories (OPT). Concomitant to this legal accountability there must also be responsibility. The international community must face up to its legal and moral obligations; it can no longer allow Israel to exist as a state above the law, subject to different standards and pervasive exceptionalism. Individual states must fulfill their legal obligation "to ensure respect" for international humanitarian law "in all circumstances." International law should be the foundation of all activity; it cannot continue to be disregarded in the name of a nebulous and elusive "peace process."

Israel has subjected the Gaza Strip to a closure policy since 1991; however, its current, most extreme form, has been applied continuously since June 14, 2007, following the Hamas takeover of the Gaza Strip. The ever-tightening closure has resulted in the economic and cultural suffocation of the local population of 1.5 million Palestinians; a population that was also subject to the illegal attacks of Israel's Operation Cast Lead, an offensive which killed over 1,400 Palestinians, and decimated the infrastructure of the Gaza Strip. The combined effect of the three-year closure and the Israeli attacks on Palestinian civilians and civilian property during Cast Lead has resulted in an entirely preventable humanitarian crisis, but perhaps more importantly, Palestinians in Gaza are experiencing an ongoing crisis of dignity, self-determination, and human rights for which they see no apparent remedy. The lack of accountability for war crimes and human rights violations committed in the OPT in general and in Gaza in particular has given Palestinians the sense that the rule of law does not apply to their suffering, that they are effectually without rights. At the same time, Israel, the main perpetrator of rights violations in Gaza, is protected by an international conspiracy of silence, resulting in a culture of impunity. As long as Israeli violations of international human rights and humanitarian law are not met with the appropriate response from the international community, Israel will continue to carry out attacks like those on the civilians on the *Mavi Marmara*. Over the course of the Israeli attacks on Gaza between December 27, 2008, and January 18, 2009, Israeli forces committed crimes against Palestinian civilians in the OPT on a scale unseen since 1967, when Israel first occupied the West Bank and Gaza Strip. Israeli forces killed 1,419 Palestinians, and wounded over 5,300. The vast majority of those killed were civilians entitled to full protection and immunity from attack under international humanitarian law (1,167 protected persons, 82.2 percent); 326 were children, and 111 were women. This figure includes the 251 noncombatant police officers killed during the offensive. However, Operation Cast Lead was merely the most brutal manifestation of Israel's longstanding illegal policy, and each of the underlying crimes have been consistent features of the occupation. The number of Palestinians killed by Israeli military forces and Israeli settlers in the West Bank and the Gaza Strip from the beginning of the second intifada in September 2000 until the end of December 2009 thus totals 6,520, including 4,955 civilians; tens of thousands of others have been wounded.

In spite of Israel's declaration of a unilateral ceasefire in Gaza on January 18, 2009, and the effective cessation of military operations by Palestinian resistance groups, Israeli forces continued to commit violations against the population of the Gaza Strip. The Gaza Strip was exposed to air bombardment, shelling from the sea and land incursions on a near-daily basis. Between the end of the offensive and the end of 2009, forty-seven Palestinians were killed, including twenty-six civilians, seven of whom were children. Twelve of these civilians were killed during times of complete calm by Israeli snipers in the "buffer zone" to the east and north of the Gaza Strip, and five others were killed when Israeli forces targeted and bombed tunnels along the border between the Gaza Strip and Egypt. In addition, at least twenty-seven patients awaiting medical treatment abroad died in 2009 due to the delays in the complicated process of applying for permission to exit Gaza for treatment.

In the West Bank, a similar reality exists, as Israel continues its settlement activities and attempts to perpetuate an apartheid system, turning Palestinian communities into isolated Bantustans. Here, Israeli forces killed eighteen Palestinians in 2009, including fifteen civilians, six of whom were children. Israeli settlers killed three Palestinian civilians, including two children. All civilian victims were killed at times when they did not pose a threat to the lives of Israeli soldiers, including during protests against the confiscation of Palestinian land or incursions into Palestinian communities.

As Jewish settlements, built on occupied territory in violation of international law, expand and the roads serving them cut through Palestinian lands, hundred of checkpoints and roadblocks obstruct the movement of Palestinians. The Israeli military controls the access points to the so-called Area A (Palestinian cities, nominally under Palestinian control) and carries out incursions every night. Armed Israeli settlers, protected by the army, continue to commit crimes against Palestinian civilians and property. Additionally, Israel continues to take measures aimed at consolidating the illegal annexation and isolation of East Jerusalem through the creation of a Jewish demographic majority in Jerusalem. This is achieved by making it extremely difficult—in effect impossible—for Palestinian Jerusalemites to obtain building permits, by demolishing "illegally" built homes, by expelling Palestinians from their homes to allow Jewish settlers to move in, and by revoking residency permits from those Jerusalemites who are unable to prove their continuous presence in the city.

In 2009, Israel continued to arrest Palestinians during house raids, especially in the West Bank, and incursions into Palestinian towns, villages, and refugee camps across the West Bank and Gaza Strip. Hundreds of Palestinians were arrested at Israeli military checkpoints and roadblocks. In 2009, Israeli forces arrested approximately 5,000 Palestinians, including 1,000 from the Gaza Strip. Arrest campaigns continued to target political leaders and representatives of the Palestinian people. At the end of 2009, Israel continued to detain at least twenty-six members of the Palestinian Legislative Council, the majority of whom are of the Change and Reform parliamentary bloc of Hamas. Israeli forces also arrested a number of civil society activists for their work in defending human rights, particularly those activists involved in peaceful protests against the construction of the Apartheid Wall and settlements. As noted above, this illegal reality is allowed to persist and to evolve as a result of Israeli impunity. In response, all national and international human rights organizations have consistently and clearly called for accountability. Most recently, this call was emphatically stated by the U.N. Fact-Finding Mission on the Gaza Conflict (in the so-called Goldstone report). Indeed, it was the realization that the "prolonged situation of impunity has created a justice crisis in the Occupied Palestinian Territories that warrants action" that formed the basis for the report's recommendations. The Fact-Finding Mission laid out specific, detailed, and practicable mechanisms through which impunity could be combated and justice pursued. Significantly, the mission also stated clearly that "justice and respect for the rule of law are the indispensable basis for peace."

These recommendations were a landmark in the history of the OPT, and they offered the tangible possibility of effective legal remedy.

However, instead of seizing this opportunity, the United States and the majority of members of the European Union failed to demand follow-up or implementation of the recommendations made by the Goldstone mission. The major world powers thus failed to enforce the rule of law and instead further fostered a culture of impunity for Israeli violations of international law. Thus, the international community helped to create an atmosphere whereby Israel is encouraged to violate the law, resulting in an increasing disregard for even the most basic and fundamental legal principles. This disregard—some might say callousness—is evidenced, inter alia, by the attack on the

Freedom Flotilla, settlement construction and expansion, and the continued collective punishment of Gaza's 1.5 million inhabitants.

The participants of the Gaza Freedom Flotilla, civil society activists from forty countries, sought to express their solidarity with the victimized population of Gaza and alleviate the suffering caused by the Israeli-imposed closure. Given the totality of the closure, a sea entrance was the only possible route. The group aimed to convey a simple message in support of the protection of civilians as outlined in the Fourth Geneva Convention, in support of the enforcement of international human rights and humanitarian law, and against human-made suffering. Their ammunition in this noble cause was made up of "prohibited" items such as food, medicine, schoolbooks, and wheelchairs.

The killings carried out in international waters during the early hours of Monday, May 31, 2010, represented a despicable form of state criminality. The nature of this act demonstrates how far the Israeli government has strayed from its obligations under international law. The threats voiced by high-ranking Israeli officials in advance of the convoy's departure show that the events were not an accident; indeed, the commandos involved had been training for the attack for at least a week. Israel and those individuals responsible must be held accountable for this war crime, in which its military forces killed and injured numerous civilians attempting to deliver humanitarian aid. In its clear response to the killings, Turkey gave the United States and the members of the European Union a lesson in accountability in its support of the rule of law. The international community must take the lead in conducting independent, impartial, and credible investigations, as demanded by the U.N. Security Council. Given Israel's track record and systematic shortcomings regarding independent investigations members of its armed forces have allegedly committed, internal Israeli investigations cannot be accepted. The underlying issues at stake in this despicable crime, which attained so much international attention, are the need to end the Israeli occupation of Palestinian territory and to realize the Palestinian right to self-determination. Yet until 'these materialize, the illegal closure of the Gaza Strip must be lifted in order to end the socioeconomic strangulation of the 1.5 million Palestinians living in the Gaza Strip. Furthermore, there must finally be accountability—otherwise the international community risks setting yet another precedent showing that Israel will be granted unconditional impunity.

If the Goldstone report had not been vetoed, if the international community had fulfilled its obligation to enforce international humanitarian law, and if the rule of law were respected, it is almost certain that the unjustifiable bloodshed in the Mediterranean could have been prevented. Had Israel been held accountable for its systematic disregard of Palestinian civilians' inherent dignity and human rights, instead of being rewarded for its violations of international human rights and humanitarian law, it surely would not have dared to violently attack, kill, and injure foreign civilians on a peaceful mission in international waters.

WHAT IS NOT ALLOWED

Richard Tillinghast

No tinned meat is allowed, no tomato paste,
no clothing, no shoes, no notebooks.
These will be stored in our warehouses at Kerem Shalom
until further notice.

Bananas, apples, and persimmons are allowed into Gaza,
peaches and dates, and now macaroni
(after the American Senator's visit).
These are vital for daily sustenance.
But no apricots, no plums, no grapes, no avocados, no jam.
These are luxuries and are not allowed.

Paper for textbooks is not allowed.
The terrorists could use it to print seditious material.
And why do you need textbooks
now that your schools are rubble?
No steel is allowed, no building supplies, no plastic pipe.
These the terrorists could use to launch rockets
against us.

Pumpkins and carrots you may have,
but no delicacies,
no cherries, no pomegranates, no watermelon, no onions,
no chocolate.
We have a list of three dozen items that are allowed,
but we are not obliged to disclose its contents.
This is the decision arrived at

by Colonel Levi, Colonel Rosenzweig, and Colonel Segal.
Our motto:
"No prosperity, no development, no humanitarian crisis."

You may fish in the Mediterranean,
but only as far as three km from shore.
Beyond that and we open fire.
It is a great pity the waters are polluted—
twenty million gallons of raw sewage dumped into the sea every day
is the figure given.
Our rockets struck the sewage treatment plants,
and at this point spare parts to repair them are not allowed.

As long as Hamas threatens us,
no cement is allowed, no glass, no medical equipment.
We are watching you from our pilotless drones
as you cook your sparse meals over open fires
and bed down
in the ruins of houses destroyed by tank shells.

And if your children can't sleep,
missing the ones who were killed in our incursion,
or cry out in the night, or wet their beds
in your makeshift refugee tents,
or scream, feeling pain in their amputated limbs—
that's the price you pay for harboring terrorists.
God gave us this land.
A land without a people for a people without a land.

4. INSIDE ISRAEL

LEXICON OF MOST MISLEADING TERMS
IN ISRAEL/PALESTINE CONFLICT

Amira Hass

- *Humanitarian crisis.* "There is no humanitarian crisis in Gaza," official Israeli spokesmen such as Defense Minister Ehud Barak and Foreign Ministry director general Yossi Gal say repeatedly. And they are correct, because a crisis is a sudden change, a deviation from a norm, while what's going on in Gaza has become the routine.

  They are right also about the "humanitarian" aspect, if what they mean is that hundreds of thousands are not dying of thirst or hunger. There is no humanitarian crisis, if you think that all a person needs is a set number of daily calories. And for someone who lives in Jerusalem or Tel Aviv, it is easy to ignore the non-crisis-like fact that 90 percent of the water produced in the Gaza Strip from its only water source—part of the coastal aquifer—is not fit for human consumption. People who do not get purified water are risking their health—high blood pressure, and kidney and intestinal diseases. Indeed, only thanks to the extended-family support system, charitable organizations, the U.N. Relief and Works Agency, international aid programs, public-sector wages, and the "tunnel economy" are people not being starved.

  But what about a person's need for freedom of movement, a person's right to create, to produce, to earn a living and study, to leave for timely medical treatment, and to travel? The spokes-people and P.R. professionals who try to prove things are fine reduce human needs to a graph containing only water, food, and shelter. These graphs tell more about their presenters than they do about human beings.

- *"Israel transfers humanitarian aid to the Gaza Strip."* This is a routine statement that leads many to conclude that Israel pays for the Gazans' food and medicine that do enter the Strip. This is a mistaken conclusion, but it might be based on an accurate perception of the situation: In prison, the warden is responsible for providing the inmates' food. But not in the 360-square-kilometer Gaza prison, which houses 1.5 million people. What we should be saying is, "Israel permits basic commodities to enter Gaza." Some are ordered, paid for, and distributed by international organizations. Most are sold to Gaza merchants, who sell them in the markets, stores, and pharmacies.

- *Closures/ "A closure was imposed"/ "A closure was lifted."* Once, before the disengagement from Gaza in 2005, these misleading definitions included the Gaza Strip. Now they refer to only the West Bank. On the eve of every Israeli holiday, the radio news reports that "a closure has been imposed on Judea and Samaria." And then it is lifted. That is also the source for the strange plural form, *closures.* A closure comes and a closure goes, and in between everything is fine.

But the *closure* has been in effect since it was declared in January 1991. Since then, all the Palestinians in the West Bank and Gaza Strip have been deprived of the right to freedom of movement. Since then, they have been subject to a complicated regime of permits that is becoming ever more sophisticated. Israel decides which categories of people get permits to move around and determines the number of people in every category. It is always a small minority that gets to move, and always under restrictive conditions. Meanwhile,

Jewish settlers in that very same territory come and go without permits.

- *"In 2002 when the West Bank was reoccupied."* One hears this fairly often from Palestinian spokesmen. This is an extremely senseless statement, even when replaced by "...when the Israel Defense Forces reoccupied the towns of the West Bank." When the Palestinian Authority was established in 1994, the Israeli occupation and its far-reaching authority was not abolished. When IDF troops left West Bank towns at the end of 1995, the presence of armed Palestinian policemen did not make the towns un-occupied. When the P.A. took responsibility for most . of the Palestinian population and its health, sewage, and education problems, it did not receive the authority and resources of a state. Israel still has these. And the sovereign has remained the IDF—in 1996, in 2002, and today.

- *A nonviolent struggle.* The IDF rejects Palestinian and international claims that the fight against the separation fence is a "nonviolent struggle." The IDF is correct. This should be immediately erased from the lexicon. *Nonviolent* is not an appropriate term for the demonstrations at Na'alin, Bil'in, Nabi Salah, Walaja, Maasra, Iraq Burin, and the others to come. But this is not due to the reasons given by the army and other Israeli officials. *Violent* has a negative connotation, of course, implying the unjustified use of force, which goes against the existing order and the values of civilization.

When we define the struggle against foreign rule as *nonviolent* or *violent*, it's as if we have asked the occupied to prove their resistance is kosher (or not). And to whom? The very foreign ruler who considers boycotting settlement products to be unkosher. The adjectives *nonviolent* and *violent* presume that the occupation is a natural state of affairs, whose violence is permitted, a civilized norm meant to tame its subjects. A *nonviolent struggle* therefore diverts attention from the fact that forced rule is based on the use of violence. Every soldier at a roadblock, every camera on the separation fence, every military edict, a supermarket in a settlement, and an Israeli diaper factory on Palestinian land—they are all part of the nonstop violence.

"NO CITIZENSHIP WITHOUT LOYALTY!"

Neve Gordon

I.

In Israel, almost all of the protests against the navy's assault on the relief flotilla took place in Palestinian space. Palestinian citizens in almost every major town and city, from Nazareth to Sachnin and from Arabe to Shfaram, demonstrated against the assault that left nine people dead and many more wounded. The one-day general strike called for by the Palestinian leadership within Israel was, for the most part, adhered to only by Arab citizens.

In Jewish space, by contrast, business continued as usual. Except for a demonstration in front of the Ministry of Defense in Tel Aviv, which brought together a few hundred activists, the only site where there was some sign of a grassroots protest against the raid was on Israeli university campuses. While numerically these protests were also insignificant—there were fewer than 2,000 demonstrators from all the different campuses, out of a student body of more than 200,000—they were extremely important both because they took place within Jewish space and because the protestors were Jews and Palestinians standing side by side.

Perhaps because of the widespread international condemnation of the attack on the flotilla, the Israeli police were relatively careful when handling these protests. Their caution is particularly striking when compared with the police reaction during the war on Gaza.

Twelve students from the Technion and Haifa University were none-theless arrested, and one at Ben-Gurion University was detained by undercover agents.

There was a visceral response to these campus protests, however, from pro-government students. Counter-demonstrations were im-mediately organized, bringing together much larger crowds that rallied around the flag. While demonstrations and counter-demon-strations are usually a sign of a healthy politics, in this case the pro-government demos revealed an extremely disturbing trend in Israeli society.

A group of opposition students from Ben-Gurion University pre-pared a big banner on the street near their off-campus apartment: 15 Dead. The Israeli government, as usual, has its reasons, and the Zionist majority, as usual, extends its support. Their neighbors spat on them and called them "cunts," "whores," and "traitors who love Arabs" until the students fled.

The following morning these students and their friends rolled the same banner down from the administration building, initiating a third wave of protests on campus. Both those opposing and those supporting the Israeli government use Facebook to tell their friends about these spontaneous demonstrations, and so within minutes a couple of hundred students from both sides of the fray had gathered and were shouting chants in the middle of campus.

A Palestinian student with a Palestinian flag was shoved and had his flag torn from him by some of the pro-government protesters, who were chanting, "No citizenship without loyalty!" In response, the Jewish and Palestinian oppositionists shouted, "No, no, it will not come, fascism will not come!" and "Peace is not achieved on the bod-ies of those killed!"

At one point a Jewish provocateur, who is not a member of any group (and could even be a police agent), raised his hand in the air: "Heil Lieberman!" The response of the pro-government students was immediate: "Death to the Arabs!" Luckily the university security managed to create a wedge between the protesters, and in this way prevented the incident from becoming even more violent.

Pro-government students interviewed in the press said they were "shocked to see faculty members, together with students from the left and Arab students shouting slogans against Israel." Their classmates posted pictures of the protests on Facebook, asking likeminded students to "identify their classroom 'friends.'"

A Facebook group was created to call for my resignation: By the end of the day more than 1,000 people had joined. As well as hoping that I die and demanding that my family be stripped of our citizenship and exiled from Israel, members of this Facebook group offer more pragmatic suggestions, such as the need to concentrate efforts on getting rid of teaching assistants who are critical of the government, since it is more difficult to have me—as a tenured professor—fired.

What is troubling about these pro-government students is not that they are pro-government, but the way they attack anyone who thinks differently from them, along with their total lack of self-criticism or restraint. If this is how students at Israel's best universities respond, what can we expect from the rest of the population?

II.

One day in June, hundreds of students demonstrated in front of Ben-Gurion University's administration building. About a third of the protestors were expressing their opposition to the government's decision to attack the relief flotilla, while the remaining two-thirds came to support the government. At one point the pro-government protesters began chanting, "No citizenship without loyalty!"

While loyalty is no doubt an important form of relationship both in the private and public spheres, unpacking its precise meaning in the Israeli context reveals that a total inversion of the democratic understanding of politics has occurred.

As Israeli citizens, Prime Minister Benjamin Netanyahu and

Foreign Minister Avigdor Lieberman want us to prove our loyalty to the flag by supporting a policy of oppression and humiliation. We must champion the separation barrier in Bil'in and in other places throughout the West Bank. We have to defend the brutal destruction of unrecognized Bedouin villages, and the ongoing land grab both inside Israel and in the Occupied Palestinian Territories. We must support the checkpoints and the silent transfer in East Jerusalem. We are also expected to bow our heads and remain silent every time government ministers, Knesset members, and public officials make racist statements against Arabs. We must support the neoliberal policies that continuously oppress Israel's poor, and we are obliged to give our blessing to the blockade and the imprisonment of Gaza Strip's 1.5 million residents.

Hearing the chants at the recent demonstration at my university, I understood that I will never be able to accept this form of loyalty. I refuse, after all, to be loyal to a policy of humiliation, racism, and discrimination. I am neither loyal to the settlers nor to house demolitions. I cannot be loyal to the silencing of opposition and to the oppression of the needy and destitute. I am not loyal to the blockade on Gaza and the expulsion of Palestinian residents in Jerusalem. And certainly, I am unwilling to be loyal to the killing of children.

And yet, loyalty is an important issue that urgently needs to be discussed because ultimately there is a firm link between the state and loyalty. The pressing questions are: What is the nature of this link? What is the meaning of loyalty? And who is supposed to be loyal to whom? Perhaps surprisingly, the answer to these questions is not particularly complex. We need to demand loyalty from the state to all of its citizens, without distinction of race, color, sex, gender, language, religion, political opinions, national or social origin, property, or birth status. In other words, I agree with the loyalty requirement, but because I am a follower of the republican rather than the fascist tradition, I am obliged to resist the Duce's logic which some of our leaders have adopted and insist, instead, that the state serve all of its citizens.

A state that is loyal to its citizens does not discriminate between Jews and Arabs, does not expropriate land from Muslims and Christians, does not humiliate and trample the lower classes, and does not brutally oppress the Palestinians in the Occupied Territories. A state of this sort protects the rights of all of its citizens and thus will not need to demand loyalty because it will receive loyalty on a silver platter.

Yes, I too understand the importance of loyalty. But the appropriate chant is not "No citizenship without loyalty!" but rather "Loyalty to every citizen!"

ISRAEL'S COMMANDO COMPLEX

Doron Rosenblum

It is impossible to understand or explain Israel's passive-aggressive responses to the flotilla crisis without reference to the ground from which its current leaders emerged. Both the prime minister and the defense minister are dyed-in-the-wool creatures of military operations. Both were steeped in the instant-heroism mentality and the commando spirit: the ethos in which a military force shows up at the height of a crisis like a deus ex machina and in a single stroke slices through the Gordian knot.

Defense Minister Ehud Barak's public image grew out of the 1972 rescue of a hijacked Sabena passenger plane, during which he was seen standing on the wing of the aircraft waving his pistol. And one cannot imagine the political career of Prime Minister Benjamin Netanyahu without Operation Entebbe and the myth-cloaked death of his brother Yoni, a mission so glorious and electrifying that its inspiring charge alone could turn his brother into a star, both as Mr. Terror and as a veteran of Sayeret Matkal, the Israel Defense Forces general staff's elite special-operations force.

Those 1970s rescue operations were seen as the continuation of the largest and most miraculous one of all, the Six-Day War. Although decades have passed since the moral high was injected into our veins, our leaders have never stopped trying to reconstruct it in order to atone for their ineffectiveness as statesmen. And the greater the number of successive failed missions, the greater the longing for the next redemptive mission that would heal the trauma and the bad trip of its predecessor. The next jackpot always appeared to be around the corner: if not in Lebanon, then in Gaza; if not in Gaza, then in Iran.

Netanyahu and Barak came into power for the second time, despite each man's record of failure, on the wings of two contradictory, or complementary, hopes: first, that in combination they would deliver the goods and create the redemptive operation to end all operations, the smartest one of all; second, that they of all people—and not civilian leaders such as Ehud Olmert, Shimon Peres or Amir Peretz, who felt a need to overreact militarily—could gain the maturity necessary for an act of diplomatic courage. But so far they haven't fulfilled either hope. They have demonstrated both a total absence of courage and inspiration in the diplomatic sphere and an absence of creativity in the use of force. So what's left?

The failure of the flotilla operation is less troubling than the national jonesing that has followed it: the frenetic flitting between the poles of reflexive victimhood ("Oy oy oy, they resisted, they had knives, swords, and other weapons, the activists who were killed were big-bodied") and of inert heroism (praise for the restraint and sensitivity that resulted in only nine and not 600 deaths; the desperate attempt to cling to the vestiges of the myths of military prowess and the increased stifling of criticism with the slogan "Quiet, we're saluting"). All of these, together with a great sense of missed opportunity: the illusion that a successful operation—difficult to define and to imagine in any event—would have relieved, even temporarily, a certain existential angst.

All these responses were more intense this week, although in fact they are constant. They are the responses of addicts who are repeatedly denied their fix: the perfect IDF operation, or the decisive war, which will stifle any question and complaints (and any need for statesmanship).

Some point to a sea change in the Palestinian, and even the Hamas, leadership, saying that they have finally discovered the advantages of propaganda and statesmanship over violence and terror. Instead of en-couraging and wholeheartedly adopting this approach, Israel, which hasn't changed its thought patterns for decades, is caught by surprise and even dismayed. (Recently an intelligence official actually called the absence of Palestinian terror a "propaganda problem.") In the ab-sence of statesmanship, all Israel can offer is another clumsy opera-tion in which it comes off looking like some relic from the 1970s and '80s with a commando knife between its teeth. Even worse: It looks like Avigdor Lieberman, Eli Yishai, Moshe Ya'alon, and all the rest.

Israel has always complained, condescendingly, that the neigh-bors it is forced to deal with are Arabs rather than Norwegians and Swedes. Now, when it is dealing with Europeans and the entire world, Israel can see how it itself is perceived—and to blush furiously. If it still can.

THE DEADLY CLOSING OF THE ISRAELI MIND

Ilan Pappé

At the top of Israel's political and military systems stand two men, Ehud Barak and Benjamin Netanyahu, who are behind the brutal attack on the Gaza flotilla that shocked the world but that seemed to be hailed as a pure act of self-defense by the Israeli public.

Although they come from the left (Defense Minister Barak from the Labor Party) and the right (Prime Minister Netanyahu from Likkud) of Israeli politics, their thinking on Gaza in general and on the flotilla in particular is informed by the same history and an identical worldview.

At one time, Ehud Barak was Benjamin Netanyahu's commanding officer in the Israeli equivalent of the Special Air Service in the British Army. More precisely, they served in a similar unit to the one sent to assault the Turkish ship last week. Their perception of the reality in the Gaza Strip is shared by other leading members of the Israeli political and military elite, and is widely supported by the Jewish electorate at home.

And it is a simple take on reality. Hamas, although the only government in the Arab world elected democratically by the people, has to be eliminated as a political as well as a military force. This is not only because it continues the struggle against the forty-year Israeli occupation of the West Bank and the Gaza Strip by launching primitive missiles into Israel—more often than not in retaliation to an Israel killing of its activists in the West Bank. But it is mainly due to its political opposition for the kind of "peace" Israel wants to impose on the Palestinians.

The forced peace is not negotiable as far as the Israeli political elite is concerned, and it offers the Palestinians a limited control and sovereignty in the Gaza Strip and in parts of the West Bank. The Palestinians are asked to give up their struggle for self-determination and liberation in return for the establishment of three small Bantustans under tight Israeli control and supervision.

The official thinking in Israel, therefore, is that Hamas is a formidable obstacle for the imposition of such a peace. And thus the declared strategy is straightforward: starving and strangulating into submission the 1.5 million Palestinians living in the densest space in the world.

The blockade imposed in 2006 is supposed to lead the Gazans to replace the current Palestinian government with one which would accept Israel's dictate—or at least would be part of the more dormant Palestinian Authority in the West Bank. In the meantime, Hamas captured an Israeli soldier, Gilad Shalit, and so the blockade became tighter. It included a ban of the most elementary commodities, without which human beings find it difficult to survive. For want of food and medicine, for want of cement and petrol, the people of Gaza live in conditions that international bodies and agencies described as catastrophic and criminal.

As in the case of the flotilla, there are alternative ways for releasing the captive soldier, such as swapping the thousands of political prisoners Israel is holding with Shalit. Many of them are children, and quite a few are being held without trial. The Israelis have dragged their feet in negotiations over such a swap, which are not likely to bear fruit in the foreseeable future.

But Barak and Netanyahu, and those around them, know too well that the blockade on Gaza is not going to produce any change in the position of the Hamas, and one should give credit to the prime minister, David Cameron, who remarked at Prime Minister's Questions last week that the Israelis' policy in fact strengthens, rather than weakens, the Hamas hold on Gaza. But this strategy, despite its declared aim, is not meant to succeed, or at least no one is worried in Jerusalem if it continues to be fruitless and futile.

One would have thought that Israel's drastic decline in international reputation would prompt new thinking by its leaders. But the responses to the attack on the flotilla indicate clearly that there is no hope for any significant shift in the official position. A firm commitment to continue the blockade, and a heroes' welcome to the soldiers who pirated the ship in the Mediterranean, show that the same politics would continue for a long time.

This is not surprising. The Barak–Netanyahu–Avigdor Lieberman government does not know any other way of responding to the reality in Palestine and Israel. The use of brutal force to impose your will and a hectic propaganda machine that describes it as self-defense, while demonizing the half-starved people in Gaza and those who come to their aid as terrorists, is the only possible course for these politicians. The terrible consequences in human death and suffering of this determination do not concern them, nor does international condemnation.

The real, unlike the declared, strategy is to continue this state of affairs. As long as the international community is complacent, the Arab world impotent, and Gaza contained, Israel can still have a thriving economy and an electorate that regards the dominance of the army in its life, the continued conflict, and the oppression of the Palestinians as the exclusive past, present, and future reality of life in Israel. The U.S. vice president, Joe Biden, was humiliated by the Israelis recently when they announced the building of 1,600 new homes in the disputed Ramat Shlomo district of Jerusalem on the day he arrived to try to freeze the settlement policy. But his unconditional support now for the latest Israeli action makes the leaders and their electorate feel vindicated.

It would be wrong, however, to assume that American support

and a feeble European response to Israeli criminal policies such as one pursued in Gaza are the main reasons for the protracted blockade and strangulation of Gaza. What is probably most difficult to explain to readers around the world is how deeply these perceptions and attitudes are grounded in the Israeli psyche and mentality. And it is indeed difficult to comprehend how diametrically opposed are the common reactions in the U.K. to such events, for instance, to the emotions that it triggers inside the Israeli Jewish society.

The international response is based on the assumption that more forthcoming Palestinian concessions and a continued dialogue with the Israeli political elite will produce a new reality on the ground. The official discourse in the West is that a very reasonable and attainable solution is just around the corner if all sides would make one final effort: the two-state solution.

Nothing is further from the truth than this optimistic scenario. The only version of this solution that is acceptable to Israel is the one that both the tamed Palestine Authority in Ramallah and the more assertive Hamas in Gaza could never ever accept. It is an offer to imprison the Palestinians in stateless enclaves in return for ending their struggle.

Thus even before one discusses either an alternative solution—a single democratic state for all, which I support—or explores a more plausible, two-state settlement, one has to transform fundamentally the Israeli official and public mindset. This mentality is the principal barrier to a peaceful reconciliation in the torn land of Israel and Palestine.

ISRAEL'S LOSS OF MORAL IMAGINATION

Henry Siegman

Following Israel's bloody interdiction of the Gaza flotilla, I called a lifelong friend in Israel to inquire about the mood of the country. My friend, an intellectual and a kind and generous man, has nevertheless long sided with Israeli hardliners. Still, I was entirely unprepared for his response. He told me—in a voice trembling with emotion—that the world's outpouring of condemnation of Israel is reminiscent of the dark period of the Hitler era.

He told me most everyone in Israel felt that way, with the exception of Meretz, a small Israeli pro-peace party. "But for all practical purposes," he said, "they are Arabs."

Like me, my friend personally experienced those dark Hitler years, having lived under Nazi occupation, as did so many of Israel's Jewish citizens. I was therefore stunned by the analogy. He went on to say that the so-called human rights activists on the Turkish ship were in fact terrorists and thugs paid to assault Israeli authorities to provoke an incident that would discredit the Jewish state. The evidence for this, he said, is that many of these activists were found by Israeli authorities to have on them $10,000, "exactly the same amount!" he exclaimed.

When I managed to get over the shock of that exchange, it struck me that the invocation of the Hitler era was actually a frighteningly apt and searing analogy, although not the one my friend intended. A million and a half civilians have been forced to live in an open-air prison in inhuman conditions for over three years now, but unlike the Hitler years, they are not Jews but Palestinians. Their jailers, incredibly, are survivors of the Holocaust, or their descendants. Of course, the inmates of Gaza are not destined for gas chambers, as the Jews were, but they have been reduced to a debased and hopeless existence.

Fully 80 percent of Gaza's population lives on the edge of malnutrition, depending on international charities for their daily nourishment. According to the U.N. and World Health Organization authorities, Gaza's children suffer from dramatically increased morbidity that will affect and shorten the lives of many of them. This obscenity is a consequence of a deliberate and carefully calculated Israeli policy aimed at de-developing Gaza by destroying not only its economy but its physical and social infrastructure while sealing it hermitically from the outside world.

Particularly appalling is that this policy has been the source of amusement for some Israeli leaders, who according to Israeli press reports have jokingly described it as "putting Palestinians on a diet." That, too, is reminiscent of the Hitler years, when Jewish suffering amused the Nazis.

Another feature of that dark era were absurd conspiracies attributed to the Jews by otherwise intelligent and cultured Germans. Sadly, even smart Jews are not immune to that disease. Is it really conceivable that Turkish activists who were supposedly paid $10,000 each would bring that money with them on board the ship knowing they would be taken into custody by Israeli authorities?

That intelligent and moral people, whether German or Israeli, can convince themselves of such absurdities (a disease that also afflicts much of the Arab world) is the enigma that goes to the heart of the mystery of how even the most civilized societies can so quickly shed their most cherished values and regress to the most primitive impulses toward the Other, without even being aware they have done so. It must surely have something to do with a deliberate repression of the moral imagination that enables people to identify with the Other's plight. Pirkei Avot, a collection of ethical admonitions that is part of the Talmud, urges: "Do not judge your fellow man until you are able to imagine standing in his place."

Of course, even the most objectionable Israeli policies do not begin to compare with Hitler's Germany. But the essential moral issues are the same. How would Jews have reacted to their tormentors had they been consigned to the kind of existence Israel has imposed on Gaza's population? Would they not have seen human rights activists prepared to risk their lives to call their plight to the world's attention as heroic, even if they had beaten up commandos trying to prevent their effort? Did Jews admire British commandos who boarded and diverted ships carrying illegal Jewish immigrants to Palestine in the aftermath of World War II, as most Israelis now admire Israel's naval commandos?

Who would have believed that an Israeli government and its Jewish citizens would seek to demonize and shut down Israeli human rights organizations for their lack of "patriotism," and dismiss fellow Jews who criticized the assault on the Gaza flotilla as *Arabs*, pregnant with all the hateful connotations that word has acquired in Israel, not unlike Germans who branded fellow citizens who spoke up for Jews as *Juden*? The German White Rose activists, mostly students from the University of Munich, who dared to condemn the German persecution of the Jews (well before the concentration camp exterminations began) were also considered "traitors" by their fellow Germans, who did not mourn the beheading of these activists by the Gestapo.

So, yes, there is reason for Israelis, and for Jews generally, to think long and hard about the dark Hitler era at this particular time. For the significance of the Gaza flotilla incident lies not in the questions raised about violations of international law on the high seas, or even about "who assaulted whom" first on the Turkish ship, the *Mavi Marmara*, but in the larger questions raised about our common human condition by Israel's occupation policies and its devastation of Gaza's civilian population.

If a people who so recently experienced on its own flesh such unspeakable inhumanities cannot muster the moral imagination to understand the injustice and suffering its territorial ambitions—and even its legitimate security concerns—are inflicting on another people, what hope is there for the rest of us?

THE MYTH OF ISRAELI MORALITY

Lamis Andoni

The Israeli attack on the international aid flotilla—killing nine and injuring dozens more—is not the first example of nonviolent resistance by Palestinians and their supporters being met by force.

Israel has, in fact, at different times reacted with repression or even extreme violence to cultural and political manifestations of Palestinian identity.

But the flotilla carnage is the first direct and officially declared attack by the Israeli Army on foreign activists—taking Israel's reaction to solidarity activities to a new and unprecedented level.

Israeli claims that Turkish activists "resisted" its takeover of the ships do not change the reality that the Israeli Army performed an illegal armed operation against activists who challenged the siege of Gaza—not with weapons, but by trying to deliver food and medical supplies to the besieged Palestinian population.

Impunity for Israel has already been shown in the cases of Western peace activists Rachel Corrie and Tom Hurndell who were killed while peacefully protesting against Israeli Army actions against Palestinian citizens.

AN ACT OF FEAR

But Israel's reaction was not merely an act of arrogance. It was also an act of fear and weakness in the face of a rising tide of Palestinian and international civic campaigns.

Israeli concerns run so deep that it has been pouring money and energy into a worldwide campaign to counter what it considers to be a drive "aimed at delegitimizing" Israel.

But Israel's own actions, such as the raid on the aid ship, only serve to reinforce the image of a state fully engaged in illegal actions in the Occupied Territories and beyond.

Israel's reaction to nonviolent protests inside and outside the Occupied Territories is part of its fear of the assertion of Palestinian identity in the historic land of Palestine.

After its establishment in 1948, Israel placed the Palestinian Arab population that remained under harsh military rule, banning the teaching of Palestinian and Arab history, poetry, and songs.

Those who defied the ban were imprisoned, or in the case of the late poet Mahmoud Darwish, forced into exile where they sought to freely express the yearnings of a dispossessed nation.

Following the Israeli occupation of the West Bank and Gaza Strip, Israel cracked down on Palestinian political leaders, who were rounded up and many simply deported to Jordan.

In 1974 Israel "authorized" municipal elections, only to deport the winners when Palestinians elected supporters of the Palestine Liberation Organization (PLO).

Israeli extremists attacked two of the elected mayors, of Ramallah and Nablus, maiming both men.

None of those elected were known to have any association with armed struggle but belonged to the Palestinian intelligentsia, including Hanna Nasser, then president of the University of Beir Zeit.

DEPORTATION, IMPRISONMENT, ASSASSINATION

Deportations and imprisonment were part of a systemic policy to preempt the emergence of an independent political leadership in the occupied West Bank and Gaza Strip, while for those outside the Occupied Territories—intellectuals in Beirut and PLO ambassadors in Europe—assassination was the order of the day throughout the 1970s.

In 1972, one of Palestine's finest novelists, Ghassan Kanafani, was killed in a car bomb and, in 1973, poet Kamal Nasser was assassinated by a Mossad hit team led by Ehud Barak, the current Israeli defense minister.

Both operations were carried out in the heart of Beirut.

Until the signing of the Oslo agreement in 1993 the raising of the Palestinian flag—and at times the public display in any form of the banner's colors—were acts that triggered punishment.

Young Palestinians, including children, were shot at and sometimes wounded or even killed for daring to display the flag in public.

Even symbolic acts suggesting recognition of Palestinian rights are not tolerated by Israel.

PEACEFUL RESISTANCE

In 1988 the PLO invited international writers, artists and activists to travel by ship along with scores of Palestinians who had been deported by Israel and representatives of refugees to make a symbolic journey "of return."

After successfully intimidating Greek vessel owners from renting a ship to the PLO, Israel then bombed a Cypriot boat a few hours before the solidarity activists, including Westerners—Christians and Jews—were to board it.

But while the 1988 bombing—at the peak of the first Palestinian intifada—aimed at blocking the journey itself, the ferocity of the armed campaign against the Gaza flotilla suggests that Israel, more than ever before, is deeply concerned about the success of peaceful means of resistance.

Israel correctly viewed the Free Gaza convoy as part of a Palestinian and international campaign not only to break the siege of the tiny Strip, but to end its occupation and to recognize legitimate Palestinian national rights.

But the idea that the use of military force can stop the campaign from spreading is ludicrous—unless Israel plans to blow up protests everywhere from the village of Bil'in in the West Bank to London, Berlin, and San Francisco.

Israel has already employed a public relations campaign to demonize and discredit the growing boycott campaign—modeled after a similar campaign against the former apartheid regime in South Africa.

It has also been engaged in a weekly campaign of arrests and increasingly the shooting and wounding of Palestinian, Western, and even Israeli activists protesting against the illegal segregation wall that has been eating up West Bank land in the villages of Bil'in and Ni'lin.

The Israeli government has been intolerant of diplomatic attempts by the Palestinian Authority to curtail the expansion of Jewish settlements in the West Bank, including East Jerusalem, and the lifting of the siege of Gaza Strip.

Benjamin Netanyahu, the Israeli prime minister, complained to George Mitchell, the American special envoy to the Middle East, that the P.A. had lobbied internationally to block the admission of Israel to the prestigious Organisation for Economic Co-operation and Development (OECD) and accused the Palestinian government of incitement for endorsing a boycott of the produce of illegal settlements.

SENDING A MESSAGE

Thus while Israel feels entitled to practice what are essentially violent acts—enforced as they are by military strength—of settlement building on confiscated Palestinian land, it wants to strip Palestinians, including the P.A., of the means by which to voice their demands peacefully.

Ironically, it was Turkey who facilitated Israel's admission into the influential OECD, only to be paid back soon after with the killing of its nationals on board the Gaza-bound flotilla.

Israel, it seems, wanted to send a message to allies and opponents alike that it does not tolerate dissent or defiance—even in a peaceful form.

When its enemies use force, Israel feels it can rely on its arsenal of tanks and bombs. But what the raid on the flotilla shows is that, when possible, it also responds with military action to nonviolent resistance.

The flotilla, sailing unprotected in international waters, appeared a good target against which Israel could exercise the plan of action it knows best—the lethal use of force.

The 2006 war on Lebanon and the 2008–2009 war on Gaza revealed the limits of Israeli military supremacy in achieving its political goals, and the attack on the flotilla has backfired disastrously.

The bullets that pierced the bodies of the activists have boomeranged, shattering the myth of Israeli morality.

In fact, the increasing calls in its wake for an immediate end to the blockade of Gaza now show that Israel has failed and the Free Gaza Movement prevailed.

A HISTORY OF IMPUNITY

Yousef Munayyer

The government of Israel has announced the launch of an investigation into the events surrounding the deadly Memorial Day flotilla raid that left nine activists dead. Many international bodies including the United Nations and the European Union, as well as human rights groups like Amnesty International, are calling for an independent and impartial, international investigation into the incident. In fact, The U.N. Human Rights Council has already called for an investigation and chosen a principle investigator. Turkey too has decided to launch its own investigation. The Mahmoud Abbas–led Palestinian Authority in Ramallah, which can in no way be construed as a pro-Hamas entity, also slammed the Israeli investigation.

There are obvious questions that arise when an alleged perpetrator, in this case the government of Israel, is left in charge of investigating themselves. To mitigate such concerns, Israel has allowed two international observers to participate. One of them, David Trimble, raises questions on his own. He has a Nobel Peace Prize on his résumé, but he is also known for having antipathy toward human rights groups, whom he has accused of aiding terrorists, and was recently part of an initiative to launch a pro-Israel campaign in Northern Ireland. The other observer, Ken Watkin, is the former head of Canada's military judiciary.

But for the sake of argument, let's assume that the international observers can keep any biases they may have out of their deliberations.

Will they be able to come up with an accurate assessment of the events? It's not likely, since any information "almost certain to cause substantial harm to [Israel's] national security or to the State's foreign relations"[1] will not be made available to the international observers. Basically, the international observers, hand-picked by the state of Israel, are only permitted to observe what the state of Israel wants them to observe. A farce, if there ever was one.

Despite this, and a vast international outcry for an impartial, international investigation, the United States has come out in support of Israel's commission, calling it an "important step" and stating that Israel's "independent public commission can meet the standard of a prompt, impartial, credible, and transparent investigation."

Many around the globe do not share these sentiments and are deeply skeptical of Israel's investigation. But this skepticism does not lie in anti-Semitism or an anti-Israel sentiment, as many Israeli government spokespeople would have us believe. Rather, a long history of flawed or nonexistent investigations into the killings of civilians at the hands of Israel's soldiers has led many to the conclusion that Israel is incapable of independently reaching justice. A brief review of some of these investigations in is order:

1953: Qibya—As a punitive and vengeful response to cross-border raids, the Israeli government decided to send a message to the Palestinians. This village, just over the Green Line, became the target. The death toll of seventy Palestinians was made up mostly of women and children, and forty-five homes were destroyed. Operational orders included commands for maximal killing and driving the inhabitants from their homes. International condemnation followed what was known to the Israeli military as Operation Rose. The United States expressed its regret for the loss of life and demanded that perpetrators "be brought to account and that effective measures should be taken to prevent such incidents in the future."[2] No credible public independent investigation was held. Those responsible included Israeli Defense

Forces Chief of Staff Moshe Dayan, Deputy Defense Minister Pinhas Lavon, and chief of staff Mordechai Meklaf. The latter appointed Ariel Sharon, who was the commander of the brigade responsible for the raid. He would go on to have a long and controversial career in Israeli political and military life. None of these officials were charged and all continued careers in public life.

1956: Kufr Qasem—In this village of Palestinians with Israeli citizenship, forty-seven were killed, of which fifteen were women, and eleven were children under the age of fifteen. Thirteen others were wounded. The IDF swiftly changed curfew hours as villagers were returning to their homes. Major Shmuel Melinki gave the order to "shoot to kill" anyone outside of their homes. During trial, Melinki claimed the order "conformed to the spirit of the times." Israeli Prime Minister David Ben-Gurion ordered an investigation. To the surprise of many Palestinians the initial court martial found Melinki guilty of killing forty-three civilians and sentenced him to seventeen years in prison. Others found guilty included Lieutenant Joubral Dahan and Sergeant Shalom Ofer, both sentenced to fifteen years. Privates Hreish and Abraham, among others, were sentenced to seven years imprisonment for killing seventeen citizens. The brigadier who directed Melinki to crack down on those breaking the curfew was found guilty of a mere technical error, and was sentenced to a reprimand and a fine of one piaster (ten cents!). Those initially sentenced by court martial for the killings had their sentences commuted by a series of civilian courts and politicians. No one found guilty for the murders ultimately served more than three years in prison. After their release, Melinki was promoted into the ranks of military intelligence and Dahan received a position in a city municipality.

1967: The USS Liberty—During the war in 1967, Israeli military aircraft and navy bombarded a United States Navy reconnaissance ship, killing thirty-four noncombatant sailors and injuring approximately

170 others. The United States reacted with outrage. At the time, Secretary of State Dean Rusk stated that the attack must be condemned and that the U. S. government expected the government of Israel to take the disciplinary measures required by international law. The Israeli position was that this was a mistake. The IDF Chief Military Prosecutor filed charges against select military personnel, but an examining judge ruled that nothing in the incident deviated "from the standard of reasonable conduct which would justify the committal of anyone for trial."[3] No official proceedings ensued.

1976: "Land Day" shootings—After announcing the confiscation of thousands of dunams of land that fell between two Palestinian villages in the Galilee, Israel braced for a reaction by declaring immediate curfews and that protests would be illegal. Palestinian citizens of Israel in the area organized strikes and demonstrations in protest of the land confiscation, part of which was privately owned Palestinian land. The crackdown that ensued involved thousands of Israeli police and tactical forces, and resulted in the killing of six unarmed Palestinian Arabs, the injury of approximately 100 more and the mass arrests of hundreds of others. No credible public investigation took place. No one was prosecuted in connection with the killings.

1978: Operation Litani—Following a PLO bus hijacking that left thirty-seven Israelis dead, Israel invaded southern Lebanon in March 1978. The result of the operation was a stunningly disproportionate response that left 1,100 Palestinian and Lebanese dead. Most of the causalities were civilians. The operation solicited ire from U.S. President Jimmy Carter. Carter noted in his book *The Blood of Abraham* that he instructed the State Department to push for condemnation of the killings in the U.N. Security Council, and that if the Israelis refused to cease the operation, he would be compelled to notify congress that U.S. weapons were being used illegally. No credible public independent investigation into the killings of civilians was held.

1982: Sabra and Shatila—The number of deaths at these Palestinian refugee camps in Lebanon is disputed to be between 400 to upwards of 3,000, mostly civilians. This massacre drew international condemnation and the U.N. General Assembly termed it an act of genocide by a vote of 123–0 with twenty-two abstentions (the United States abstained). An outcry in Israel led to the establishment of an investigation led by Yitzhak Kahan, then President of the Israeli Supreme Court. The Kahan Commission found that Israel was indirectly responsible for the massacre and that Ariel Sharon (whose career had continued unabated after the Qibya massacre) bore personal responsibility. The Kahan Commission recommended Sharon be dismissed from his post as defense minister and never hold a ministerial position again. After much debate, Sharon stepped down as defense minister but maintained a minister-without-portfolio position in the government. It was during these years that President Ronald Reagan drew the conclusion that Sharon was a "bad guy who seemingly looks forward to a war." Sharon would go on to be elected prime minister.

1996: Qana—During fighting in southern Lebanon between Israel and Hezbollah, approximately 800 Lebanese civilians sought shelter in a United Nations compound in Qana. Israeli forces shelled the U.N. compound, killing 106 and injuring 116 more. Israel claimed that the attack was a grave error. The investigation conducted by the Israeli Army determined mapping errors were behind the shelling. The United Nations disagreed, stating that evidence from the scene of the massacre showed that the Israeli claims were untrue and that "it is unlikely that the shelling of the United Nations compound was the result of gross technical and/or procedural errors."[4] While the international outcry that followed the killings led to increased diplomatic efforts to end the fighting in southern Lebanon, no one was prosecuted in connection with the massacre.

2000: October Events—After Ariel Sharon's controversial visit to the

Temple Mount, an event thought to have sparked the second intifada, numerous protests throughout Israel and the Occupied Territories took place. The Israeli repression of these protests led to several incidents of killings of unarmed, civilian Palestinian protesters. Within a few weeks, twelve Palestinian citizens of Israel and a Palestinian from Gaza were killed. An Israeli commission was established to investigate the killings headed by Israeli Supreme Court Judge Theodor Or. The Or Commission's 860-page report, released in 2003, found that the demonstrators were merely exercising their rights as citizens to protest. The report criticized Israeli commands to authorize the use of snipers without a security threat and criticized Israeli police for failing to collect evidence surrounding the killings. As a result, no officers were prosecuted.

2002: Jenin—During the second intifada and under the leadership of Israeli Prime Minister Ariel Sharon, Israel declared Jenin a closed military zone on April 1, 2002. Raids and fighting in the camp left many dead and wounded as well as significant damage to civilian infrastructure. The death toll is in dispute and media and observers were not permitted into the camp until nearly a week after the battle ended, leading to widespread accusations of a massacre cover-up. The United Nations puts the death toll at fifty-two, of "whom up to half may have been civilians."[5] Much international uproar followed, and the United States pressured Israel to account for their actions through an international investigation. Initially Israel complied with a U.N. investigation before retracting. No Israeli investigations took place, and Israel did not cooperate with the U.N. investigation. No prosecutions followed the events in Jenin.

2008–09: Operation Cast Lead—A twenty-three-day Israeli operation in the Gaza Strip, with the stated objective of halting Hamas rocket fire, resulted in the deaths of approximately 1,400 Palestinians, most of whom were civilians. The scores of civilian dead, the use of controversial weapons such as white phosphorus in civilian areas and the destruction of U.N. facilities and civilian infrastructure, led to an international outcry. A now-infamous U.N. investigation led by Judge Richard Goldstone found that Israeli actions may amount to war crimes. Israel refused to cooperate with the U.N. commission, and, to date, one Israeli soldier has been prosecuted for stealing and charging items on a Palestinian's credit card. Other recent reports indicate that one or two more soldiers may be charged in connection with shooting unarmed civilians. No other charges have been brought forth. The Israeli defense minister that oversaw the operation, Ehud Barak, remains in the same position today.

A number of other events could be added to this list, but the trend is clear. Where there have been allegations of war crimes or the killing of civilians, Israel has often failed to investigate or to cooperate with independent investigations. In the instances where Israeli investigations have been carried out and soldiers or commanders have been found responsible, sentences were significantly commuted and/or the recommendations of the commission have been completely ignored by the heads of state empowered to enforce them. One must wonder how the course of history may have been altered had Ariel Sharon, who played a role in a number of these events, been discharged and imprisoned after Qibya in 1953, or even prevented from holding a ministerial level position as the Kahan Commission had recommended after the Sabra and Shatila massacre. Instead, Sharon went on to ascend to the premiership and presided over the most significant expansion of illegal Israeli settlements since the Menachem Begin era in the late 1970s. Indeed, it was only failed health, not the Israeli judicial system, that ended Sharon's long career in public life.

It's in this historical context that Israel begins an investigation into the raid on the flotilla that left nine dead. Pardon me for not holding my breath.

Notes

1. See: "Government establishes independent public commission," Israel Ministry of Foreign Affairs, June 14, 2010 (http://www.mfa.gov.il/MFA/Government/Communiques/2010/Independent_Public_Commission_Maritime_Incident_31-May-2010.htm)

2. See: "The Qibya (Israel-Jordan) Incident: United Nations Security Council Resolution, November 24, 1953" (http://avalon.law.yale.edu/20th_century/mid009.asp)

3. See: "Exhibit 21" (http://ussliberty.org/report/exhibit%252021.pdf)

4. See: "Letter dated 7 May 1996 from the Secretary-General addressed to the President of the Security Council" (http://domino.un.org/UNISPAL.NSF/0/62d5aa740c14293b85256324005179be?OpenDocument)

5. See: "Report of the Secretary-General prepared pursuant to General Assembly resolution ES-10/10" (http://www.un.org/peace/jenin/index.html)

THE ISRAELI MEDIA'S FLOTILLA FAIL

Max Blumenthal

If the raid of the Gaza Freedom Flotilla was a disaster for the Israel Defense Forces, its aftermath demonstrated an equally bewildering performance by the Israeli media. The IDF Spokesman's Office churned out one misleading claim after another, each one more implausible than the next, seeking to implant in the public's mind a version of events that bore little relation to reality. To a degree, this was to be expected; but it was startling to see how some of Israel's most respected reporters lined up to serve as military stenographers, barely challenging the IDF's rapidly changing versions of events. IDF claims about the flotilla passengers' links to Al Qaeda, anti-Semitic statements shouted at the Israeli Navy, and terrorist intentions were eagerly broadcast by the Israeli media without a second thought. When independent reporters forced the IDF to retract or "clarify" all of these claims, Israeli news outlets refused to correct their errors, or covered them up without acknowledgment.

It so happened that I arrived in Israel for a research trip the day after the flotilla raid. As a result, I was able to do something which I always thought to be a very basic journalistic practice, so basic it's supposed to be applied routinely: asking an implicated party in a story to produce evidence for its claims. What I found bewildering is that at least judging from Israeli media reports, few, if any, mainstream reporters applied this practice, and when a visiting colleague did their job for them—nobody bothered to correct or withdraw their original report.

On June 2, the IDF disseminated a press release titled "Attackers of the IDF soldiers found to be Al Qaeda mercenaries." The accusation was not accompanied by any conclusive evidence—the IDF reported that *Mavi Marmara* passengers were equipped with night-vision goggles. This did not stop *Yedioth*'s Ron Ben-Yishai, who was embedded with the navy commandos, from amplifying the baseless charge. Citing an "interrogation" of *Marmara* passengers—"lynchers," he called them—Ben-Yishai wrote the same day, "Some among the [flotilla passengers] are believed to have ties with World Jihad groups, mainly Al Qaeda." The article made no reference to any efforts on part of Ben-Yishai to investigate this claim, nor did he seem to think to ask why the IDF was about to release dangerous operatives of Osama bin Laden—presumably they would attack again, wouldn't they?

On June 3, Israeli journalist Lia Tarachansky of the Real News Network and I placed calls to the IDF Spokesman's Office to demand further evidence of the *Marmara*'s Al Qaeda ties. We received identical responses from spokespeople from the IDF's Israel and North America desks: "We don't have any evidence. The press release was based on information from the National Security Council." Hours later, the IDF retracted its claim, changing the title of its press release to "Attackers of IDF Soldiers Found Without Identification Papers." Despite the official retraction, Ben-Yishai's article remains uncorrected.

On June 4, the IDF released an audio clip purporting to consist of transmissions between the *Mavi Marmara* and a naval warship. "Go back to Auschwitz!" a *Marmara* passenger shouted, according to the IDF. YNet and Haaretz reported on and reproduced the audio clip without investigating its authenticity. Forget that the voice uttering the anti-Semitic slur sounded like a mentally disturbed teenager; had reporters performed a cursory search of the IDF Spokeman's Office website, they would have found a longer clip released on May 31 that featured a dramatically different exchange with the *Marmara* with no mention of Auschwitz. Further, the voice of flotilla organizer Huwaida Arraf was featured in the "Auschwitz" clip, yet Arraf was not aboard the *Marmara* (she was on the *Challenger One*). Could the IDF have doctored audio to exploit public hysteria surrounding the issue of anti-Semitism?

On my blog, I pointed out the discrepancies in the IDF's footage and raised the question of doctoring. The next day, the IDF conceded that it had in fact doctored the footage, releasing a "clarification" and a new clip claiming to consist of the "full" exchange between the navy and the flotilla. Unfortunately, the authenticity of the new clip was impossible to verify.

Despite the IDF's admission, YNet and *Haaretz* have not corrected their original reports, though *Haaretz* has at least altered its headline. Once the doctoring was exposed, the *New York Times* covered the episode in detail, directing international attention to the triumph of independent online reporting and the apparent failure of Israel's parochial press corps.

On June 7, *Haaretz*'s Anshel Pfeffer reported on an IDF press release claiming without evidence that five flotilla passengers had links to international terror. The press release was larded with highly implausible claims, including that Ken O'Keefe, who runs an aid organization with Tony Blair's sister-in-law, was planning to train a Hamas commando unit in the Gaza Strip. When I called the IDF Spokesman's Office, I learned that once again, no evidence was available to support their press release. "There is very limited intelligence we can give in this specific case," Sargeant Chen Arad told me. "Obviously I'm unable to give you more information." Did Pfeffer demand more evidence? If he did and was answered in the same manner as I did, why did *Haaretz* publish an unsubstantiated spin as fact?

Joined by *Haaretz* military correspondents Avi Isacharoff and Amos Harel, Pfeffer became a channel for another daytime deception by the IDF. On May 31, the three reporters produced an article based exclusively on testimony from naval commandos—the flotilla passengers' side of the story was ignored—claiming they had faced live fire and lynching attempts from *Marmara* passengers. Since the story was published, the IDF has produced scant evidence to support either accusation. The article was accompanied by a suspicious photo from the IDF Spokesman's Office depicting a bearded Muslim man brandishing a knife and surrounded by photojournalists. Daylight beams in from a window behind the man. *Haaretz*'s caption, which was sourced to the IDF, asserted that the photo was taken "after" the commandos had boarded the *Marmara*. However, the commandos raided the ship at night, while the photo was taken during the day. Once again, the IDF's story was fishy.

I called Sargeant Arad at the IDF Spokesman's Office to investigate. He told me he had no evidence to support the photo's questionable caption. Soon after our phone conversation, *Haaretz* quietly altered the caption, removing its claim that the photo was taken "after" the commando raid. For nearly a week, the false photo caption had remained intact. Why did *Haaretz* suddenly change it? The only plausible explanation is that the paper received a tip from the IDF Spokesman's Office. If true, the tip-off suggests a scandalous level of coordination between the Israeli military and the country's media.

In the wake of the flotilla raid, Israeli journalists had a unique opportunity to lead the global media's investigation into the bloodbath that occurred on the deck of the *Mavi Marmara*. After all, no one had better access to the military or the eyewitnesses aboard the flotilla. Instead, too many among the Israeli press corps allowed themselves to be conscripted into the IDF's hapless information war, leaving the important task of investigating the raid to independent reporters who remembered to view claims by any nation's military with extreme skepticism.

So why do well-connected, experienced reporters follow the IDF baton so willingly, and fail to follow up when IDF claims are retracted? Is it simple bias, a desire to present their military in the best possible light, a desire so strong they abandon their duty to their readers to verify their information? Are they afraid of sanctions, of losing contacts and access to information? Do they fear personal reprisals? Their readers, and the world media that still relies on Israeli journalism as a vital source of information, need to know.

NO VILLA IN THE JUNGLE

Raja Shehadeh

It depends how far back we travel. Ten years ago, Israeli citizens were not forbidden by law from entering Palestinian cities in the West Bank, nor was the Gaza Strip under siege as it is now. It is much easier to impose your definition of the people living behind the ghetto walls when you don't allow your citizens to find out for themselves. If we go back some seventy years, we find a number of mixed Jewish-Arab towns, both cities and villages, in Palestine under the British Mandate. And if we go farther still, we will find that the entire Eastern Mediterranean under the Ottoman Empire was without borders demarcating either Arab nation states—Syria, Jordan, Lebanon—or the Jewish state of Israel.

The present is a very different reality. To cross from Ramallah, where I live, to Haifa, where my grandmother was living before 1948, I have to go through five different Israeli barriers. Palestine/Israel has become like a babushka doll, with borders within borders within borders. Driving in the Jordan Valley, I mainly saw borders, barbed wire, and watchtowers. At one such border, on a hillside near the entrance to the Jordan bridge terminal in the West Bank, Israeli officials had used small stones to mark out the Star of David and nearby the insignia of the Israeli police, attempting to claim the land by adorning it with their symbols. Like the seal stamped on our documents, this was just another way of indicating that the area was no longer considered occupied territory but is an integral part of the Jewish state.

"We aren't North America or Western Europe," Ehud Barak, Israel's Defense Minister, told the commandos who participated in the deadly raid on the Gaza-bound Freedom Flotilla last Monday; "we live in the Middle East, in a place where there is no mercy for the weak and there aren't second chances for those who don't defend themselves."

The same Barak is fond of describing Israel as "a villa in the jungle." Israeli politicians like him appear congenitally incapable of conceiving of another way of life for their country than as a fortress state with a strong army living by the gun in an area of millions of Arabs with whom Israel makes no effort to construct bridges, communicate peacefully, learn the language, find a place for itself, or integrate except by force and the language of power and violence.

But just as Israel's present leaders are fond of distinguishing between the untamed Middle East resembling a jungle, they indulge in their favorite fantasy that their country is part of the West. Why should they have open borders that would allow in their "terrorist neighbors"? Better keep the country sealed while retaining the aerial link to the West, over the sea.

The events on the high sea on May 31, 2010 disturbed this false equilibrium. Traveling on the ships that came to challenge the Israeli policy of keeping Gaza under siege were hundreds of Westerners, many of them famous for their contributions to the best the West can offer: writers, politicians, and defenders of human rights. Israeli propagandists should have thought twice before describing them as terrorists. Still they did. They could not afford to do otherwise.

Not surprisingly, this did not go well. If it is possible to ascribe the qualities of wild beasts to those behind walls because the victim's voices cannot be heard, even the accomplished and highly experienced Israeli *hasbara* could not convince the world that the Americans, British, Irish, and Swedes on the boats were all as Israel described them, terrorists, and even worse, members of Al Qaeda.

One of the justifications offered for attacking the boats was that they were challenging Israel's policy toward Gaza. But then this was precisely the declared objective of the organizers. They were members of civil society who had despaired of their governments meeting their responsibilities in enforcing international law and protecting the human rights of a besieged population of 1.5 million people. They decided to take action on their own.

Israel cannot be unaware of the power of mass movement. This, and the fact that the use of force against anyone challenging its policies toward the Occupied Palestinian Territories, goes a long way in explaining why it struck hard at the flotilla, killing a number of the passengers on these ships and injuring others. It was the same reaction as the leaders of Israel had after the Palestinians' first uprising: "Break their bones," Prime Minister Rabin ordered his army, so that unarmed protestors would cower and stay home. The policy did not work then, nor would it this time round.

Wherever in the world we might be, we humans live in our own small worlds. In Palestine, however, the walls that surround us are constructed against our will. Yet there are those auspicious moments when in the course of our confined existence the heavens seem to open and the sky becomes the limit. Then in the precious moment when we discover that the rest of humanity does care about the injustice in our small confined spaces and has come to our rescue, Barak is proven wrong. And those who believed themselves to be living in the villa are found out to be inhabiting the depths of the jungle.

It is at a moment like this in the open sea when ships carrying activists from around the world are approaching Gaza that we get a second chance at redeeming our humanity and discovering how our world can be a welcoming place.

5. OLD FRIENDS, NEW THINKING

TURKEY AFTER THE FLOTILLA

Murat Dagli

After the bodies of the nine Turkish activists killed by Israeli forces on the *Mavi Marmara* on May 31, 2010, returned home, tens of thousands participated in the funerals and burials in two of Istanbul's major mosques the following day and during Friday prayers. The anger toward Israel only intensified after surviving passengers began recounting the extent of the atrocities during Israel's attack on the Gaza Freedom Flotilla and the abuse they suffered during detention.

Israel, with the usual support from Washington, continues to deny any wrongdoing and claims that the interception was fully legitimate and the loss of lives was the unfortunate result of acts of self-defense by its commandos who were "attacked."

Meanwhile, Turkish flags and posters of Prime Minister Recep Tayyip Erdoğan are prominent in demonstrations around the world. Erdoğan's profile and popularity were already high in the Arab world due to his televised confrontation with Israeli President Shimon Peres at the World Economic Forum in 2009 over Israel's attack on Gaza earlier that year.

After years of disappointment with successive Arab regimes, Turkey appears to be taking a regional leadership role. While better and closer relations between Turkey and the Arab world are welcome developments, and there is hope for a momentum building up for the Palestinian cause, the ambiguities of the Turkish stance are apparent and raise important questions.

Should the current crisis with Israel be interpreted as a singular event in which Turkey gave a strong response or as the inevitable culmination of a completely new foreign policy orientation?

In the midst of the heightened pace of activism, diplomatic activity, and political maneuvering, it is important to analyze the dilemmas of the Turkish political scene, and to distinguish rhetoric from political realities.

Within days of the flotilla crisis starting, influential Turkish newspapers such as *Hürriyet*, *Vatan*, and *Milliyet* expressed reservations about escalating the tension with Israel.

Underlying these reservations are a variety of concerns from the economic repercussions of a prolonged political crisis to the danger of turning this tension into a permanent "blood feud." More importantly, the foundations of these cautionary remarks are based on the deep-seated convictions about Turkey's foreign policy model.

Even though "peace at home, peace in the world" is said to be the guiding principle of Turkish foreign policy since the foundation of the republic in 1923, Turkey's foreign policy has in fact consistently been Western oriented. The Ministry of Foreign Affairs, seen as the most Westernized institution in Turkey and a leading force in Western-oriented aspirations of the Turkish Republic, has also continuously sought a significant degree of autonomy from domestic political changes.

In this context, the appointment of Ahmet Davutoğlu, a professor of International Relations and an intellectual figure close to the Justice and Development Party (AKP), initially created a good deal of tension and resistance within the ministry. Therefore, Ankara's further involvement, let alone explicit claim for leadership in the Middle East, can be expected to be a cause of great concern for a considerable portion of the Turkish establishment.

Further aggravating this sense of urgency are long-established popular Turkish misconceptions about the Middle East as backward, underdeveloped, and uncivilized. Hence, the sense that Turkey's turn to the East and away from the West will be seen as a step backward by some of Turkey's elites.

Even though an undeniable shift in Turkish foreign policy has occurred over the past decade, it is still unclear whether these changes are truly substantial or if the anxieties of a complete reversal in foreign policy are the result of a worldview that fears that Turkey can only be oriented in one direction or the other.

A key element of Turkey's new foreign policy is the search for more autonomy. As a result of the new power configurations in the region after the end of the Cold War (including wars in Iraq and the Caucasus), Turkey, especially under Davutoğlu's tenure as foreign minister, has sought to assert its position as the major power broker in the region.

In this respect, neither Erdoğan's confrontation with Peres at Davos in 2009 nor the recent nuclear brokerage between Iran and Brazil are singular events. Rather, they should be seen as expressions of a newfound self-confidence and willingness to act autonomously.

The fact that Israel found itself as the main "target" in these instances reveals more about Israel's uncompromising desire to dictate its political and military will rather than a complete sea change in Turkish foreign policy.

An ever more isolated Israel is prone to view any deviation from the norms that have been established in the region in the last fifty years as a major threat to its "security." Given the context of the changing power dynamics, Israel's brutal interception of the flotilla could be seen as a planned strategy to teach a lesson to a new opponent, rather than a quarrel between old friends.

At the same time, one of the most important questions is the extent to which Turkey's new foreign policy initiatives are merely political maneuverings for a domestic audience. Despite the harsh condemnations of Israel by the prime minister, the parliament, as well as President of the Republic Abdullah Gül, Ankara has so far followed a careful diplomatic strategy.

Turkey's ambassador to Israel has been recalled, plans to transport water and natural gas to Israel have been put on halt, and a couple of military maneuvers have been cancelled. Yet no major military deals have been revoked so far.

Even more than these discrepancies between rhetoric and reality, the AKP's political discourse and practices reveal the structural dilemmas in Turkish politics and their impact on how the Palestinian cause is perceived and represented.

While the loss of lives understandably turned the attention to Turkey, it should be remembered that the flotilla was not an active state policy but a civil and international initiative. Moreover, relations between the AKP and the human rights and relief group Insani Yardim Vakfi (IHH), which participated in the flotilla, have not always been cordial.

However, the AKP appears to be attempting to seize and ride the tide of sympathy and concern for the passengers. Although visiting the wounded activists in their hospital bed can be seen as an act of concern and support, the fact that senior party officials welcomed the returning activists at Istanbul airport can also be seen as an attempt to co-opt the movement.

Turkey, with its well-established state tradition, has masterfully followed the traditional diplomatic route of attempting to protect and defend its citizens from breaches of international law by working within the appropriate international institutions.

Yet this same state tradition weighs heavily on state–civil society relations, as the state almost reflexively seeks to dominate any autonomous civil initiative. In this sense, the AKP's political maneuvers are not to be seen merely as party strategy, but are also manifestations of deeply internalized state discourses and practices of Turkish political culture.

In this respect, the widespread arguments in Turkish media and of political parties across the board that Israel has made its biggest mistake so far, and that relations have reached a point of no return, owe more to a nationalist discourse.

This nationalist discourse emphasizes (and exaggerates) the prominence of the Turkish state in place of offering a long-term analysis of Israeli policies in the region. It appropriates the popularity of movements initiated by nongovernmental organizations while at the same distrusting their independence. Thus it risks diverting attention away from generating tangible solidarity and understanding for the Palestinian cause and reducing the issue to a crisis between Turkey and Israel.

Rather than taking part in the worldwide support for Palestinian rights, and supporting civil society initiatives, the AKP's statist reflexes may actually serve to weaken the international dimension of the support and make it more vulnerable to propaganda attempts that portray Israel's illegal acts as a righteous struggle against a radical Islamist threat.

In addition to these deep-seated features of Turkish political culture, there may also be more immediate reasons why the AKP government may want to use this crisis for its own political purposes. Despite the rhetoric of making changes and taking some reluctant steps, the AKP government has to date hardly delivered on its promises. Two major factors stand out: the perennial Kurdish problem and the recent change of leadership in the main opposition Republican People's Party (CHP).

The resumption of attacks by the Kurdistan Worker's Party (PKK) has left more than thirty soldiers dead in the last two months. As a result, the AKP has come under increasing criticism both from the Kurdish parties and groups as well as opposition political parties.

As the AKP tries to play the leadership card in the Middle East, those who are critical of the party argue that there are more pressing and immediate domestic problems and accuse the AKP of using foreign policy adventures to mask its failure at home. While this isolationist discourse is partly motivated by the above-mentioned prejudices about the "backwardness" of Middle Eastern politics, and suspicions of a possible alliance between Israel and the PKK, it remains true that the Kurdish problem is the Achilles' heel not only for the AKP but also for the Turkish polity.

However, in spite of the AKP's highly dubious record, there is no reason why the two objectives, that is, further democratization at home and a more active foreign policy in the Middle East, should be seen as mutually exclusive rather than compatible and reinforcing political objectives.

As for the most recent developments in the main opposition party, a sex scandal involving the former leader of the CHP, Deniz Baykal, led to a significant change in the party's leadership. Although there was a wave of enthusiasm among the supporters of the CHP, it remains to be seen if the emergence of a new leadership also corresponds to a substantial change in party ideology.

The new CHP leader, Kemal Kılıçdaroğlu, hinted at broadening the party's base from the mostly urban middle and upper-middle classes to the underprivileged groups of the suburbs. Yet an initial rise in popularity has been short-lived in the face of the recent crisis. Instead, the AKP has tried to make the most of Erdoğan's charismatic leadership and wrest the momentum away from the CHP, at least for now.

It is only natural to expect the AKP to turn the recent crisis to their advantage. It is also an opportunity to test the leadership qualities of those in power. However, it is worth noting that the charismatic leadership easily turns into a cult of personality and, as such, can become an impediment for a more democratic and participatory political culture, as can be learned from examples such as Russia's Vladimir Putin or Italy's Silvio Berlusconi. Erdoğan is also quick to assume the role of undisputed chief and personalize politics rather than act as the leader of collective decision-making. The personalization of politics and the cult of personality have rarely been helpful in establishing the foundations of a solid and viable political structure.

As an Islamist political party and movement, the AKP also faces a dilemma in its contradictory attitudes toward Egypt and Sudan, to give only two relevant examples. While Israel's policies toward Gaza are harshly condemned both by the state and civil initiatives, there is silence over Egypt's blockade. While the rhetoric of solidarity and humanitarian aid against Israel's oppressive policies in Palestine fly high, no major statement has been made or protest held against Egypt's own contradictory policies toward Israel.

Furthermore, while the Sudanese government has been accused of genocide by the International Criminal Court, the AKP's policies toward Sudan have been accommodating, to say the least. In this respect, critics are quick to point out that conservative and Islamist movements in Turkey have not displayed the same degree of sensitivity when it came to a variety of human rights violations either at home or in other countries in the Middle East. In this regard, many warnings have already been voiced in order not to turn an important occasion to mobilize mass support against Israeli state policies into an anti-Semitic discourse, which, taking into consideration past practices toward minorities in contemporary Turkey and widespread ignorance about the historical background of the Palestinian plight, is always a present danger.

Finally, another tendency prevalent in both the Turkish media and the political discourse of the AKP is the reduction of the Palestinian problem to the predicament of Gaza by exclusively concentrating on conditions in the besieged territory. Since the specific purpose of the Freedom Flotilla was to draw attention to the Israeli blockade in Gaza, it is only natural that Gaza has been the center of attention in the weeks after the attack. However, the exclusive emphasis on Gaza is not confined to the latest developments but is the culmination of a longer process that was only intensified by the latest events.

In this sense, it should be recognized that unless the question of "who speaks for the Palestinians" is always kept in mind and discussed unfailingly, the broader dimensions of the Palestine issue—in all its aspects, from the right of return, to the realities on the ground in the West Bank, to the crisis of Palestinian leadership—can be replaced with reductionist views and expectations.

Many people hope that loss of lives on the flotilla was not in vain, that they mark an new phase in a worldwide mobilization to put more pressure on Israel to end its occupation and oppression of the Palestinian people.

What is at stake is to preserve this hope, building on the momentum gained through painful sacrifices, and turn them into concrete policies. While nurturing hope it is even more important not to fall for false promises, and to be alert against the excesses of political rhetoric.

It is true that Turkey's involvement can prove to be highly valuable to further the Palestinian cause. But Turkey's involvement and potential are preconditioned on recognizing its own internal dilemmas. Apart from taking the necessary steps for further democratization and creating the conditions for a more participatory public sphere at home, this means refraining from appropriating civil initiatives for narrow party interests, moderating statist reflexes and strictly nationalist discourses, and resisting the cult of the leader.

Turkish involvement must be constructed in terms of cooperation and solidarity, and must be seen as a learning process rather than one-dimensional help of a regional power seeking to play a leadership role. Instead of reviving the anachronistic and useless rhetoric of an Ottoman golden age, which can easily give way to the condescending attitude of those who see themselves as the heirs of a great empire, it would be more promising to demonstrate genuine willingness to learn from Palestine and the Palestinians. The Palestinian mirror is, after all, a litmus test for those who really want to engage in a struggle for justice, peace, and equality.

SMEARING THE IHH

Marsha B. Cohen

The IDF (Israeli Defense Forces) has backed down from the claim that forty activists on the Gaza flotilla, who had resisted the ship's interception by Israeli commandos in international waters on Monday, are "Al Qaeda mercenaries."

Some participants in the Gaza convoy are members of *Insan Hak ve Hürriyetleri İnsani Yardım Vakfı* (IHH)—the Foundation for Human Rights, Liberties, and Humanitarian Relief. IHH is a Turkish non-governmental organizaion (NGO) established in the early 1990s. Its mission is to provide humanitarian relief in regions of conflict or that have experienced natural disasters. For the past six years, IHH has held Special Consultative status as an NGO in the United Nations Economic and Social Council.

According to Max Blumenthal,[2] when he and Lia Tarachansky, an Israel-based freelance journalist fluent in Hebrew, called the IDF requesting more conclusive evidence of Al Qaeda affiliation than possession of bulletproof vests and night-vision goggles, they were each told, "We don't have any evidence." The IDF press release had been based on information emanating from Israeli Prime Minister Benjamin Netanyahu's National Security Council.

The next day, Blumenthal notes with satisfaction, the IDF's press office changed the headline to "Attackers of the IDF Soldiers Found Without Identification Papers,"[3] although the browser retains the original accusation of a link with Al Qaeda. The rewritten story, which still bears the date June 2, 2010, and the original time it was posted, omits any mention of a connection of the group with Al Qaeda.

However, the condemnation of IHH participants now ricocheting around the blogosphere isn't about to go away anytime soon. The sad truth, with all due respect to Max (and a great deal is due!), is that the IDF gave in on the paltry evidence gleaned from photos of night-vision goggles and bulletproof vests because they believe they have a weapon much more powerful—a pro-Israel blogosphere where no Israeli Jew can do anything wrong, and no Muslim can do anything right. And the claim that there is a link between "Islamic terrorism" and the participants in the Gaza flotilla doesn't need any pictures—a thousand words will do.

The link goes back to a strategy crafted in the aftermath of the events of September 11, 2001. In the wake of the destruction of the World Trade Center and an attack on the Pentagon by Islamic extremists, Israelis expressed the hope that Americans might view their plight more sympathetically. Israeli leaders anticipated that that they would be invited not only to join, but to be in the forefront of the impending war against Muslim fundamentalism. The U.S. priority, however, was enlisting and involving "moderate Arab states" in the "coalition of the willing" in the global fight against terrorism.

The timing was not particularly auspicious for Israel. Then–Prime Minister Ariel Sharon was struggling to keep his own coalition together. Its right-wing partners were demanding that he get tough with terrorists, expel Palestinian leader Yasir Arafat, and reject once and for all the idea of a Palestinian state in the West Bank and Gaza. Israeli aims and actions were on a collision course with the dynamics of U.S. foreign policy.

Israel's foreign minister, Shimon Peres (now the president), proposed that Israel affirm its agreement with U.S. aims in the "war on terror." Several cabinet ministers agreed with the ingenious suggestion that the Palestinian Authority (P.A.) be presented as "Israel's Taliban," and Sharon announced that the P.A. would be considered as a state that harbors terrorists.

The fairly rapid routing of the Taliban (with unacknowledged cooperation from Iran) and a spate of suicide bombings in Israel occurred in the weeks leading up with Sharon's "working visit" to the White House on November 21, 2001. According to the statement by the White House press secretary on that date, the topic of the meeting between Sharon and George W. Bush was to be "the international campaign against terrorism and the pursuit of peace in the Middle East." Analysts expected little from the meeting. They were surprised. Sharon came away not only with the inclusion of Israel in the frontline of the "war on terror," but with the unprecedented American affirmation of Israel's right to act both defensively and proactively in dealing with terrorists—a right that has gone almost unchallenged for nearly nine years. "Link to terror" became an elixir, believed to possess the almost magical property of being able to immunize Israeli policies from criticism.

So it's not surprising that, as the Gaza debacle unfolded on Monday, a link between the IHH and Al Qaeda was discovered. Appropriately perhaps, it was announced by the Israeli ambassador to Denmark, which is called the land of fairy tales. The French news agency AFP reported:

> Israeli Ambassador to Denmark Arthur Avnon said on Monday that his country only attacked the Gaza-bound aid flotilla earlier in the day after receiving reports that it had links to Al-Qaeda.
>
> "The people on board were not so innocent... and I can not imagine that another country would react any differently," the ambassador added. Avnon lamented the loss of life, but said that Israeli soldiers were attacked when they boarded the ship.[4]

Although mainstream media sites largely ignored the claim, it was picked up by Fox News[5] and then swirled through the right wing "pro-Israel" blogosphere.[6] A 2006–2007 working paper by Evan F. Kohlmann, "The Role of Islamic Charities in International Terrorist Recruitment and Financing," published by the Danish Institute for International Studies (DIIS), mysteriously surfaced.[7]

It is noteworthy, although it has not been pointed out by most of those circulating Kohlmann's twenty-three-page monograph, that it bears a disclaimer which clearly states that papers like Kohlmann's, which were published as part of DIIS's "Countering Radicalisation through Development Assistance" series, "do not reflect the views of the Danish Ministry of Foreign Affairs or any other government agency, nor do they constitute any official DIIS position."[8]

It is also worth noting that Kohlmann's status as an "anti-terrorism expert" is open to question. Tom Mills, writing for Spinwatch (April 29, 2008), called attention to the fact that Kohlmann was an eighteen-year-old freshman at Georgetown University when he began monitoring Islamist groups from the Internet. An intern for the Investigative Project, a Washington think tank, in 1998, Kohlmann was still an undergraduate when he began writing articles on terrorism for *The Journal of Counterterrorism & Security*.[9] Kohlmann's mentor, Steven Emerson, who had set up the Investigative Project, was the producer of the 1994 *Frontline* television special "Jihad in America" and the author of, among other anti-terrorism tracts, *Jihad Incorporated: A Guide to Militant Islam in the United States*, both of which have been recognized as unfairly profiling Muslims.[10]

When Kohlmann finished law school, he set up his own business as a consultant on terrorism, and secured a position as commentator for MSNBC. Mills wrote, "With no expertise beyond undergraduate qualifications and an internship at a dubious think tank, Kohlmann became a consultant to the U.S. Department of Defense, the Department of Justice, the FBI, the Crown Prosecution Service and Scotland Yard's SO-15 Counter Terrorism Command."[11] Mills noted that

Like other 'terrorism experts,' Kohlmann tends to demonise Islamist groups, and to link disparate groups and individuals into an encompassing narrative of international terrorism. His 'expertise' are therefore very useful to prosecutors who seek to demonstrate the malevolent intent of a defendant in the absence of convincing evidence of their preparation or planning of acts of terrorism.[12]

Professor of Sociology David Miller, of Strathclyde University, explained in the *Guardian* (May 13, 2008) that the lack of qualifications of self-styled terrorism experts like Kohlmann is only half the problem. "The real issue is one of independence: many of the expert witnesses to have appeared for the prosecution have been associated with rightwing or pro-Zionist organizations," Miller told John Grace. "Under these circumstances, how can their expertise not be in some way contaminated?"[13]

According to Kohlmann's working paper, IHH is an example of an Islamic charity which diverted funds intended for humanitarian relief and used them to buy weapons:

Turkish authorities began their own domestic criminal investigation of IHH as early as December 1997, when sources revealed that leaders of IHH were purchasing automatic weapons from other regional Islamic militant groups. IHH's bureau in Istanbul was thoroughly searched, and its local officers were arrested. Security forces uncovered an array of disturbing items, including firearms, explosives, bomb-making instructions, and a "jihad flag." After analyzing seized IHH documents, Turkish authorities concluded that "detained members of IHH were going to fight in Afghanistan, Bosnia, and Chechnya."[14]

Kohlmann cites a French intelligence report which claimed that the terrorist infiltration of IHH extended to its most senior ranks.

Kohlmann claims the report, written by famed counterterrorism magistrate Jean-Louis Bruguière, had charged IHH President Bulent Yildrum with having conspired in the mid-1990s to "recruit veteran soldiers in anticipation of the coming holy war [*jihad*]," and transferring cash, firearms, knives, and explosives, parenthetically on behalf of IHH.[15] Furthermore, Kohlmann said that an examination of IHH's phone records in Istanbul showed repeated telephone calls in 1996 to "an al-Qaeda guesthouse in Milan."

Bruguière had been called as an expert witness at the Seattle trial of Ahmed Ressam, the would-be "Millennium bomber" who had targeted Los Angeles International Airport in 1999. Bruguière, according to Kohlmann, testified that IHH had played an important role in the plot. Under "repeated questioning" from federal prosecutors, according to the trial transcript as rendered by Kohlmann (one can't help wondering why the questioning would need to be repeated), Bruguière depicted IHH as an NGO whose humanitarian work served as a cover for more nefarious activities.

As Kohlmann's report began circulating in support of Israeli charges that the participants in the Gaza flotilla were linked to terrorism in general and to Al Qaeda in particular, Alfred de Montesquiou of the Associated Press decided to phone Bruguière and verify Kohlmann's assertions in a telephone interview, which was published under the eye-grabbing headline "Interview: Turkish Aid Group Had Terror Ties."[16] Bruguière, currently the E.U.'s coordinator in a joint E.U.–U.S. terrorism finance tracking program, told de Montesquiou, "Elements within the charity supported jihadi operations in the 1990s." Nonetheless, Bruguière added that he didn't know whether they continued to do so. Nor did Bruguière mention the current head of IHH, Bulent Yildrum. Rather, Bruguière told de Montesquiou, "Some members of an international terrorism cell known as the *Fateh Kamel* network then worked at the IHH." Kamel was an Algerian-Canadian who Bruguière claimed had ties to then nascent Al Qaeda.

As an aside, it's ironic—but unnoticed by Kohlmann or anyone citing him—that Bruguière was also the judge who ordered the raids on the Mujehidin e-Kalk Organization (MEK, also abbreviated MKO) in Paris in June 2003.[17] An odd hybrid of Marxism and radical Islamism at the time of the Iranian revolution, MEK (which also operates under the name NCRI—National Council of Resistance of Iran) broke with the Khomeini regime after the latter had gained control of Iran in 1979.[18] During the Iran-Iraq war in the 1980s, MEK fought on the side of Saddam Hussein. Although it has engaged in terrorist acts and has the status of a quasi cult centered on its leader, Maryam Rajavi, MEK has nonetheless been championed as a possible instrument for regime change in Iran by prominent pro-Israel neoconservatives. Many MEK members are presently detained at Camp Ashraf in Iraq, where U.S. policy-makers debate how useful these terrorists might be in achieving American strategic goals. Unlike IHH, MEK is indeed considered to be a terrorist organization by the U.S. State Department government, despite the repeated efforts of some members of Congress to rehabilitate MEK's reputation. At the time of the 2003 raid, Bruguière said he had uncovered a "criminal conspiracy with the intent to prepare acts of terrorism and financing of a terrorist enterprise." (Shouldn't neocons supporting the MEK also be exposed for their own "links to terrorism"?)

In response to Bruguière's accusations that IHH had been tied to terrorism in the past, IHH board member Omer Faruk Korkmaz insisted IHH was a legal organization: "We don't know Ahmed Ressam or Fateh Kamel," Kormaz told de Montesquiou. "We don't approve of the actions of any terrorist organization in the world." Fatma Varol, an IHH volunteer at IHH's Istanbul headquarters, also challenged Bruguière's Seattle testimony about the organization to the *Christian Science Monitor* correspondent Iason Athanasiadis: "IHH was not related to jihadis but formed to help people who need help, such as the Muslims of Bosnia who were suffering from the Serb genocide," she says. "It's only a humanitarian aid foundation bringing help to needy people wherever there's conflict."[19]

Whatever Bruguière may (or may not) have testified about IHH, the French government doesn't consider it a terrorist group. Despite rumblings in the right-wing blogosphere that the CIA is hinting at members of Gaza flotilla's terrorist ties, it's not on the U.S. State Department's list of foreign terrorist organizations either, nor on Great Britain's. As Athanasiadis points out, Israel is the only country in the world to ban the IHH as a terrorist organization—and only since 2008, primarily because of its sympathy for the Palestinian cause and Hamas. Athanasiadis also notes, "The current Turkish government has publicly supported the organization and hinted that it might send an armed escort with the next ship or ships running the Israeli blockade of Gaza."

Bulent Yildrum himself was among the participants in the Gaza convoy and was inteviewed by BBC News on June 3. BBC reported that the activists, speaking on their return home, asserted that, in addition to the nine deaths caused by shots fired by the IDF, the Israeli commandos had also administered electric shocks and beaten passengers during their assault on the *Mavi Marmara*:

> Upon his arrival back in Turkey, he admitted some of the activists had grabbed the guns off soldiers in self-defence.
>
> "Yes, we took their guns. It would be self-defence even if we fired their guns. We told our friends on board: 'We will die, become martyrs, but never let us be shown... as the ones who used guns'. By this decision, our friends accepted death, and we threw all the guns we took from them into the sea."
>
> He described how a doctor and a journalist were both shot at close range, and said another activist was shot as he was surrendering.
>
> "I took off my shirt and waved it, as a white flag. We thought they would stop after seeing the white flag, but they continued killing people," he said. [20]

English-language Turkish news site *Zaman* interviewed Yildrum upon his return to Istanbul. Yildrum said everyone was shocked when the Israeli Navy attacked the *Mavi Marmara*, from the air and from the sea. "We thought maybe they were putting on a show for us. If we were in their waters, under Palestinian jurisdiction, then we would have imagined that they would attack us. They suddenly dropped people onto the ship. Our friends only put up civilian resistance. The entire press corps was there."[21]

> He said he told Israeli authorities during his interrogation that they were managing the process badly. "Then they asked us, 'Didn't you attack us with iron bars and axes?' I told them what I did was only self-defense. This was defense against helicopters and assault boats, against well-trained commandos. They lie when they say they were given permission to use real bullets after the 35th minute. They threw in gas bombs, which injured our friends. Only two of the initially fired bullets were rubber. The others were nail-like bullets. Our friend Cevdet was martyred. He is a member of the press. He was only taking pictures as the Israelis fired on us. They smashed his brain into pieces from exactly one meter away."[22]

Perhaps the least likely statement to come from an alleged "Al Qaeda sympathizer" or "anti-Semite" or operative comes at the end of Yildrum's Zaman interview:

> Yildrum vowed to fight the blockade of Gaza until it is lifted, "or we will come with bigger fleets from Egypt and from the sea. Let statesmen figure out what will happen then. We will pay a price, but so will you. All the conscientious people of the world stand united. We are not afraid of anything," he said.
>
> He also responded to allegations that the flotilla attacked by Israel was of an "Islamist nature." Yildrum said: "Had it

been Muslims killing Jews, I would again go with a flotilla. We are against all cruelty."[23]

The 600 to 700 participants—and the thousands behind the movements they represent—are a remarkably diverse, if unlikely, mélange. It's not just Turks like Bulan Yildrim, who probably have attracted the attention of the CIA and U.S. military intelligence because he had been an outspoken critic of the U.S. invasion of Iraq in 2003. The "Free Gaza" movement in Britain—its co-founders and its legal communications team, are English women between sixty-five and eighty-five—including a Jewish Holocaust survivor named Hedy Epstein.[24] The Gaza flotilla has brought together Greeks and Turks, who for over a century have viewed one another as enemies. Only from the Greek press does one learn that two of the six Gaza ships and three dozen activists in the convoy were Greek.[25]

Not unlike the FBI's attempts to discredit the American civil rights movement as a tool of Soviet communism half a century ago, the Israeli government's *hasbarah* network is branding the global outcry against Israeli policies and actions as a manifestation of "terrorism." But in an age of very real terror threats, the vague and vacuous "link to terror" elixir—a drink-me brew Israel believes makes it appear more powerful or more vulnerable, but always in the right and beyond censure—may finally have reached its expiration date.

Notes

1. (http://mondoweiss.net/2010/06/terror-smear-against-ihh-springs-from-a-familar-source.html#more-19867)

2. Max Blumenthal, "Under Scrutiny, IDF Retracts Claims About Flotilla's Al Qaeda Links," June 3, 2010. (http://maxblumenthal.com/2010/06/under-scrutiny-idf-retracts-claims-about-flotillas-al-qaeda-links/)

3. "Attackers of the IDF Soldiers Found Without Identification Papers," June 2, 2010. (http://webcache.googleusercontent.com/search?q=cache:qNY9voVo06 IJ:dover.idf.il/IDF/English/News/today/10/06/0201.htm)

4. AFP, "Israeli Diplomat says Al-Qaeda Linked to Gaza Aid Fleet," May 31, 2010. (http://nowlebanon.com/NewsArchiveDetails.aspx?ID=173171 #ixzz0ppM2hi00)

5. Fox News, "Israeli Officials Claim Aid Flotilla had Ties to Al Qaeda, PM Gives Military 'Full Support," May 23, 2010. (http://www.foxnews.com/world/2010/05/30/reports-israeli-ships-attack-aid-flotilla-dead/)

6. See "Israel: Gaza Freedom Flotilla Organizers Linked To Worldwide Terrorism," May 29, 2010. (http://www.israelnewsagency.com/gazafreedompeaceflotilla-hamasshipsisraelidfihhpalestineislamicjihadterrorismalqaedaturkeyturkishre-liefhumanitarianrelieffoundation48052910.html)

7. Evan F. Kohlmann, "The Role of Islamic Charities in International Terrorist Recruitment and Financing." Danish Institute for International Studies Working Paper, DIIS Working Paper 2006/7, January 2006, ISBN: 87-7605-126-9. (http://www.diis.dk/sw19083.asp)

8. Ibid.

9. Tom Mills, "Evan Kohlmann: the Doogie Howser of Terrorism?" April 29, 2008. (http://www.spinwatch.org.uk/-articles-by-category-mainmenu-8/74-terror-spin/4850-evan-kohlmann-the-doogie-howser-of-terrorism)

10. Profile, Steven Emerson. (http://www.rightweb.irc-online.org/profile/Emerson_Steven/)

11. Tom Mills, "Evan Kohlmann: the Doogie Howser of Terrorism?"

12. Ibid.

13. John Grace, "Status of Terrorism Experts Questioned," *Guardian*, May 13, 2008 (http://www.guardian.co.uk/education/2008/may/13/highereducation.academicexperts)

14. Evan F. Kohlmann, "The Role of Islamic Charities in International Terrorist Recruitment and Financing."

15. Jean-Louis Bruguière and Jean-Francois Ricard, *"Requisitoire Definitifaux aux Fins de Non-Lieu. De Non-Lieu partiel. De Requalification. De Renvoi devant le Tribunal Correctionnel, de mantien sous Controle Judiciaiare et de maintien en Detention."* Cour D'Appel de Paris; Tribunal de Grande Instance de Paris. No. Parquet: P96 253 3901.2. All five of Kohlmann's citations from this document claim to be drawn from a single page of this document—page 112.

16. Alfred de Montesquiou, "AP Interview: Turkish Aid Group had Terror Ties." (http://news.yahoo.com/s/ap/20100602/ap_on_re_eu/eu_gaza_ships_terror_ties)

17. Henri Astier, BBC News Online, Europe, "Profile: France's Top Anti-Terror Judge," July 1, 2003. (http://news.bbc.co.uk/2/hi/3031640.stm)

18. (http://www.fas.org/irp/world/para/mek.htm)

19. Iason Athanasiadis, "Targetted by the Israeli Raid: Who is the IHH?" *Christian Science Monitor*, June 1, 2010. (http://www.csmonitor.com/World/Middle-East/2010/0601/Targeted-by-Israeli-raid-Who-is-the-IHH)

20. BBC News, "Activists Describe Israeli Raid on Gaza Aid Convoy," June 3, 2010. (http://news.bbc.co.uk/2/hi/world/middle_east/10206802.stm)

21. Today's *Zaman*, "IHH Chief Tells of Violence, Chaos on International Aid Ship," June 4, 2010. (http://todayszaman.com/tz-web/news-212070-ihh-chief-tells-of-violence-chaos-on-international-aid-ship.html)

22. Ibid.

23. Ibid.

24. Robert Booth, "Grey Power for Gaza," *Guardian*, June 3, 2010. (http://www.guardian.co.uk/world/2010/jun/03/grey-power-free-gaza)

25. *Kathimerini*, "Israeli Raid on Ships Rocks Greek Relations," June 1, 2010. (http://www.ekathimerini.com/4dcgi/_w_articles_politics_100003_01/06/2010_117407)

VICTIMHOOD, AGGRESSION, AND TRIBALISM

Glenn Greenwald

One of the primary reasons the Turkish government has been so angry in its denunciations of the Israeli attack on the flotilla is because many of the dead were Turkish citizens. That's what governments typically do: object vociferously when their citizens are killed by foreign nations under extremely questionable circumstances. Needless to say, that principle—as all principles are—will be completely discarded when it comes to the U.S. protection of Israel.

From Fox News:

> A U.S. citizen of Turkish origin was among the nine people killed when Israeli commandos attacked a Gaza-bound aid flotilla.... An official from the Turkish Islamic charity that spearheaded the campaign to bust the blockade on Gaza identified the U.S. citizen as 19-year-old Furkan Dogan.... Dogan, who held a U.S. passport, had four bullet wounds to the head and one to the chest.... ("American Citizen Among Those Killed in Flotilla Raid," June 3, 2010)

Will the fact that one of the dead at Israel's hands was an American teenager with four bullet wounds to his head alter the Obama administration's full-scale defense of Israel? Does that question even need to be asked? Not even American interests can undermine reflexive U.S. support for anything Israel does; even the Chief of the Mossad acknowledged this week that "Israel is progressively becoming a burden on the United States." One dead nineteen-year-old American with four bullet holes in his head (especially one of Turkish origin with a Turkish-sounding name) surely won't have any impact.

On June 1, newly elected British Prime Minister David Cameron became the latest world leader to unequivocally condemn Israel, saying the attack was "completely unacceptable" and demanding an end to the blockade. But on Charlie Rose's show on June 2, Joe Biden defended Israel with as much vigor as any Netanyahu aide or *Weekly Standard* polemicist. Biden told what can only be described as a lie when, in order to justify his rhetorical question "What's the big deal here?" he claimed that the ships could have simply delivered their aid to Israel and Israel would then have generously sent it to Gaza. ("They've said, 'Here you go. You're in the Mediterranean. This ship—if you divert slightly north you can unload it and we'll get the stuff into Gaza.'") In fact, contrary to the Central Lie being told about the blockade, Israel prevents all sorts of humanitarian items having nothing whatsoever to do with weapons from entering Gaza, including many of the supplies carried by the flotilla.

One can express all sorts of outrage over the Obama administration's depressingly predictable defense of the Israelis, even at the cost of isolating ourselves from the rest of the world, but ultimately, on some level, wouldn't it have been even more indefensible—or at least oozingly hypocritical—if the United States had condemned Israel? After all, what did Israel do in this case that the United States hasn't routinely done and continues to do? As even our own military officials acknowledge, we're slaughtering an "amazing number" of innocent people at checkpoints in Afghanistan. We're routinely killing civilians in all sorts of imaginative ways in countless countries, including with drone strikes, which a U.N. official just concluded are illegal. We're even targeting our own citizens for due-process-free assassination. We've been arming Israel and feeding them billions of dollars in aid and protecting them diplomatically as they (and we) have been doing things like this for decades. What's the Obama administration supposed to say about what Israel did: We condemn the killing of unarmed civilians? We decry these violations of international law? Even by typical standards of government hypocrisy, who in the U.S. government could possibly say any of that with a straight face?

What this really underscores is that the mentality driving both Israel and the United States is quite similar, which is why those two countries find such common cause, even when the rest of the world recoils in revulsion. One of the more amazing developments in the flotilla aftermath is how a claim that initially appeared too self-evidently ludicrous to be invoked by anyone—Israel was the victim here and was acting against the ship in self-defense—has actually become the central premise in Israeli and (especially) American discourse about the attack (and as always, there is far more criticism of Israeli actions in Israel than in the United States).

US VERSUS THEM

A prime cause of this inversion is the distortion in perception brought about by rank tribalism. Those whose worldview is shaped by their identification as members of a particular religious, nationalistic, or ethnic group invariably overvalue the wrongs done to them and greatly undervalue the wrongs their group perpetrates. Those whose world view is shaped by tribalism are typically plagued by an extreme persecution complex (*The whole world is against us!!! Everyone who criticizes us is hateful and biased!!!*). *Haaretz* reports on June 2 that "Jewish Republicans and Democrats in the U.S. gave a rare demonstration of unity on Wednesday when they backed Israel's raid of a Gaza-bound humanitarian aid flotilla." Gee, whatever could account for that "rare demonstration of unity" between these left-wing Jewish progressives and hard-core, Jewish right-wing war cheerleaders who agree on virtually nothing else? My, it's such a mystery.

I can't express how many e-mails I've received over the last week, from self-identified Jewish readers (almost exclusively), along the lines of: I'm a true progressive, agree with you on virtually every issue, but hate your views on Israel. When it comes to Israel, we see the same mindset from otherwise admirable Jewish progressives such as Anthony Weiner, Jerry Nadler, Eliot Spitzer, Alan Grayson, and (after a brief stint of deviation) Barney Frank. On this one issue, they magically abandon their opposition to military attacks on civilians, their defense of weaker groups being bullied and occupied by far stronger factions, their belief that unilateral military attacks are unjustified, and suddenly find common cause with Charles Krauthammer, the *Weekly Standard*, and the Bush administration in justifying even the most heinous Israeli crimes of aggression.

It will never cease to be mystifying (at least to me) that they never question why they suddenly view the world so differently when it comes to Israel. They never wonder to themselves: *I had it continuously drummed into my head from the time I was a small child, from every direction, that Israel was special and was to be cherished, that it's fundamentally good but persecuted and victimized by Evil Arab forces surrounding it, that I am a part of this group and should see the world accordingly. Is this tribal identity that was pummeled into me from childhood—rather than some independent, dispassionate analysis— the reason I find myself perpetually sympathizing with and defending Israel?*

Doesn't the most minimal level of intellectual awareness—indeed, the concept of adulthood itself—require that re-analysis? And, of course, the *self-hating* epithet, with which I've naturally been bombarded relentlessly over the last week, is explicitly grounded in the premise that one should automatically defend one's "own group" rather than endeavor to objectively assess facts and determine what is right and true.

This tribalism is hardly unique to Israel and Jews; it's instead universal. As the Bush years illustrated, there is no shortage of Americans who "reason" the same way: *I was taught from childhood that America is right and thus, even in adulthood, defend America no matter what it does; my duty as an American is to defend and justify what America does, and any American who criticizes the U.S. is "self-hating" and anti-American; the wrongs perpetrated by Us to Them pale in comparison to the wrongs perpetrated by Them on Us.*

Or listen to Fox News fearmongers declare how Christians in the United States and/or white males—comprising the vast majority of the population and every power structure in the country—are the Real Persecuted Victims, from the "war on Christmas" to affirmative action evils. Ronald Reagan even managed to convince much of the country that the true economic injustices in America were caused by rich black women driving their Cadillacs to collect their welfare checks. This kind of blinding, all-consuming tribalism leads members of even the most powerful group to convince themselves that they are deeply victimized by those who are far weaker, those whose necks have been under the boots of the stronger group for decades, if not longer.

That's just the standard symptom of the disease of tribalism, and it finds expression everywhere, in every group. It's just far more significant—and far more destructive—when the groups convincing themselves that they are the Weak and Bullied Victims are actually the strongest forces by far on the planet, with the greatest amount of weaponry and aggression, who have been finding justifications for so long for their slaughtering of civilians that, as Israeli Amos Oz suggested this week about his country, there are virtually no limits left on the naked aggression that will be justified. Thus, even when Israel attacks a ship full of civilians and wheelchairs in international waters and kills at least nine human beings, this is depicted by its tribal loyalists as an act of justified self-defense against the Real Aggressors.

SCHUMER'S *SIPPENHAFTUNG*

Juan Cole

"Gaza" is an abstraction to most Israelis and to most blind partisans of Israel like Senator Charles Schumer of New York. A majority of the 1.5 million Gazans is not even from Gaza, but rather from what is now Israel.

Americans do not know, and perhaps do not care, that 68 percent of Palestinians in Gaza are refugees living in eight refugee camps, who were ethnically cleansed and violently expelled from their homes in what is now Israel in 1947 and 1948. And no, they were not for the most part combatants, just civilians caught up in a civil war of sorts. They lost massive amounts of property and their homes, which would now be worth billions, but have never received a dime from the Israelis in reparations or compensation. Then in winter of 2008–2009, the Israeli military destroyed one in every eight Palestinian homes, rendering even more people homeless.

The website Think Progress revealed that recently Schumer made these remarks to an Orthodox Jewish audience in New York:

> The Palestinian people still don't believe in the Jewish state, in a two-state solution. More do than before, but a majority still do not. Their fundamental view is, the Europeans treated the Jews badly and gave them our land—this is Palestinian thinking [...] They don't believe in the Torah, in David [...] You have to force them to say Israel is here to stay. The boycott of Gaza

to me has another purpose—obviously the first purpose is to prevent Hamas from getting weapons by which they will use to hurt Israel—but the second is actually to show the Palestinians that when there's some moderation and cooperation, they can have an economic advancement. When there's total war against Israel, which Hamas wages, they're going to get nowhere. And to me, since the Palestinians in Gaza elected Hamas, while certainly there should be humanitarian aid and people not starving to death, to strangle them economically until they see that's not the way to go, makes sense.

So anything short of "starving to death," i.e., mass extermination in the camps, is all right as long as it convinces the enemy?

How about something short of starving to death, such as 10 percent of children being stunted from malnutrition? Would that be worth it? Or a majority of Gazans being "food insecure," according to the United Nations? Both are the current situation, which is supported by Schumer. How about Gaza children looking for food in garbage? Some 56 percent of Gaza Palestinians are children, who hardly voted for Hamas but whom Schumer wishes to punish economically.

Meanwhile, Schumer doesn't recognize a Palestinian state, but he nevertheless gets three solid meals a day.

Schumer accuses the Palestinians of not "recognizing" Israel, which is sort of like accusing the pelicans in the Gulf of Mexico of not "recognizing" BP. If Schumer wants the recognition and good will of the Gaza Palestinians, he should arrange for them to be paid for the homes and farms out of which they were chased by the Israelis, who made them homeless refugees in a kind of vast concentration camp in Gaza and are now half-starving them.

As Think Progress explained, nothing Schumer said in his address is true. A majority of Palestinians favors a two-state solution. Moreover, Palestinians are Christians and Muslims, who do in fact acknowledge the Torah (the Hebrew Bible, which the Quran praises as full of guidance and light) and David (whom the Quran calls "Da'ud"). Schumer is shamelessly ignorant about Palestinian culture, but it is true that they do not draw from David's existence or from the Quran's praise of the Torah or Bible the same conclusion as contemporary political Zionists or Jewish nationalists, that Jews have a right to expel local people from Palestine and usurp their property without compensation. But then virtually no Jews drew such a conclusion in the United States until after World War II, and most diaspora Jews rejected such an idea until that era.

Although Israeli propaganda, which goes by the Hebrew term *hasbara*, maintains that the siege of Gaza comes as a response to Muslim militants firing small homemade rockets into nearby Israeli towns (most of them landed uselessly in the desert), this argument holds no water. The blockade was instituted only after the fundamentalist party, Hamas, came to power, and was intended to weaken the party and overthrow it, as leaked Israeli memos have demonstrated. As Schumer's remarks show, the blockade was intended to produce a political result, the "recognition" of Israel by the Gaza Palestinians, which in essence would be a formal relinquishment of their claims to their families' property taken from them by Israelis in 1948 and their right to return home to Israel. In exchange, they would receive nothing but the lifting of the blockade.

As despicable as Schumer's comments were, the Israeli blockade of Gaza is not even the central issue. If it were, then any Israeli loosening of the blockade would seem to be an advance.

In fact, the blockade is a symptom of the underlying issue, which is Palestinian statelessness. The Palestinians of Gaza have no state. What the Israelis deign to call the "Hamas regime" is no such thing because it lacks sovereignty, over its borders, air, sea, imports, and exports. (The idea that Israel is "at war" with its own occupied territory is laughable.) The Israeli "withdrawal" of 2005 simply removed a few thousand colonists and withdrew troops to the borders (except for occasional raids and air strikes). But it did not allow the creation of a sovereign state. Gaza Palestinians are excluded from a third of their own farmland by Israeli restrictions on where people can live. That so many Palestinians are unemployed, that their industries have collapsed, that most lack clean water to drink, and that malnutrition is causing stunting in 10 percent of children—all these outrages derive from their lack of a sovereign state to look out for their interests.

The problems inflicted on Gaza Palestinians by the Israeli blockade will only be resolved by the bestowal of citizenship on Gazans, either by a Palestinian state (which does not exist and would have to be created) or by Israel (which does not want the Gazans as citizens but may end up being stuck with them).

A Palestinian state is important because the Palestinian people are stateless. Being without citizenship in a state leaves people vulnerable and without rights, since there is no state that will defend their rights. If someone just moved into your house while you were out watching a movie, you could ask the police of your town to remove them, with reference to the property deed that you filed with your municipal authorities. But if Israelis take over Palestinian land, the Palestinians have no one to complain to. The Israeli courts favor the colonizers and don't recognize Palestinian rights. Palestinians, being stateless, do not have the right to have rights. (Sociologist Margaret Somers has pointed out that former U.S. Supreme Court Chief Justice Warren Burger defined citizenship as "the right to have rights.")

As such, the Palestinians are the most oppressed people in the world. There are other peoples who feel that they have the wrong citizenship and would like to secede, but at least they have a government and rights within that government's framework. No one can just throw them off their farms, claiming that they do not exist. They have someone to give them a passport, which Palestinians do not. There are other peoples that are in conflict and being killed in fair numbers. A not-insignificant number of Palestinians have been killed by the Israelis, whether through often indiscriminate and disproportionate violence or through food and services blockades. Of course there are other groups that are killed in larger numbers. But I would argue that the psychological toll taken by the imposition of statelessness on a people is more debilitating than the knowledge that some of the group has been killed by oppressors.

European Jews themselves were made stateless by Nazi decree, as were millions of other Europeans. It was a trend in the 1930s and 1940s—leftists were denaturalized by Franco in Spain, for example. In the post–World War II world, citizenship has become recognized as key to basic human dignity and civil rights. There are only about 12 million stateless now, and the Palestinians are the single largest group of them.

What I cannot understand is how Israel, the United States (including Senator Schumer), and the European Union expect this thing to end. In the West Bank there are three political processes. First, there are the proximity talks between Palestine Authority President Mahmoud Abbas and the Israelis (talks about the conditions for talks). Second, there are municipal elections this summer in the West Bank. Third, the Fayyad Plan calls for the Palestine Authority to have some 20,000 trained security forces in the West Bank by summer 2011, at which point Salam Fayyad, the appointed prime minister of the Palestine Authority, and his government could well declare an independent state.

But in Gaza there is no political process and no prospect of one. The fundamentalist party, Hamas, won the January 2006 parliamentary elections in the Palestine Authority. But Israel and the United States immediately rejected its victory, kidnapped parliamentarians and disrupted the government, and then supported a coup in the West Bank by Fatah, the secular nationalist party of President Abbas. An attempt to extend the coup to the Gaza Strip failed, so Hamas remained in power there. The Israelis have attempted to overthrow and dislodge Hamas, including through the blockade on ordinary civilians and through the 2008–2009 Gaza War, but so far have failed.

Unless a way can be found to hold legitimate elections in Gaza, it will remain isolated, both politically and economically, even from other Palestinians in the West Bank, so that the lives of its inhabitants will continue to be hell. The Israeli far right, now in power politically, will use the isolation of Gaza to argue that there is no single Palestinian representative with whom they can negotiate, and that they therefore do not need to negotiate and can go blockading Gaza and stealing the land of West Bank Palestinians.

To repeat: The Israeli blockade of Gaza is a war crime and it is harming the health and well-being of the Gaza Palestinians. But it is not in and of itself the problem, such that easing the blockade solves anything fundamental. Incorporation of Gaza residents into a sovereign state, such that they have citizenship and can exercise popular sovereignty, is the key to any real advance.

Washington and Tel Aviv no longer have infinite time to resolve the issue. The blockade of civilians is backfiring on the Israelis by provoking international civil society to take steps, whether dockworkers in Stockholm and Oakland, California, who decline to offload Israeli ships for a day or a week, or consumer boycotts of goods produced by Israeli squatters in the Palestinian West Bank, or further aid flotillas mounted by humanitarian groups aiming to rescue the children of Gaza from the Scrooges like Senator Schumer.

The international community has to stop dithering and intervene to end this Israeli lawlessness in Gaza, and provide a path for Gaza Palestinians to citizenship in some sovereign state. The consequences of not doing so are now potentially explosive.

Palestinian statelessness is a sad throwback to the inhumane policies of European governments of the 1930s and 1940s, as is Senator Schumer's logic that all Gaza Palestinians, including children, should be economically punished until they agree with Schumer's Zionism. Since the children of Gaza did not vote for Hamas, there is only one way that position makes sense. If they are being punished for Hamas's crimes, then it must be because they are related to Hamas members.

Punishing people because they are related to enemies of the state is called in German *Sippenhaft* or *Sippenhaftung*. I don't usually like such analogies from the 1930s and 1940s in Europe to contemporary Zionist thinking, because they inevitably offend even a sympathetic Jewish audience. But it should be noted that *Sippenhaftung* was implemented against gentile German family members of dissidents such as those involved in the plot to assassinate Hitler, and that Stalin also deployed the tactic of punishing relatives of perceived dissidents. And there is no other way to read Schumer's prescription for putting Gaza's children on a diet than as a contemporary form of *Sippenhaftung*.

It is shameful, and he and others who speak this way deserve the comparison for these inhumane sentiments.

DEFENDING THE INDEFENSIBLE: A HOW-TO GUIDE

Stephen M. Walt

Powerful states often do bad things. When they do, government officials and sympathizers inevitably try to defend their conduct, even when those actions are clearly wrong or obviously counterproductive. This is called being an "apologist," although people who do this rarely apologize for much of anything.

Some readers out there may aspire to careers in foreign policy, and you may be called upon to perform these duties as part of your professional obligations. Moreover, all of us need to be able to spot the rhetorical ploys that governments use to justify their own misconduct. To help students prepare for future acts of diplomatic casuistry, and to raise public consciousness about these tactics, I offer as a public service this handy twenty-one-step guide: "How to Defend the Indefensible and Get Away With It." The connection to recent events is obvious, but such practices are commonplace in many countries and widely practiced by non-state actors as well.

Here are my twenty-one handy talking points when you need to apply the whitewash:

1. We didn't do it! (Denials usually don't work, but it's worth a try.)
2. We know you think we did it but we aren't admitting anything.

3. Actually, maybe we did do something but not what we are accused of doing.

4. OK, we did it but it wasn't that bad. ("Waterboarding isn't really torture, you know.")

5. Well, maybe it was pretty bad but it was justified or necessary. ("We only torture terrorists, or suspected terrorists, or people who might know a terrorist…")

6. What we did was really quite restrained, when you consider how powerful we really are. I mean, we could have done something *even worse.*

7. Besides, what we did was technically legal under some interpretations of international law (or at least as our lawyers interpret the law as it applies to us).

8. Don't forget: The other side is much worse. In fact, they're evil. Really.

9. Plus, they started it.

10. And remember: We are the good guys. We are not morally equivalent to the bad guys no matter what we did. Only morally obtuse, misguided critics could fail to see this fundamental distinction between Them and Us.

11. The results may have been imperfect, but our intentions were noble. (Invading Iraq may have resulted in tens of thousands of dead and wounded and millions of refugees, but *we meant well.*)

12. We have to do things like this to maintain our credibility. You don't want to encourage those bad guys, do you?

13. Especially because the only language the other side understands is force.

14. In fact, it was imperative to teach them a lesson. For the nth time.

15. If we hadn't done this to them they would undoubtedly have done something even worse to us. Well, maybe not. But who could take that chance?

16. In fact, no responsible government could have acted otherwise in the face of such provocation.

17. Plus, we had no choice. What we did may have been awful, but all other policy options had failed and/or nothing else would have worked.

18. It's a tough world out there and Serious People understand that sometimes you have to do these things. Only ignorant idealists, terrorist sympathizers, craven appeasers, and/or treasonous liberals would question our actions.

19. In fact, whatever we did will be worth it eventually, and someday the rest of the world will thank us.

20. We are the victims of a double standard. Other states do the same things (or worse) and nobody complains about them. What we did was therefore permissible.

21. And if you keep criticizing us, we'll get really upset and then we might do something really crazy. You don't want that, do you?

Repeat as necessary.

TREAT ISRAEL LIKE IRAN

Stephen Kinzer

Quick, name the rogue state in the Middle East. Hints: It has an active nuclear-weapons program but conducts it in secret; its security organs regularly kill perceived enemies of the state, both at home and abroad; its political process has been hijacked by religious fundamentalists who believe they are doing God's will; its violent recklessness destabilizes the world's most volatile region; and it seems as deaf to reason as it is impervious to pressure. Also, its name begins with *I*.

How you answer this riddle depends in part on where you sit. From an American perspective, the obvious answer is Iran. Iran seems alone and friendless, a pariah in the world, and deservedly so given its long list of sins. In Washington's view, Iran poses one of the major threats to global security.

Many people in the world, however, see Iran quite differently: as just another struggling country with valuable resources, no more or less threatening than any other, ruled by a regime that, while thuggish, wins grudging admiration for standing up to powerful bullies. They are angrier at Israel, which they see as violent, repressive, and contemptuous of international law, but nonetheless endlessly coddled by the United States.

The way American diplomats have spent the days following the Israeli raid on a flotilla of ships bringing relief aid to Gaza shows how differently the United States treats Israel and Iran. After Monday's deadly attack, a U.S. envoy, George Mitchell, flew to Tel Aviv and then traveled to Ramallah. He urged Israeli and Palestinian leaders to salvage whatever possible from the debacle and look for common ground, even though prospects for peace are remote.

American diplomats at the United Nations, meanwhile, are working intensely to win support for punishing new sanctions on Iran. Their message about Iran is the precise opposite of the one Mitchell is preaching to Israelis and Palestinians: Negotiations are hopeless, oppressive regimes understand only force, and all compromise equals appeasement.

It is always difficult to compare the danger one country poses to global security with that posed by another, and it is natural to treat old friends differently from longtime enemies. Israel is a far more open and free society than Iran. Millions of Americans feel personally tied to its fate. Nonetheless the contrast in American attitudes toward the two countries is striking. Toward Israel the attitude is: You may be rascals sometimes, but whatever pranks you pull, you're our friend and we'll forgive you. Toward Iran, it's the opposite: You are our implacable enemy, so nothing you do short of abject surrender will satisfy us.

This dichotomy is now on especially vivid display. Israel's raid on the Gaza flotilla, like the Gaza occupation itself, has evoked only mild clucks of disapproval in Washington. But when Turkey and Brazil worked out the framework of a possible nuclear compromise with Iran a couple of weeks ago, American officials angrily rejected it.

Instead of treating Israel and Iran so differently, the West might try placing them in the same policy basket, and seeking equivalent concessions from both.

It is easy to denounce Israel and Iran as disturbers of whatever peace exists in the Middle East, and to lament that the region will be in turmoil as long as they keep behaving as they do. More important is the fact that both countries are powerful, and can upset any accord to which they are not a party. Punishing, sanctioning, and isolating them would be emotionally satisfying, but it is not likely to help calm the region.

Instead of pushing Israel and Iran into corners, making them feel besieged and friendless, the world should realize that without both of them, there will be no peace in the Middle East. This requires a new, more creative approach to the challenge of protecting Israel over the long term. It also requires a willingness to engage Iran. As Lyndon Johnson famously reasoned when he reappointed J. Edgar Hoover to head the FBI, "It's probably better to have him inside the tent pissing out than outside the tent pissing in."

Treating Israel and Iran more equally would also mean judging their nuclear programs by equivalent standards. If Israel and Iran are placed under the same set of rigorous nuclear safeguards, the Middle East will quickly become a safer place.

In the same spirit of equality, the world should do whatever possible to encourage higher human rights standards in Israel and Iran. Ruling groups in both countries treat some honest critics as traitors or terrorists. They rule without the tolerance that illuminates Jewish and Persian history.

Israel and Iran have come to pose parallel challenges. They are the region's outcasts—yet the region will never stabilize until they are brought back out of the geopolitical cold. Rather than stoke their escalating hostility, the United States should work to reduce tensions between them. Holding them to the same standards would be a start.

THE VICTIM THAT IS ISRAEL

Arun Gupta

Amid the continuing fallout over the deadly confrontation on the Gaza aid ship *Mavi Marmara*, there is a critical historical lesson: There is only one real victim, and that is Israel. Sure, the "small, isolated" (*Wall Street Journal*, June 1, 2010) nation may *appear* to have been the aggressor, having surrounded a humanitarian convoy in international waters with naval assault boats and helicopters before storming in with heavily armed elite forces, killing and wounding dozens of civilians, but it was the one acting in self-defense.

Appearances are deceiving because understanding Israel's eternal victimhood requires the proper mindset. First, the *New Republic* lets us know, the incident involved "a ship of terrorists" attempting "to open an arms importation route to Gaza" (June 9, 2010). With that fact established, the *Atlantic Monthly*'s Jeffrey Goldberg, who has been hanging "around a lot of Israeli generals lately," kindly advises us that there should be "no particular pain felt for the dead on the boat."

On the other hand, "There's real pain in Israel…pain at the humiliation of the flotilla raid, pain on behalf of the injured soldiers, and pain that the geniuses who run this country could not figure out a way to outsmart a bunch of Turkish Islamists and their useful idiot fellow travelers" (June 1, 2010). The White House sees no point in condemning Israel's killing of civilians in the flotilla because "nothing can bring them back" (briefing by U.S. press secretary Robert Gibbs, June 1, 2010). Hillary Clinton (*Village Voice*, December

6, 2005) provides further insight, explaining how benighted Arabs who "are not sure what democracy means" should look to Israel—"a beacon of democracy"—as an example. Clearly, Israelis are the only true humans worthy of our sympathy, a point the *Washington Post* understands, stating, "We have no sympathy for the motives of the participants in the flotilla" (June 1, 2010).

Why should one try to ease suffering in Gaza? Israel is a "peace-loving society" (*Educational Review Journal*, forthcoming) that offered to escort the flotilla of "naïveté and malice" (Slate, June 4, 2010) to the "Ashdod Port and arrange for the delivery of their supplies to Gaza after security checks, over land" (*Jerusalem Post*, June 1, 2010). It was just trying to prevent "the flow of seaborne military supplies to Hamas," the Israeli ambassador wrote in the *New York Times* (June 2, 2010). After all, Israel was only asking to search the flotilla's cargo for banned "war materiel" (*New York Times*, June 6, 2010) such as coriander, ginger, nutmeg, dried fruit, fabric for clothing, nuts, musical instruments, chickens, donkeys, horses, fishing rods, and newspapers (*Economist*, June 1, 2010).

Washington Post columnist Charles Krauthammer comprehends that "the point understood by the blockade-busting flotilla of useful idiots and terror sympathizers… is to deprive Israel of any legitimate form of self-defense" (June 4, 2010). Krauthammer deduces brilliantly, "The world is tired of these troublesome Jews, 6 million—that number again—hard by the Mediterranean, refusing every invitation to national suicide. For which they are relentlessly demonized, ghettoized and constrained from defending themselves, even as the more committed anti-Zionists—Iranian in particular—openly prepare a more final solution." As night follows day, if Israel let the aid flotilla reach Gaza, a second Holocaust would result.

Only Israel has "legitimate security needs," as Hillary Clinton explains (Reuters, June 1, 2010), whereas Palestinians' "legitimate needs" are limited to "sustained humanitarian assistance and regular access to reconstruction materials." Because Palestinians "are not sure what democracy means," their needs do not include an end to the siege, basic human rights, or a viable state.

Reports about Israel's years-long siege of Gaza—where "more than 60 percent of families do not have enough food to eat, there are daily electricity cuts, and the water network is operating far below capacity" (Oxfam press release, May 31, 2010)—are irrelevant. Sure, Israeli policy may be to "put the Palestinians on a diet" (*Guardian*, May 16, 2006), fulfilling army chief General Rafeal Eitan's longing to turn Arabs into "drugged cockroaches in a bottle" (*Washington Report on Middle East Affairs*, February 2005), but in actuality the "humanitarian situation in Gaza is good and stable" (Agence France-Presse, May 26, 2010), and people there dine out on "beef stroganoff and cream of spinach soup." In any case, "concern for Gaza and Israel's blockade is so out of balance," counsels Thomas Friedman (*New York Times*, June 1, 2010). He suggests we focus instead on the bombings of mosques of an Islamic sect in Pakistan, the killings of activists in Iran, and the trashing of a children's summer camp in Gaza.

But noble-minded Israel still shows concern. Just as it is always seeking peace with hostile Arab neighbors bent on annihilating it, Israel was willing to deliver supplies that are in abundance in Gaza (*Jerusalem Post*, June 1, 2010) despite the "Gazan terrorists [in charge] who proclaim their goal is to destroy Israel" (Daily Beast, May 31, 2010). So "if anyone goes without food, shelter or medicine, that is by the choice of the Hamas government" (*New York Times*, June 2, 2010). But the flotilla sabotaged Israel's goodwill.

It's another example of how Israel is victimized, just as when it selflessly disengaged from Gaza in 2005. But Israel's generosity, including firing more than 7,700 artillery shells into northern Gaza in less than a year after its withdrawal (Human Rights Watch, June 19, 2006), was met with Hamas rockets (*Democracy Now!*, January 5, 2009), which is why one senior Israeli official threatened Palestinians with a "bigger shoah" (*Haaretz*, February 29, 2008). Then there are "Hamas sympathizers" (*Wall Street Journal*, June 7, 2010) who ask why, if Israel disengaged from Gaza, does it still control its coast, airspace, borders, commerce, fuel, water, and electricity (PLO Negotiations Affairs Department website); why have Israel and the United States rejected Palestinian and Arab offers of a two-state solution based on the 1967 borders for some forty years (*Democracy Now!*, November 27, 2007); and why has Israel sabotaged virtually every ceasefire (*Haaretz*, December 3, 2006) Fatah and Hamas have agreed to in recent years, even unilateral ones.

These misperceptions persist because those who hold them fail to comprehend that Israel only "responds" (TomDispatch.com, February 26, 2008) to attacks from the subhuman Arabs. Now we can correctly perceive the confrontation between Israel and the Gaza aid flotilla. The United States and United Kingdom understand the issue as Israel's right to defend itself. The question we should be asking is how naive little Israel was outsmarted by "Islamists and their useful idiot fellow travelers," who were responsible for and welcomed the bloodshed. The flotilla "aimed to provoke a confrontation" and was intended "'to break' Israel's blockade of Gaza," noted Leslie Gelb (Daily Beast, May 31, 2010), the dean of the U.S. foreign policy establishment, echoing the line from Fox News (Newsbusters, May 31, 2010) to the *Washington Post* (June 1, 2010). The paper of record (*New York Times*, June 1, 2010) indicated that organizers wanted to provoke a "violent response from Israel," agreeing with the *Jerusalem Post* (June 1, 2010), which stated that the "'peace militants'… attacked the soldiers who boarded the ship with guns, iron bars, and knives and led to the dire results they were looking for." This fact did not escape the Obama White House, with one "senior" official saying, "the organizers of the flotilla were clearly seeking a confrontation—and tragically they got one" (Reuters, June 1, 2010).

Ever restrained, the *Jerusalem Post* (June 1, 2010) connects the dots. Because the "peace militants'… hatred towards Israel knows no bounds," and they "wanted to cause some damage, no matter the cost for them," they are like suicide bombers because "the aim justifies the means." If the lesson is still unclear, Max Boot, Leslie Gelb's colleague on the Council of Foreign Relations, spells it out in the *Wall Street Journal* (June 1, 2010). The "blood was on the hand of the pro-Hamas activists," because "Israel, like the United States and other democratic nations, is at a severe disadvantage trying to combat a ruthless foe willing to sacrifice its own people to score propaganda points." Boot may be too generous in calling the activists "pro-Hamas," however. The Israeli ambassador reveals they are actually Hamas' "sponsors [who] cower behind shipments of seemingly innocent aid" (*New York Times*, June 2, 2010).

Although the passengers included European legislators, U.S. diplomats, a Nobel Peace Prize laureate, Israelis, doctors, clergy, and journalists from around the world, Israel was not battling civilians on a "mission of mercy," writes the great humanitarian Marty Peretz (*New Republic*, June 1, 2010). In fact, the Turkish sponsor, the Humanitarian Relief Fund, "is said to have ties to Al Qaeda. Which would be logical since Al Qaeda is an ally of Hamas." Furthermore, Peretz illuminates, Hamas is the "Gazan outpost of the global jihad" and "second cousin once-removed of Hezbollah." Thus, in stopping the aid flotilla, Israel was really combating a branch of the devious global jihad that hates the West without reason. (Hamas is also "an Iranian pawn" (*New York Times*, January 12, 2009), which may seem confusing because Iran and Al Qaeda are fierce enemies, as are Hamas and Al Qaeda (*Guardian*, August 15, 2009), but such are the complexities of the Middle East that only experts like Peretz can divine.)

Prior to the deadly attack, there were eight previous attempts (*Christian Science Monitor*, May 28, 2010) to deliver aid by sea, including ships that Israel chose not to confront and which delivered goods to Gaza without incident (Palestine Free Voice, August 2008). The Israeli Navy spent "many weeks... preparing to meet the flotilla" (*Haaretz*, June 1, 2010), the military admitted three days before the raid that it planned to use violence (MaxBlumenthal.com, June 4, 2010), and the Israelis warned the captains of each ship while in international waters that "lethal force would be used if they persisted" (*Democracy Now!*, June 9, 2010). Despite this, we learn from the *Wall Street Journal*, Israel "walked into a trap set by a flotilla of Hamas sympathizers" (June 7, 2010); from the *New York Times*, it "blundered" (June 2, 2010) into a trap; from the *Los Angeles Times*, it "fell into a trap" (June 2, 2010); from the *Financial Times*, it "sail[ed] into a Turkish trap (June 6, 2010); and from the *Guardian*, it was "lure[d] … into a trap" (June 1, 2010).

If it seems curious that prominent media all conclude that golden-hearted Israel was duped, such is the "blatant double standard" (*New York Times*, June 1, 2010; the South African *Mail & Guardian*, June 9, 2010; *Wall Street Journal*, June 3, 2010) applied to the Jewish state that "is destined and compelled, like a puppet on a string, to react the way it did" (*Guardian*, June 1, 2010).

The task at this point would appear to be disentangling what happened during the actual raid. For instance, why were the "outnumbered, under-equipped and incorrectly prepared commandos" (*Jerusalem Post*, June 1, 2010)—who also happen to be "the best trained and most effective in the world" (*Haaretz*, June 1, 2010)—"taken off guard by a group of Arabic-speaking men" (Associated Press, May 31, 2010) when the soldiers rappelled onto the deck? Or why has one journalist, Max Blumenthal, been able to force Israeli officials to admit they doctored photos and audio clips released after the raid or show they falsely claimed that five passengers on the *Mavi Marmara* were "active terror operatives"?

Why have eyewitnesses on the *Mavi Marmara* said "live ammunition was fired before any Israeli soldier was on deck," and "The Israeli navy fired on the ships five minutes before commandos descended from ropes that dangled from helicopters" (FreeGaza.org, June 7, 2010)? There are also the eighty-one questions that Israeli peace activist Uri Avnery has compiled, such as why is Israel claiming Gaza's territorial waters are part of Israel's territorial waters when it has "separated" from it; why were five people on the *Mavi Marmara* shot in the back; "what is the source of the lie that the Turks called out 'Go back to Auschwitz'"; and "who invented the story that the activists had brought with them deadly weapons" (Ma'an News Agency, June 12, 2010)?

All these questions miss the point. Israel is still the victim, even if it's a "self-inflicted wound," so say the *New York Times* (June 1, 2010) and *Los Angeles Times* (June 2, 2010). You see, Israel made the mistake of trying to justify its actions with evidence. It forgot that reality has a well-known terrorist bias. When the facts sympathize with Hamas, terrorists, and drugged cockroaches, Israel needs to dispense with the facts. Because we know Israel is the eternal victim, that is all we need to know. All that matters is how Israel says it perceives the situation.

Arie "Lova" Eliav, one of the "granddaddies of the Israeli Left" and a founder of Labor Party, who died literally hours before the raid on the flotilla, put it best in an interview six years ago, saying, "We acted as they would have done to us" (*Jerusalem Post*, June 1, 2010). While he was speaking about Israel's founding war of aggression, the statement justifies every Israeli atrocity since 1947 and any future one. Since Israel is confronting "ruthless, indiscriminate animals" (CNN, July 20, 2006), its response is only limited by the imagination. After all, according to the Obama administration, "the president has always said it will be much easier for Israel to make peace if Israel feels secure" (ABC News online, June 1, 2010). And how does Israel feel? "Israel has long seen itself as the Alamo, a fortress under the siege," a former U.S. ambassador to Israel explains (*Washington Post*, June 6, 2010).

We come to one of the most important principles of the Middle East conflict: While we should treat Israeli perceptions as reality, Palestinians' reality is just perception that is up for debate. For example, "Palestinians say the restrictions on food imports and construction materials have created a humanitarian crisis" (*BusinessWeek*, June 7, 2010).

So the next time there is news about Israel killing activists, massacring children, bombing a refugee camp, or perhaps obliterating an entire country, there is no need to pay attention to the "facts." The only reality you should consider is that Israel, the eternal victim that will never feel secure, is just responding to some terrorist's outrage. And once the last "ruthless, indiscriminate animal" is exterminated, there will be "peace."

NO DIRECTION HOME

Daniel Luban

On the morning of May 31, Americans woke up to a flood of media reports about a deadly Israeli raid on a Gaza-bound humanitarian flotilla, and Israel's liberal supporters in the United States immediately found themselves in a familiar bind. On one hand, pro-Israel hardliners called on liberal Zionists to take a firm stand in support of Israel's actions, warning—as one neoconservative critic put it[1]—that to do otherwise would mark them as "at best, fair-weather friends and, at worst, little different from open anti-Zionists who implicitly support [Hamas]'s goal of eliminating the Jewish state." On the other hand, critics of Israel's ongoing blockade of Gaza called on these liberals to denounce not merely the tactical wisdom of the raid but the morality of the blockade itself. Most liberal Zionists proved characteristically unwilling to get behind either alternative. While a few spoke out[2] against the siege of Gaza, the majority restricted themselves to familiar admonitions that the raid was "unwise" and "counterproductive" even if the intentions behind it were blameless.

It was a classic illustration of the liberal Zionist predicament. In recent weeks this predicament has received an increased amount of attention, due in large part to a bracing and much-discussed essay[3] by Peter Beinart,[4] in which he sounded the alarm on the plummeting levels of support for Israel among younger American Jews. "For several decades, the Jewish establishment has asked American Jews to check their liberalism at Zionism's door," Beinart wrote, "and now, to their horror, they are finding that many young Jews have checked their Zionism instead." Similar concerns led to the formation in 2008 of J Street, a lobby group that aims to represent the views of liberal Jews and serve as a counterweight to traditionally right-leaning groups like AIPAC. If current trends continue, American Jewish attitudes toward Israel may ultimately be transformed in a way unseen since the bulk of the community first got on board with Zionism, in the wake of the 1967 Six-Day War.

How can liberal Zionism be saved? It is tempting to blame its decline on Israel's own shift to the right in recent years—epitomized by the rise of Foreign Minister Avigdor Lieberman—a shift aided and abetted by a right-leaning institutional leadership of the American Jewish community that refuses to criticize Israel under any circumstances. But *can* liberal Zionism, at least in the form that has dominated American Jewish life for decades, be saved at all? And should it be? These are harder questions but may ultimately be more important ones. It may be emotionally satisfying to posit a blameless liberal Zionism betrayed by outside forces, or to suppose that younger Jews are reacting only against the right and not liberal Zionism itself, but it is not clear that either claim is true. For one thing, Benjamin Netanyahu and Avigdor Lieberman undoubtedly make good villains, but the aspects of Israeli politics that have alienated U.S. liberals go deeper than the current right-wing government. (To take only the most recent example, it was not the nefarious Netanyahu or the loathsome Lieberman who brought us the attack on Gaza, but rather the supposed "good guys": Ehud Olmert, Ehud Barak, and Tzipi Livni.)

More generally, the apparently impending collapse of mainstream liberal Zionism in the United States is no accident. Some of the phenomenon may be attributed to a generation growing up farther removed from the looming presence of the Holocaust and without memories of the 1967 and 1973 wars. But we cannot adequately understand this collapse without understanding the compromises and contradictions that liberal Zionism became involved in over a period of decades.

***

Let me drop the pretense of disinterestedness for a moment. I am a member of the "younger generation" whose attitudes have become the subject of so much discussion, and in many ways I am typical of it. I held a set of views fairly typical of American liberal Zionism. I was largely uninformed about the Israel/Palestine conflict, but I was against the occupation and the settlements, and I considered myself sympathetic to Palestinian suffering. Still, I did not really question the basic Israeli narrative of the conflict ("We want peace, but they only want to annihilate us").

I considered myself a Zionist, in the sense that I supported Israel's "right to exist," which I took to mean that I did not want the state to be violently destroyed and its inhabitants driven into the sea. Only later did I come to understand that this was not the meaning of Zionism at all, and equally that non-Zionism had nothing to do with wanting to drive the Jews into the sea; I then realized that I had probably never been a Zionist in any real sense at all. (I now suspect that this is a common phenomenon, and that many if not most American Jews who call themselves Zionists are not so in any strict ideological sense—a misunderstanding encouraged by a pro-Israel establishment that is eager to equate non-Zionism with anti-Semitism.)

I can't pinpoint exactly when or how my views shifted. I started paying closer attention to the conflict and its history. I suspect the general disillusionment of the George W. Bush years also pushed me to the left on the Israel/Palestine issue, as it did to so many people on so many issues, and the Iraq War in particular (which I had opposed, but far from wholeheartedly) made me reconsider the merits of "serious liberalism" as an overall foreign policy stance. The fact that so many of Israel's most vocal supporters were among the leading proponents of the Iraq debacle forced me, like many others, to confront exactly what support for Israel entailed.

But of course, blaming Bush and Iraq does not explain why one should reconsider Israel and Zionism; even blaming the neocons or the Likud does not explain why one should reconsider mainstream liberal Zionism. To do so, it is necessary to examine some features of the liberal debate over Israel as it has been conducted in recent years in the bastions of mainstream Jewish opinion—in the *New York Times* and on NPR, in campus Hillels and suburban synagogues.

* * *

The first notable feature of the debate was its heavily emotive and tribal character. Rather than taking a measured look at the situation in Israel and the Palestinian territories, participants spent an inordinate amount of time fighting to claim the "pro-Israel" mantle and squabbling over who could be said to love Israel more. Hardliners contend that a "true friend" would never criticize Israel publicly; liberals argue that a "true friend" must help Israel avoid becoming an international pariah.

It is not difficult to see, however, that the liberal Zionists in these debates will always be at an inherent disadvantage. After all, Netanyahu and the rest of the Israeli political establishment are more than happy to weigh in on who they think their "true friends" are—and not surprisingly, it is the friends who are willing to hawk for war against Iran and turn a blind eye to West Bank settlements. Liberal Zionists will never really be able to convince the public that they know Israel's long-term interests better than Israel itself, no matter if it is true, and therefore will always have trouble answering the charge that they are, as Sarah Palin put it,[5] "second-guessing" Israel's own decisions. Thus the competition over who can appear to love Israel more is one that, unjustly or not, the liberals will generally lose.

More to the point, by constantly reaffirming their undying love for Israel, by couching every argument in terms of Israeli needs and

Israeli security, the liberals sacrifice the most effective advantage they have: their power to make moral arguments. Thus we hear frequently that a two-state solution would be "good for Israel" by solving the "demographic problem," or that the Gaza assault was "bad for Israel" by harming the country's international standing. Less frequently do we hear that the real value of the two-state solution would be in ending the misery and injustices of the occupation, or that the Gaza assault was bad, first and foremost, for the people of Gaza. Because they are afraid to make these arguments, the liberals have no good answers when the hardliners reply that the two-state solution imposes intolerable risks to Israeli security, or that the Gaza incursion was a successful response to the rocket fire into southern Israel.

The second feature of the debate was the obsessive focus on the motives of Israel's critics. On the one hand, there was the need to ensure that all criticism was restricted to "true friends" of Israel—always Jews, who must constantly reaffirm their Zionist credentials. On the other hand, there were the unhinged (one might say disproportionate) attacks directed at any critics who were deemed to be "outsiders"— generally Gentiles (and if Jewish, easily tarred as "self-haters"), who failed to abide by the rules of acceptable debate and therefore had to be made examples of.

Recent years have seen any number of examples, from Jimmy Carter to Tony Judt to John Mearsheimer and Stephen Walt to, mostly recently, Richard Goldstone. In each case, much of the crime was to step outside the prescribed limits of "acceptable" criticism: to say not merely that the perpetuation of the occupation would be regrettable, but that it would bring "apartheid" (Carter[6]); not merely that the window for a two-state solution is closing, but that it has closed (Judt[7]); not merely that the Israel lobby is bad for Israel, but that it is bad for the United States (Mearsheimer and Walt[8]); not merely that Israel made unspecified "mistakes" in Gaza, but that it committed outright war crimes (Goldstone[9]). But in each case, the problem was more with the messenger than the message. Thus both Ehud Olmert[10] and

Ehud Barak,[11] for instance, have reiterated Carter's "apartheid" rhetoric without arousing much visible outrage. Similarly, Beinart is only the latest in a line of mainstream liberal Zionists who have conceded the basic truth of the Mearsheimer/Walt thesis without acknowledging it by name. (I should disclose here that John Mearsheimer teaches in the political science department of the University of Chicago, in which I am a doctoral student, although we work in different fields.)

If the debate over Israel has shifted noticeably to the left over the last several years, this fact therefore owes almost nothing to the "responsible" liberal Zionists and almost everything to those whom the responsible liberal Zionists have tarred as anti-Semites. Yet the mainstreaming of once-taboo positions has not brought a respite in the tone or frequency of attacks; on the contrary, Israel's defenders seem to have doubled down. It has gotten to the point that when Harvard's Alan Dershowitz recently compared[12] Goldstone to the Nazi vivisectionist Josef Mengele—an objectively shocking analogy—few observers so much as batted an eye.

This pattern of behavior has by now become so familiar that we rarely stop to ask the obvious question, Why? Why focus so obsessively on delineating "acceptable" from "unacceptable" criticism and attempting to annihilate anyone who crosses the line?

Many of those responsible for enforcing ideological conformity on the issue were neoconservatives; their behavior could at least be read as a rational attempt to further their political goals. After all, they liked the status quo as it was. But many of the enforcers were liberals, or at least claimed to be. They professed their support for the two-state solution, their opposition to the settlements, their discomfort with (although never outright opposition to) the attacks on Lebanon and Gaza. Their professed goals actually differed little from those of many of their targets; after all, most of the hated figures mentioned above are fairly moderate proponents of a two-state solution, not one-staters or anti-Zionists. One might reasonably expect that if the liberal enforcers were serious about their "pro-peace" agenda, they would have found a way to make common cause with these critics rather than trying so fervently to destroy them. Instead, they followed a typical pattern: a few perfunctory words in favor of "peace" and against the settlements, followed by torrents of invective directed at anyone who was actually engaged in concrete action to further these goals. If these so-called liberals had devoted one-tenth of the time they spent policing the bounds of the debate to actually ending the occupation, the entire situation might be very different today.

* * *

At some point, I simply got tired of these fratricidal and self-absorbed debates, tired of the endless rhetorical dance. I stopped caring much about the "pro-Israel" label, or whether others would consider me a true "friend of Israel," or whether I was abiding by the strictures of "acceptable criticism." In the face of so much evident misery and injustice, these considerations came to seem self-indulgent and irrelevant. I continue to believe that the policies I support would ultimately be in the best interest of the people of Israel, but I recognize that only a minority of Israelis agree with me, and I frankly have little interest in squabbling with the Likudniks and neoconservatives over the right to call myself "pro-Israel."

Either the Gaza blockade is just, or it is not; either the Lebanon war was wise, or it was not; either the U.S. should bomb Iran, or it should not; either the two-state solution remains viable, or it does not. To reply to these questions with invocations of Judaism or anti-Semitism or the Holocaust is sheer non sequitur, and when someone does so it is generally a sign that they have no good answers. As for the charge of self-hatred, it may once have had bite, but today it has lost its sting. It comes off as desperate, even silly, and I can't find it in me to muster an answer to it.

If I am more representative than defenders of the status quo would like to admit, then it is naive to think that the old post-1967 liberal Zionism can be revived simply by speaking out more forcefully against

Avigdor Lieberman and the settlers. It is likely that American liberal Zionism was always destined to founder eventually on its own intellectual contradictions and political compromises, and those who are nostalgic for it should consider the possibility that at this point we simply can't go home again. The way forward can only come if we shed the pathologies that have stunted thinking to this point, and take a hard and pragmatic look at what concrete steps could lead to a better future.

Notes

1. (http://www.commentarymagazine.com/blogs/index.php/tobin/303796)

2. (http://www.thedailybeast.com/blogs-and-stories/2010-06-01/israel-flotilla-disaster-gaza-embargo-us-supporters-to-blame/)

3. (http://www.nybooks.com/articles/archives/2010/jun/10/failure-american-jewish-establishment/?pagination=false)

4. (http://www.tabletmag.com/tag/peter-beinart/)

5. (http://www.haaretz.com/news/palin-u-s-shouldn-t-second-guess-defensive-military-steps-taken-by-israel-1.253703)

6. (http://www.amazon.com/Palestine-Peace-Apartheid-Jimmy-Carter/dp/0743285026)

7. (http://www.nybooks.com/articles/archives/2003/oct/23/israel-the-alternative/)

8. (http://www.lrb.co.uk/v28/n06/john-mearsheimer/the-israel-lobby)

9. (http://www2.ohchr.org/english/bodies/hrcouncil/specialsession/9/FactFindingMission.htm)

10. (http://www.haaretz.com/news/olmert-to-haaretz-two-state-solution-or-israel-is-done-for-1.234201)

11. (http://www.guardian.co.uk/world/2010/feb/03/barak-apartheid-palestine-peace)

12. (http://www.ynetnews.com/articles/0,7340,L-3885999,00.html)

SOMETHING'S GOT TO GIVE

Alia Malek

As they learned of the Israeli raid on the Gaza flotilla, many Arab Americans reacted with a sense of horror that they had become accustomed to, and many uttered a phrase they had said before: *Something has got to give.*

Seasoned watchers of the Israel/Palestine conflict have learned to keep hope in reserve, having believed many times before that some other event would finally shock the conscience of the world and serve as a catalyst for change, only to see instead the event fade with the news cycle and the situation for the Palestinians continue to deteriorate with each passing year.

For nearly a century, events like the flotilla raid have seemed to prove that the injustice of Palestine is too great to remain unaddressed and unchanged. Yet despite repeated opportunities to gain momentum and positive change out of horrible occurrences, the Palestinian situation has only worsened with time. Among other things, this is a constant reminder of what little impact Arab Americans have had on their country's debate and policy on the question of Palestine.

This cycle was set in motion as long ago as the Balfour Declaration of 1917. At the time, Arab Americans—a small community with underlying divisions—mobilized and mounted an effort to persuade the administration of President Woodrow Wilson to reject the declaration that called for the awarding to the overwhelming minority of Jews present in Palestine the vast majority of the land.

Arab Americans wrote articles, engaged political and government officials, staged demonstrations, attended the 1919 Paris Peace Conference, appealed directly to the U.S. Secretary of State, and testified in front of the House Committee on Foreign Affairs, constantly emphasizing the principles of self-determination in their repeated call for a neutral commission to determine the will of the people of Palestine before endorsing the declaration. They (naively) expressed confidence that there was no way their country—the champion of democracy—would support a declaration that to them was patently unjust and un-American.

The United States ultimately did support Balfour, championing self-determination for the colonizers as opposed to the colonized.

It was a bruising early foray into U.S. foreign policy in the Middle East for Arab Americans, who nonetheless continued to speak up after each new event in the Middle East that would seem to beg for something to give, whether the wars in 1948, 1967, 1973, and 2009; the invasions or bombardment of Lebanon in 1982 and 2006; the occupation and its devices (settlements, checkpoints, mass imprisonment, collective punishment, the wall); the intifadas of 1987 and 2000; the massacres at Sabra and Shatila in 1983 or in Jenin in 2002; or the murder of American activists like Rachel Corrie in 2003, to name some of the major markers of this gruesome timeline.

And despite their efforts, these violations of international and human rights laws have fairly consistently been met in the United States with an embrace of the Israeli narrative even when it flies in the face of reality, with an intellectually and morally dishonest dismissal of the Palestinian narrative, and with tacit when not open support of Israeli policies. This inability to yield much influence only deepened in the years after 9/11, when the Bush administration ignored the peace process and the legitimate Palestinian cause was lumped in with the likes of Al Qaeda. Islamophobia made Muslim suffering easier to rationalize (the majority of Palestinians are Muslim, though significant

Palestinian Christian populations continue to live in the West Bank and Gaza Strip).

Thus, the psyche of one who watches the Palestine horizon for a messianic event that will finally save and transform the region is frequently battered.

In addition, the primary reason for the political exclusion of Arab Americans in this country is their dissent and activism on the Palestinian question. One need only remember that Arab American financial contributions have been publicly rejected by both Republicans and Democrats at different times. Or consider that the murder of Palestinian-American activist Alex Odeh, who was killed in 1985, remains unprosecuted to this day, while the U.S. government spent the better part of twenty years (1987–2007) trying to prosecute and then deport the L.A. Eight, activists who were distributing leaflets on behalf of one of the Palestinian political factions. The recent prosecutions, like that of Sami al-Arian or various Palestine-focused U.S. charities, whether justified or not, similarly send chilling messages to Arab Americans to stay out of U.S. policy development in the region.

Even for Arab Americans who for whatever reasons don't particularly care about the politics of the Middle East, the perceptions of the region and its people are nonetheless relevant in their lives. These events define not only the contours of the conflict but also affect significantly the racializing of Arabs in the American imagination and subsequently, the formation of Arab-American identity. After all, because Arab Americans have been virtually shut out of narratives of U.S. history and contemporary society (whether in textbooks, the media, or pop culture), the vacuum has been filled by images of Arabs from the Middle East, which until 9/11 and the invasion of Iraq, were dominated by the Palestine/Israel conflict, seen through less than flattering lenses.

So what significance will May 31, 2010, hold for Arab Americans? It is impossible to fully know since we are still in the throes of the raid and its aftermath. But a few observations follow.

Barack Obama—a president Arab American voters helped put in power—proved in the immediate afterwards to be as flaccid as many of his predecessors, his White House releasing a statement regarding Arab American Helen Thomas that showed much more indignation over her controversial words than for Israel's murder of nine people, one of whom was an American. In the longer term, it still remains to be seen what his presidency will deliver.

The proliferation of alternative forms of media (from networks who were on board to Twitter to handheld digital video cameras) has meant that the monopoly on the narrative that Israel has had when it comes to interpreting events in the region has begun to erode. Thus there might be hope that Palestinians will someday finally be humanized in the mainstream American consciousness and that subsequently Arab Americans might begin to be included in how mainstream America imagines itself. This process is again in relative infancy.

There is also an interesting dynamic emerging amongst Jewish Americans, the people against whom Arab American trajectory is often compared and measured. Israel's recent excesses—as demonstrated by the raid and subsequent blatant and tone-deaf attempts to propagandize it—have created a space were American Jews can more comfortably distance themselves from Israel, and be more openly critical of it, in a fashion similar to how Arab Americans increasingly do not feel the burden of apologizing for Arab regimes. This progression is also in gestation.

What is immediately clear is that actors outside of the mainstream Arab American organizations, actors who have not had decades of access to elected officials and who have never claimed the mantle of the voice of a community, have proven themselves to be quite relevant and potentially much more effective. Of course these activists did not come out of nowhere, but the flotilla itself announces their arrival in the most compelling of terms.

As of this writing, Israel was forced to succumb to international outcries and the blockade seems reduced to a degree. These are achievements to applaud, especially considering that they were set in motion not by armed states but by mere people acting on their conscience, like American civil rights or anti-apartheid activists before them.

If possible, perhaps this can offer some consolation to the families of those who gave their lives aboard the *Mavi Marmara*. In the excruciatingly protracted suffering of Palestine, something might finally be ready to give.

EVER FEWER HOSANNAS

Norman Finkelstein

Polling data of Americans and Europeans, both Gentiles and Jews, suggest that the public has become increasingly critical of Israeli policy over the past decade. "The increased and brutal frequency of war in this volatile region has shifted international opinion," the British *Financial Times* editorialized one year after Operation Cast Lead, "reminding Israel it is not above the law. Israel can no longer dictate the terms of debate."[1] One poll registering the fallout from the Gaza attack of 2008-09 in the United States found that American voters calling themselves supporters of Israel plummeted from 69 percent before the attack to 49 percent in June 2009, while voters believing that the United States should support Israel dropped from 69 percent to 44 percent.[2]

Confident that it could control or intimidate public opinion, Israel carried on in Gaza as if it could get away with mass murder in broad daylight. But while official Western support for Israel held firm, the carnage set off an unprecedented wave of popular outrage throughout the world.[3] Whether it was because the assault came on the heels of the devastation Israel wrought in Lebanon, or because of Israel's relentless persecution of the people of Gaza, or because of the sheer cowardice of the assault, the Gaza invasion appeared to mark a turning point in public opinion reminiscent of the international reaction to the 1960 Sharpeville massacre in apartheid South Africa.

In the Jewish diaspora official communal organizations with

longstanding ties to Israel predictably lent blind support. But, at the same time, newly minted progressive Jewish organizations distanced themselves to a lesser or greater degree. Whereas in the past mainstream Jews actively supported Israeli wars, most registered ambivalence during the invasion, apart from a contracting older minority that came out swinging in Israel's defense, and an expanding younger minority that scathingly denounced it. Between the increasing estrangement of younger Jews from Israeli bellicosity and the increasing qualms of Jews generally about supporting it, the Gaza massacre of 2009 signaled the break-up of hitherto blanket Jewish support for Israeli wars.

In addition, whereas the antiwar demonstrations in most Western countries were ethnically heterogeneous (including significant numbers of Jews), the "pro"-Israeli demonstrations were composed almost exclusively of Jews. The fact that active opposition to Israeli policy, say, on college campuses, has spread beyond the Arab-Muslim core toward the mainstream, whereas active support for Israel has shrunk to a fraction of the ethnic Jewish core, is a telling indicator of where things are headed.

The era of the "beautiful" Israel has passed, it seems irrevocably, and the disfigured Israel that in recent years has replaced it in the public consciousness is a growing embarrassment. It is not so much that Israel's behavior is worse than it was before, but rather that the record of that behavior has, finally, caught up with it. The truth can no longer be denied or dismissed.

The documentation of the Arab/Israeli conflict set out by respected historians fundamentally conflicts with the version popularized in the likes of Leon Uris's *Exodus*. The evidence of Israeli human rights violations compiled by respected mainstream organizations cannot be reconciled with its vaunted commitment to "purity of arms." The deliberations of respected judicial and political bodies cast severe doubt on Israel's avowed commitment to a peaceful resolution of the conflict.

For a long while Israel's "supporters" deflected the impact of this accumulating documentary record by wielding the twin swords of the Holocaust[4] and the "new anti-Semitism."[5] It was purported that Jews could not be held to conventional moral/legal standards after the unique suffering they endured during World War II, and that criticism of Israeli policy was motivated by an ever resurgent hatred of Jews. However, apart from the inevitable dulling that comes of overuse, these weapons proved much less efficacious once criticism of Israel broke into the mainstream of public opinion.

According to a 2007 poll by the Anti-Defamation League (ADL), the favorable opinion of Americans toward Israel is markedly less than their favorable opinion toward Great Britain and Japan, while roughly equal to their favorable opinion of India and Mexico. Nearly half of the respondents believe that the United States should work with "moderate" Arab states "even at the expense of Israel."[6] Half or more of Americans polled held Israel and Hezbollah equally to blame for the summer 2006 Lebanon War and supported a (more) neutral U.S. stance.[7] In addition, in recent years, influential religious constituencies such as the Presbyterian Church USA, the World Council of Churches, the United Church of Christ, and the United Methodist Church have all supported initiatives, including corporate divestment, to force an end to Israel's occupation.[8]

A 2005 survey by respected Jewish pollster Steven M. Cohen found that "the attachment of American Jews to Israel has weakened measurably in the last two years…, continuing a long-term trend."

Respondents were less likely than in comparable earlier surveys to say they care about Israel, talk about Israel with others, or engage in a range of pro-Israel activities. Strikingly, there was no parallel decline in other measures of Jewish identification, including religious observance and communal affiliation. The survey found 26 percent who said they were 'very' emotionally attached to Israel, compared with 31 percent who said so in a similar survey conducted in 2002. Some two-thirds, 65 percent, said they follow the news about Israel closely, down from 74 percent in 2002, while 39 percent said they talk about Israel frequently with Jewish friends, down from 53 percent in 2002.... Israel also declined as a component in the respondents' personal Jewish identity. When offered a selection of factors, including religion, community and social justice, as well as 'caring about Israel,' and asked, 'For you personally, how much does being Jewish involve each?' 48 percent said Israel matters 'a lot,' compared with 58 percent in 2002. Just 57 percent affirmed that 'caring about Israel is a very important part of my being Jewish,' compared with 73 percent in a similar survey in 1989.[9]

"In the long run," Cohen predicts "a polarization in American Jewry: a small group growing more pious and attached to Israel, while a larger one drifts away."[10]

Ambivalence toward Israel verging on disaffection can also be discerned among influential sectors of American society, the bellwethers of U.S. intellectual life, and the reading public. A recent poll found that a majority of opinion leaders in the United States view support for Israel as a "major reason for discontent with the U.S." around the world.[11] In a 2003 *New York Review of Books* essay, noted Jewish historian Tony Judt asserted that "Israel today is bad for the Jews," and he doubted both the viability and desirability of a Jewish state.[12] John J. Mearsheimer of the University of Chicago and Stephen M. Walt of the Harvard Kennedy School coauthored an influential paper in 2006 debunking the idealized image of Israel's history and asserting that Israel has become a "strategic liability" for the United States.[13] A book by former U.S. President Jimmy Carter, provocatively titled *Palestine Peace Not Apartheid*, deplored Israeli policy in the Occupied Palestinian Territory and put the blame for the impasse in the peace process squarely on Israel.[14]

Although the Israel lobby launched vitriolic counterattacks to these interventions, its usual smears alleging anti-Semitism and Holocaust denial did not adhere. When in 2006 the lobby's pressures led to cancellation of one of Tony Judt's speaking engagements, he became an instant cause célèbre in American intellectual circles.[15] His critics, such as Abraham H. Foxman of the ADL, were derided for "slinging the dread charge of anti-Semitism" and for being an "anachronism."[16] Carter, meanwhile, was said to be a plagiarist, in the pay of Arab sheikhs, an anti-Semite, an apologist for terrorism, a Nazi sympathizer,[17] and a borderline Holocaust denier.[18] Yet his book landed on the *New York Times* bestseller list and remained there for months, selling an estimated 300,000 copies in hardback. Although snubbed by Brandeis University's president, Carter still received standing ovations from the student body when he came to speak at the historically Jewish institution. (Half the audience walked out when Harvard law professor Alan M. Dershowitz rose to answer Carter.)[19] Mearsheimer and Walt negotiated a book deal with the prestigious publishing house Farrar, Straus, and Giroux, and their book, *The Israel Lobby and U.S. Foreign Policy*, also went on to become a *Times* bestseller.[20] It is further testament to Israel's waning fortunes that, during Prime Minister Ehud Olmert's term of office, even Foxman and perennial Israel supporter Elie Wiesel took to publicly rebuking Israel for its failure to pursue peace.[21]

Unsurprisingly Israel's apologists attributed the widespread outrage at the Gaza invasion of 2008-09 to anti-Semitism.[22] It might be posited as a general rule that the lower the depths to which Israel's criminal conduct sinks the higher the decibel level of the shrieks of anti-Semitism. Jews are confronting "an epidemic, a pandemic of anti-Semitism," Abraham H. Foxman declared. "This is the worst, the most intense, the most global it's been in most of our recent memories."[23] Such fearmongering was nothing new from Foxman, who had portended back in 2003 that anti-Semitism was posing "as great a threat to the safety and security of the Jewish people as the one we faced in the 1930s."[24] Just as in the past,[25] poll data used to substantiate these exaggerations tallied "indicators" of "the most pernicious notions of anti-Semitism," such as the finding that "large portions of the European public continue to believe that Jews still talk too much about what happened to them in the Holocaust."[26] According to Parisian media philosopher Bernard-Henri Lévy, anyone doubting that the Nazi holocaust was a "moral watershed in human history" should be reckoned an anti-Semite.[27] Few of the alleged anti-Semitic incidents in Europe went beyond merely unpleasant manifestations, such as emails and graffiti,[28] while European anti-Semitism, notwithstanding the hype, paled beside anti-Muslim bias. (A rise in animus toward Jews and Muslims—in recent years the two curves tend to correlate—appears partly due to a resurgence of ethnocentrism among older, less educated, and politically conservative Europeans.[29])

Nonetheless it is most probably true that the execution by a self-proclaimed Jewish state of consecutive murderous rampages in Lebanon and Gaza, and the vocal support lent these rampages by official Jewish organizations around the world, caused a regrettable—if entirely predictable—"spillover,"[30] whereby Jews generally were in some quarters held culpable. If, as the Israeli Coordination Forum for Countering Anti-Semitism asserted, there was "a sharp rise in the number and intensity of anti-Semitic incidents" during the Gaza massacre; and if "with the ceasefire there has... been a marked decline in the number and intensity of anti-Semitic incidents"; and if "another flare-up in the region, similar to the Gaza operation, will probably lead to an even more severe outbreak of anti-Semitic activity against communities worldwide," then an efficacious method to fight anti-Semitism would appear to be for Israel to stop committing massacres.[31]

In the liberal Jewish intellectual milieu only perennial apologists for Israel, most of whom came on board right after the June 1967 war and are now in their seventies, ventured a full-throated defense of the invasion. It was obvious to moral philosopher Michael Walzer that

Israel had exhausted nonviolent options before it attacked and that Hamas bore responsibility for the ensuing civilian deaths. To Walzer the only "hard question" was whether Israel did all it possibly could to reduce these casualties.[32] It was obvious to Alan M. Dershowitz that Israel made "its best efforts to avoid killing civilians" and that it failed because Hamas pursued a "dead baby" strategy of forcing Israel to kill Palestinian children in order to garner international sympathy.[33] It was obvious to *New Republic* editor Martin Peretz from his scrutiny of the Palestinians' footwear that the Israeli blockade of Gaza was benign: "You have to look closely at the sneakers, seemingly new and, of course, costly."[34] It was obvious to writer Paul Berman that if a "possibility" exists that Hamas might threaten Israel someday in the future with genocide "if Hamas were allowed to prosper unimpeded, and if its allies and fellow-thinkers in Hezbollah and the Iranian government and its nuclear program likewise prospered," then Israel would have the right to launch an attack now.[35] On such an accumulation of hypotheticals stacked on conditionals, it is hard to conceive what country in the world would be safe from arbitrary attack, and what country would not be justified in arbitrarily launching an attack.

The generational metamorphosis regarding Israel was most evident on college campuses. "A shift toward more visible pro-Palestinian or anti-Israel sentiment has been profound on some campuses," *Inside Higher Ed* reported, "prompted, in part, by the winter war in Gaza."[36] Large halls filled to overflow for lectures deploring the Gaza massacre. Whereas "pro"-Israel groups used to protest inside or outside such lectures, they were now barely seen. Students at Cornell University lined pathways with 1,300 black flags commemorating the dead in Gaza. (The display was later vandalized.) Students at the University of Rochester, the University of Massachusetts, New York University, Columbia University, Haverford College, Bryn Mawr College, and Hampshire College held petition drives, protests, and sit-ins demanding financial support for Palestinian students and divestment from arms companies and companies doing business with the illegal

Jewish settlements. Hampshire College students successfully pressured the college's trustees to divest from American corporations that directly profit from the occupation.

Although "pro"-Israel organizations alleged that "college and university campuses...have become hotbeds of a virulent new strain of anti-Semitism,"[37] at many campuses Jewish students have played a leading role on the local "Students for Justice in Palestine" committees, and creative and dedicated young Jewish activists in Birthright Unplugged and Anarchists Against the Wall, alongside individuals such as Anna Baltzer, author of the memoir *Witness in Palestine*,[38] have gone from school to school offering personal testimony on the daily horrors unfolding in Palestine. The bonds of solidarity being forged between young Jews and Muslims opposing the occupation—the core group on many campuses consists of secular Jewish radicals and observant Muslim women—give reason for hope that a just and lasting peace may yet be achieved.

Notes

1. "Israel's Revealing Fury towards EU," *Financial Times* (December 13, 2009).

2. "Poll Shows Dip in American Voters' Supporting Israel," *Jewish Telegraphic Agency* (June 16, 2009).

3. Andrew England and Vita Bekker, "Criticism of Israel's Conduct Mounts," *Financial Times* (January 10, 2009; http://tinyurl.com/8kyhoa).

4. I use the term Nazi holocaust to denote the actual historical event, and The Holocaust to denote the ideological instrumentalization of that event. See Norman G. Finkelstein, *The Holocaust Industry: Reflections on the exploitation of Jewish suffering* (New York: 2000; second expanded paperback edition, 2003), p. 3 and chapter 2.

5. See Norman G. Finkelstein, *Beyond Chutzpah: On the misuse of anti-Semitism and the abuse of history* (Berkeley: 2005; expanded paperback edition, 2008), chapters 1–3.

6. Anti-Defamation League, "American Attitudes towards Israel, the Palestinians and Prospects for Peace in the Middle East: An Anti-Defamation League survey" (October 19, 2007).

7. ABC/Washington Post Poll (August 3-6, 2006); Los Angeles Times/Bloomberg Poll (July 28, August 1, 2006); USA Today/Gallup Poll (July 21-23, 2006; www. pollingreport.com/israel.htm); "Zogby Poll: U.S. should be neutral in Lebanon war" (August 17, 2006; http://tinyurl.com/y99y86z).

8. The Amman Call: Issued at WCC International Peace Conference, "Churches Together for Peace and Justice in the Middle East" (June 18-20, 2007; http:// tinyurl.com/ya479wl); Toya Richards Hill, "GA Overwhelmingly Approves Israel/Palestine Resolution" (June 21, 2006; http://tinyurl.com/ycmeh99); "United Methodists Urged to Divest from 20 Companies Supporting in a Significant Way Israel's Occupation of Palestinian Land" (June 21, 2007; http:// tinyurl.com/ybusx68);"Seeking a Just Peace in the Middle East, Synod Adopts Economic Leverage Resolution" (July 5, 2005; http://tinyurl.com/yb4zj6p).

9. Steven M. Cohen, "Poll: Attachment of U.S. Jews to Israel falls in past 2 years," *Forward* (March 4, 2005).

10. American Jewish Committee, 2007 Annual Survey of American Jewish Opinion (November 6, November 25, 2007); "Second Thoughts," *Economist* ("long run"). See also M. J. Rosenberg, "Another Kiss of Death," *Haaretz* (April 25, 2008).

11. "America's Place in the World 2005: Opinion leaders turn cautious, public looks homeward," *Pew Research Center for the People and the Press* (November 17, 2005), pp. 6, 11, 74.

12. Tony Judt, "Israel: The alternative," *New York Review of Books* (October 23, 2003).

13. John J. Mearsheimer and Stephen M. Walt, "The Israel Lobby," *London Review of Books* (March 23, 2006).

14. Jimmy Carter, *Palestine: Peace Not Apartheid* (New York: 2006).

15. Mark Lilla and Richard Sennett, "The Case of Tony Judt: An open letter to the ADL," *New York Review of Books* (November 16, 2006), and "A Statement in Support of Open and Free Discussion about U.S. and Israeli Foreign Policy and Against Suppression of Speech," Archipelago (n.d.; http://tinyurl.com/ yaguewd).

16. James Traub, "Does Abe Foxman Have an Anti-Anti-Semite Problem?" *New York Times* (January 14, 2007).

17. Ezra HaLevi, "Exclusive: Jimmy Carter interceded on behalf of Nazi SS guard," israelnationalnews.com (January 18, 2007).

18. Deborah Lipstadt, "Jimmy Carter's Jewish Problem," *Washington Post* (January 20, 2007).

19. Philip Weiss, "Jimmy Carter's Book Stirs a Critical Debate," *American Conservative* (February 26, 2007); David Abel and James Vaznis, "Carter Wins Applause at Brandeis," *Boston Globe* (January 24, 2007). See also Hinda Mandell, "Brandeis Students at Odds over Israel," *Boston Globe* (May 8, 2008), reporting the student senate's vote to not congratulate Israel on its sixtieth anniversary.

20. John J. Mearsheimer and Stephen M. Walt, *The Israel Lobby and U.S. Foreign Policy* (New York: 2007).

21. Orly Halpern, "Foxman, Wiesel Upbraid Israel for Pace of Peace Effort," *Forward* (May 18, 2007).

22. Yael Branovsky, "Report: Gaza war reverses drop in anti-Semitism," *Haaretz* (January 15, 2009); "Europe Fears Spike in Anti-Semitism over Gaza," ynetnews.com (January 7, 2009; http://tinyurl.com/dcd7oq).

23. Anti-Defamation League, "ADL Leader: Gaza war unleashed 'pandemic of anti-Semitism'" (February 12, 2009; http://tinyurl.com/c9vc9m).

24. Abraham H. Foxman, *Never Again? The Threat of the New Anti-Semitism* (San Francisco: 2003), p. 4.

25. Finkelstein, *Beyond Chutzpah*, chapters 2–3.

26. Anti-Defamation League, "ADL Survey in Seven European Countries Finds Anti-Semitic Attitudes Steady" (February 10, 2009; http://tinyurl.com/blzx2w).

27. Jewish People Policy Planning Institute, Annual Assessment 2008, p. 40.

28. European Union Agency for Fundamental Rights, Anti-Semitism: Summary overview of the situation in the European Union 2001–2008 (February 2009). The quality of this publication can be gleaned from the fact that the only authority it cites on anti-Semitism is the German professional anti-anti-Semite Henryk Broder (p. 24), who wrote an unctuous preface for the German edition of Alan Dershowitz's *The Case for Israel*.

29. Pew Global Attitudes Project, "Unfavorable Views of Jews and Muslims on the Increase in Europe" (September 2008).

30. Finkelstein, *Beyond Chutzpah*, pp. 81–85.

31. The Coordination Forum for Countering Anti-Semitism, Anti-Semitism in the Wake of Operation Cast Lead (January 2009).

32. Michael Walzer, "On Proportionality," *New Republic* (January 8, 2009; http://tinyurl.com/93azy7).

33. Alan M. Dershowitz, "Hamas' Dead Baby Strategy," *Washington Times* (January

16, 2009); Alan M. Dershowitz, "Israel's Policy Is Perfectly 'Proportionate,'" *Wall Street Journal* (January 2, 2009).

34. Martin Peretz, "The Truth about Gaza," *New Republic* blog ("The Spine") (January 1, 2009).

35. Michelle Sieff, "Gaza and After: An interview with Paul Berman," *Z Word* (March 2009; http://tinyurl.com/cz3ght); Philip Weiss, "Paul Berman Says Gaza Assault May Have Been Necessary to Avert 'Genocide,'" *Mondoweiss* (February 26, 2009; http://tinyurl.com/cjln6b).

36. Elizabeth Redden, "On Israel, Shifted Ground," *Inside Higher Ed* (March 6, 2009; http://tinyurl.com/ag8t8r). Samuel Freedman, "In the Diaspora: Suspended agitation," *Jerusalem Post* (March 19, 2009).

37. Jewish People Policy Planning Institute, Annual Assessment 2008, p. 13.

38. Anna Baltzer, *Witness in Palestine: A Jewish American woman in the Occupied Territories* (Boulder, CO: 2007). Her website is www.AnnaInTheMiddleEast.com.

6. PALESTINE ON OUR MINDS

INTERNATIONAL SOLIDARITY UNDER ATTACK

Mike Marqusee

From small beginnings and with few resources, the international movement in solidarity with the Palestinians has grown into a force that Israel perceives as a major threat. The assault on the Gaza aid flotilla was a lethal escalation in what has become an increasingly bitter campaign against that movement, whose constituents now range from dockworkers in South Africa refusing to offload Israeli goods to students at Berkeley demanding divestment.

The brutality of the flotilla attack was a measure of the extent to which the Israeli polity has grown to fear and loathe this global grassroots movement. In a way, the violence was a perverse tribute to a band of voluntary campaigners who are massively outstripped by Israel in money, institutional resources, and access to the media, but who nonetheless have put more pressure on Israel than the world's most powerful governments. Indeed, it's the long-term collusion of those governments with Israel that has prompted the growth of citizen's initiatives, such as the Freedom Flotilla, to redress the balance.

People from very differing societies have come to the politics of international solidarity with Palestine via many routes. Nearly always, their commitment to the cause, the commitment that led the passengers on the boats to take such risks and suffer such punishment, is an expression of a wider aspiration for social justice, and above all a belief that this justice must be global in nature if it is to mean anything.

One of the primary objects of the Israeli media barrage that followed the assault was to discredit and divide this movement. In particular, it sought to isolate and demonize an "Islamist" or "jihadi" element among the activists. (This was presaged by the especially vicious treatment meted out to those passengers identified by Israeli armed forces as Muslims.) The "Turkish boat" was said be the source of all the trouble. At one point it was claimed that an "Al Qaeda" team had been on board. The IHH was traduced. People in the West with sympathies for the Palestinians were being warned: There was a type of person involved here with whom they would never want to make common cause.

Unfortunately, in France, a section of the left, driven by a misconceived interpretation of secularism, seemed to agree. They refused to join a protest against the assault on the flotilla on the grounds that other participants would include Muslim clerics. Under the guise of a dedication to universal values, this refusal was actually a restriction of those values: the expression of human solidarity was subjected to ideological conditions. Elsewhere the movement has prospered by its embrace of pluralism. This pluralism has been forged not by making a special case for the Palestinians but by universalizing their struggle: founding it on a commitment to human rights and common standards of justice. Far from "singling out Israel," as is routinely claimed, the movement has begun, at long last, to expose how Israel singles itself out, demanding (and receiving) exemptions from those standards.

The diversity of the passengers on the flotilla was always its greatest strength. It meant that a much wider circle of people felt some kind of connection with the events in the Mediterranean, and also that they would have access to sources of information not trammeled by the Israeli state line. Transcending the boundaries of nation, religion, and language, the passengers represented a growing global public that feels itself compelled to act because its governments will not. Like the motley delegation of foreigners who pledged their support for the French Revolution to the National Assembly in 1790, they were "ambassadors of the human race." Of course, far from deterring Israel, this status made them a threat which had to be countered with a show of extreme violence.

True to form, Israeli spokespersons described the killings on board the *Mavi Marmara* as "self-defense" by Israeli soldiers threatened with "lynching." The ensuing arguments about "violence" and who was responsible for it recapitulated a long history in which Israel has identified every denial of Palestinian rights or annihilation of Palestinian life as "self-defense." Conversely, every assertion of those rights and every attempt to preserve those lives is deemed illegitimate, denounced as "aggression" or "terrorism."

Here the Israelis tapped into a long-established bias in the Western media. A study by Arab Media Watch of the mainstream British press from January to June 2008 found that violent Israeli actions were almost always portrayed as "retaliating" to Palestinian aggression. Rocket attacks were represented as a "provocation" to Israel five times more often than the Gaza blockade was represented as a "provocation" to Palestinians. Forty years of occupation were portrayed as a provocation to Palestinians on only one occasion and settlement-building twice. Where debate arises within the mainstream media, it tends to revolve around the "proportionality" of Israeli action, thus evading the underlying questions of Palestinian rights and Israeli domination.

Unlike the solidarity movements which grew up in response to the struggles in Vietnam or South Africa, the Palestine movement faces an opponent with its own international network, preaching its own form of solidarity (with Israel), very much a movement in its own right, however reliant on state support. Its rhetoric and tactics may be cynical in the extreme, but there's no denying its emotional fervor. Building opposition to South African apartheid never involved the kind of on-the-ground contest with ideologically motivated, well-resourced opponents that pro-Palestinian activists routinely engage in.

Just as the Palestinian cause is a global magnet for victims of discrimination and dispossession, so the cause of Israel is a magnet for the privileged, the entitled, the beneficiaries of Western and white supremacy. The rich and powerful see themselves as under siege from the poor and powerless and in Israel's self-portrayal they recognize themselves. The gated communities of the world rally around the gated nation. The increasingly wealthy Indian elite—which has vigorously pursued governmental and business exchanges with Israel—sees in Israel not only an ally in a struggle against "Islamic terror" but a stepping stone to a closer relationship to the United States, and in a wider sense an entry into the exclusive club of the affluent and powerful.

Thus the highly particularist ideology of Zionism—which rests on the assertion of eternal ownership of a specified territory by a specified people—becomes a broader "civilizational" cause. This ideology underpins the ever-widening Israeli definition of "self-defense." To those for whom the maintenance of a Jewish supremacist state in Palestine is the sine qua non of Jewish survival, any assertion of Palestinian rights is an "existential" threat—a negation that must itself be negated. As a state for all Jews, Israel embraces a global mission and enjoys special prerogatives. In the contemporary world only the United States claims a wider remit of self-defense, insisting that it can strike anywhere to protect its perceived interests. Israeli exceptionalism finds a mirror and enabler in U.S. exceptionalism, which in turn has its roots in the long history of Western colonialism, whose stock-in-trade was, for centuries, acts of piracy on the high seas.

Through many years of grassroots education, agitation, and organization, not to mention a steadfast defiance of intimidation, the solidarity movement has begun at last to have a real effect on the balance of power. But there is so much further to go. Governments around the world joined in the condemnation of the Israeli attack on the flotilla, but many of these same governments continue to provide essential means for Israel to pursue its destruction of the Palestinian people. In that context, those who consider themselves, in Thomas Paine's words, "citizens of the world" are called upon to redouble their efforts to secure boycott, divestment, and sanctions. If Israel continues to act with impunity, if Palestine instead of Israel is subject to isolation, then the powerful everywhere will have their options strengthened.

OUR SOUTH AFRICA MOMENT

Omar Barghouti

Since July 9, 2005, when the historic call for boycott, divestment, and sanctions (BDS) against Israel was launched[1] by an overwhelming majority of Palestinian unions, political parties, community networks, and NGOs, there has never been a period with as many BDS achievements as the last few months. This is particularly true after the bloodbath on the Gaza-bound Freedom Flotilla, which rudely awakened a long dormant sense of international moral responsibility for Israel's exceptional status for decades as a state above the law. World-renowned legal experts, literary giants, top performing artists, major church groups, large trade unions, and many more international civil society organizations, especially in the West, seem to have crossed a threshold in their views of Israel. Crucially, many are now committed to challenge Israel's impunity and counter, in diverse forms, its perceived menace to world security.[2]

Moral indignation at Israel's latest attack was bound to be channeled into more effective pressure measures—such as the BDS campaign, which empowers creative, practical action—rather than expressing itself in typical protests that parrot the same old demands, only to be ignored again by Israel and its hegemonic partners. Mahmoud Darwish's famous cry of "besiege your siege" suddenly acquired a different meaning. Since convincing a colonial power to heed moral pleas for justice or to voluntarily give up its privileges is, at best, delusional, many people of conscience felt it was time to end Israel's deadly siege by "besieging" it, by adopting BDS measures to isolate Israel as a world pariah, thus drastically raising the price of its siege, occupation, colonization, and apartheid policies.[3]

The Palestinian-led global BDS movement adopts a rights-based, not a solution-based, approach. It identifies the fundamental rights that correspond to the three main segments of the indigenous people of Palestine. Based on international law and universal principles of human rights, the call urges various forms of boycott against Israel until it fully complies with its obligations under international law by:

1. Ending its occupation and colonization of all Arab lands occupied since 1967 and dismantling the Wall;
2. Recognizing the fundamental rights of the Arab-Palestinian citizens of Israel to full equality; and
3. Respecting, protecting, and promoting the rights of Palestinian refugees to return to their homes and properties as stipulated in U.N. Resolution 194.

By avoiding the prescription of any particular political formula, the BDS call insists, instead, on the necessity of including the three basic, irreducible rights above in any just and legal solution. It presents a platform that not only unifies Palestinians everywhere in the face of accelerating fragmentation but also appeals to international civil society by evoking the same universal principles of freedom, justice, and equal rights that were upheld by the anti-apartheid movement in South Africa and the civil rights movement in the United States, among many others.[4]

This approach is bearing fruit. Consider how the United Nations' response to the attack was uncharacteristically firm and echoed BDS aims. The Human Rights Council voted with an overwhelming majority (thirty-two to three) to strongly condemn Israel's actions against the flotilla and to dispatch an independent, international probe into violations of international law resulting from it. Only Italy and the

Netherlands joined the United States in voting against this simple measure of accountability.[5] Usually cautious not to denounce Israel lest it irks the United States, U.N. Secretary General Ban Ki-moon and his top assistants condemned the attack and called on Israel in unambiguous terms to immediately end its illegal siege of Gaza.[6] The clearest and most principled voice in the U.N. officialdom was that of Special Rapporteur for Human Rights in the Occupied Palestinian Territories, Professor Richard Falk,[7] who stated, "It is essential that those Israelis responsible for this lawless and murderous behavior, including political leaders who issued the orders, be held criminally accountable for their wrongful acts." He added, "The worldwide campaign of boycott, divestment, and sanctions against Israel is now a moral and political imperative, and needs to be supported and strengthened everywhere."

At the official sanctions level, several governments reacted swiftly to the attack. Nicaragua suspended its diplomatic relations with Israel.[8] South Africa recalled its ambassador to Tel Aviv.[9] Turkey also recalled its ambassador to Tel Aviv for "consultations,"[10] while the Turkish parliament voted *unanimously* to "revise the political, military and economic relations with Israel" and to "seek justice against Israel through national and international legal authorities,"[11] a move that alarmed Israel considerably, given Turkey's status as the second-largest importer of Israeli weapons, after India. Norway's minister of education and head of the Socialist Left party, Kristin Halvorsen, reconfirmed Norway's arms ban on Israel and called all other states to "follow the Norwegian position which excludes trading arms with Israel."[12]

The Palestinian BDS National Committee (BNC), the largest coalition of Palestinian civil society entities supporting the Israel boycott, reacted to the flotilla attack by calling on June 1 for intensifying BDS, arguing as follows:

Israel's impunity is the direct result of the international community's failure to hold it accountable for its ongoing occupation, colonization, and apartheid against the Palestinian people. Israel's most recent war crimes committed in Gaza and documented in the Goldstone report as well as crimes committed in 2006 against the Lebanese people did not trigger any U.N. or official sanctions, entrenching Israel's feeling of being above the law. In fact, Israel's grave violation of international law was recently rewarded when the OECD voted unanimously to accept its membership. The BNC urges international civil society to end this deep and fatal complicity.[13]

Inspired by the historic example set by the South African Transport and Allied Workers Union (SATAWU) in Durban in February 2009,[14] when it refused to offload an Israeli ship, the BNC and, a few days later, the entire Palestinian trade union movement called on transport and dockworkers' unions around the world to "block Israeli maritime trade in response to Israel's massacre of humanitarian relief workers and activists aboard the Freedom Flotilla, until Israel complies with international law and ends its illegal blockade of Gaza."[15]

The response from trade unions surpassed all expectations.

SATAWU called upon its members "not to allow any Israeli ship to dock or unload" and urged fellow trade unionists "not to handle them."[16] The Swedish Dockworkers' Union decided[17] to blockade all Israeli ships and cargo to and from Israel and started[18] implementing that weeklong boycott on June 23.

The South African trade union federation COSATU, which played a key role in abolishing apartheid in South Africa, called for "greater support for the international boycott, divestment, and sanction campaign against Israel," urging "all South Africans to refuse to buy or handle any goods from Israel or have any dealings with Israeli businesses."[19]

The South African Municipal Workers Union (SAMWU) unanimously endorsed a motion to immediately work toward making every municipality in South Africa an "Apartheid Israel free zone,"[20] an idea that has started to inspire BDS activists in Europe and elsewhere.

In the United Kingdom, a key market for Israeli goods, the largest trade union, UNITE, unanimously voted at its first policy conference, in Manchester, to boycott *all* Israeli companies.[21] UNISON, the second-largest union, reportedly adopted[22] in its recent annual conference similar boycott measures against Israel, including the suspension of bilateral ties with Histadrut, the Israeli labor body that justified Israel's flotilla attack[23] just as it had the war of aggression on Gaza earlier.[24] The British academics' union, UCU, representing 120,000 members, issued a strong condemnation of the Israeli attack, demanding that "the U.K. government does not change the rules on universal jurisdiction to impede bringing the people responsible for these murders to justice." It is worth mentioning that just a day before the flotilla attack, the UCU had made BDS history when it voted with an overwhelming majority to sever all links with Histadrut.[25]

LO, Norway's largest trade union federation, comprising almost one-fifth of the entire Norwegian population, called on the State Pension Fund, the third largest sovereign fund in the world, to divest from all Israeli companies.[26] A poll taken after the attack showed more than 42 percent of all Norwegians supporting a comprehensive boycott of Israeli goods.[27]

On June 20, in the port of Oakland, California, union members and community activists set a historic precedent by blocking the offloading of an Israeli ship for 24 hours.[28]

At its annual conference, the Northern Illinois Conference of the United Methodist Church (UMC) voted[29] to "divest all holdings in three international corporations that profit from the occupation of Palestine," explaining that "this action is in response to a plea by Palestinian Christians for action, not just words."[30]

With a 79.5 percent majority, the student body of Evergreen State College in the United States voted to divest[31] from companies that profit from the Israeli occupation, following the precedent-setting decision by Hampshire College[32] in February 2009, in the aftermath of the Israeli atrocities in Gaza.

Endorsing the widely popular[33] cultural boycott of Israel called for by the Palestinian Campaign for the Academic and Cultural Boycott of Israel (PACBI)[34] since 2004, world-renowned British writer Iain Banks wrote in the *Guardian*[35] that the best way for international artists, writers, and academics to "convince Israel of its moral degradation and ethical isolation" is "simply by having nothing more to do with this outlaw state." Stéphane Hessel, co-author of the Universal Declaration of Human Rights, Holocaust survivor, and former French diplomat, endorsed[36] Banks's position in a Huffington Post opinion piece.

The world-renowned Swedish writer, Henning Mankell, who was on the Freedom Flotilla when it was attacked, called for South Africa–style global sanctions against Israel in response to its brutality.[37]

Many British literary and academic figures published a letter[38] in the *Independent* that said, "We… appeal to British writers and scholars to boycott all literary, cultural, and academic visits to Israel sponsored by the Israeli government, including those organized by Israeli cultural foundations and universities."

BDS also reached mainstream Western papers. *Aftonbladet*, Sweden's largest tabloid, called for a boycott of Israel.[39] A main editorial in the Irish *Sunday Tribune* stated,[40] "The power of a people's movement lies in its ability to challenge national or international policies that are inherently unjust. A boycott of Israeli goods by Irish people may seem like gesture politics, but it could achieve two aims. It would show solidarity with the people of Gaza and it would also register collective displeasure at what the Israelis are doing."

In the high-visibility realm of performing arts, famous bands reacted to the flotilla attack by canceling scheduled gigs in Israel, causing more exacerbation and triggering more introspection in the Israeli public, almost all of which supported the attack (92 percent),[41] as they did the Israeli war of aggression on Gaza (94 percent).[42] The Klaxons and Gorillaz Sound System withdrew first,[43] followed by the Pixies.[44] The latest cancellation came from U.S. folk singer Devendra Banhart. While holding on to the ill-conceived and historically discredited notion that, in a situation of grave violations of human rights, a musician can simply entertain the oppressor community and "share a human not a political message" with them, Banhart justified his withdrawal by saying that "it seems that we are being used to support views that are not our own."[45] Israeli media outlets had tried to portray his scheduled gig as a political message of support for Israel at a time of increasing isolation. A *Washington Post* article titled "Israel's feeling of isolation is becoming more pronounced"[46] captured the mood in Israel well. And an article in *Billboard*, the leading music industry publication, also highlighted the growing controversy surrounding performing in Israel in light of the flotilla attack.[47]

In the weeks and months before the flotilla attack, artists of the caliber of Elvis Costello, Gil Scott-Heron, and Carlos Santana all cancelled[48] scheduled performances in Israel after receiving appeals from Palestinian and international BDS groups. Increasingly, Tel Aviv is being compared to the South African resort, Sun City, which was boycotted by world artists during apartheid. An artist who performs in Israel today is viewed, by Palestinians and supporters of just peace around the world, just like those who violated the boycott against apartheid South Africa, as putting personal gain ahead of moral principles. Israel, attempts to lure international performers as part of its "Brand Israel"[49] campaign, which by design hides its violations of human rights and international law under a deceptive guise of artistic and scientific glamour.

Despite the promise of lucrative remuneration, many top artists refuse to perform in Israel. The *Forward*, the leading Jewish daily in New York, cites a "music insider" saying that "in recent months he had approached more than 15 performing artists with proposals to give concerts in Israel. None had agreed. The contracts offered high levels of compensation. He called them 'extreme, big numbers that could match any other gig.'"[50]

Many cultural figures, well before the flotilla attack, explicitly supported the Palestinian cultural boycott of Israel. A statement by 500 Artists Against Apartheid in Montreal[51] is the latest, perhaps most impressive, of these efforts. Earlier, in 2006, the famous British author and artist, John Berger, issued a statement[52] explicitly endorsing the cultural boycott of Israel, collecting ninety-three endorsements from prominent writers and artists. Intellectuals and artists who have endorsed BDS[53] include Ken Loach, Judith Butler, Naomi Klein, The Yes-Men, Sarah Schulman, Aharon Shabtai, Udi Aloni, Adrienne Rich, John Williams, and Arundhati Roy, among others.

Some cultural figures have refused to participate in Israel's official celebrations and festivals without explicitly adopting the boycott. In 2008, for instance, countering Israel's Sixtieth Anniversary celebrations, PACBI collected tens of signatures of prominent artists and authors for a half-page advertisement[54] that was published in the *International Herald Tribune*. The list included luminaries like Mahmoud Darwish, Augusto Boal, Roger Waters, Andre Brink, Vincenzo Consolo, and Nigel Kennedy. Some of the signatories on that ad later adopted the boycott explicitly.

A third category is of artists who accept to play Israel and then cancel after being approached by PACBI and its partners around the world, including the Israeli group, Boycott From Within,[55] which plays a significant role in convincing performers to stay away from Israel due to its violation of Palestinian rights. This category includes[56] Bono, Björk, Jean-Luc Godard, Snoop Dogg, and others.

Whether in culture, academia, business, or mere image, Israel is feeling the heat like never before. A fast spreading BDS campaign has caused fury in Israel, prompting twenty-five Members of Knesset, including from ruling and opposition parties, to put forth a bill[57] that would criminalize advocating, justifying, or support the boycott by Palestinians, Israelis, and internationals alike. This latest sign of desperation, more than anything else, proves that Israel fears the global reach and effectiveness of a morally consistent, well-argued, civil, nonviolent campaign of resistance—especially one based on international law and universal human rights—in "besieging" its siege, occupation, and apartheid. In many ways, it confirms the analysis that the "South Africa moment"[58] has arrived for Palestine.

Notes

1. (http://bdsmovement.net/?q=node/52)

2. (http://www.msnbc.msn.com/id/17474900/) and (http://news.xinhuanet.com/english/2009-10/04/content_12181647.htm#)

3. For a comprehensive study that reveals how Israel's regime over the Palestinian people constitutes occupation, colonization, and apartheid, according to the U.N. definition of the term, see: (http://www.hsrc.ac.za/Document-3202.phtml) and (http://bdsmovement.net/files/English-BNC_Position_Paper-Durban_Review.pdf)

4. For more on the origins, logic, and progress of the BDS movement see: (http://al-shabaka.org/policy-brief/civil-society/bds-global-movement-freedom-justice)

5. (http://www.ohchr.org/EN/NewsEvents/Pages/DisplayNews.aspx?NewsID=10095&LangID=E)

6. (http://www.un.org/apps/news/story.asp?NewsID=34863&Cr=gaza&Cr1=)

7. (http://gulfnews.com/news/world/other-world/israeli-leaders-should-be-brought-to-justice-un-rights-expert-1.635049)

8. (http://www.ynetnews.com/articles/0,7340,L-3897773,00.html)

9. (http://www.bloomberg.com/apps/news?sid=a_vBbjBZJ6LM&pid=20601087)

10. (http://www.todayszaman.com/tz-web/news-212110-100-ambassador-celik-kol-back-in-ankara-for-consultations.html)

11. (http://www.news-gazette.com/news/news/2010-06-02/turkeys-parliament-wants-review-israeli-ties.html)

12. (http://www.swedishwire.com/nordic/4809-norway-calls-for-boycott-on-arms-to-israel)

13. (http://bdsmovement.net/?q=node/710)

14. (http://www.satawu.org.za/international/10-international)

15. (http://bdsmovement.net/?q=node/712)

16. (http://groups.google.com/group/cosatu-press/msg/a2ff0baff48201c4?pli=1)

17. (http://ibnkafkasobiterdicta.wordpress.com/2010/06/03/the-swedish-dockers-union-decides-on-a-blockade-against-israeli-ships-and-goods/)

18. (http://bandannie.wordpress.com/2010/06/23/press-release-from-the-swedish-dockworkers-union-section-4-gothenburg/)

19. (http://www.cosatu.org.za/show.php?include=docs/pr/2010/pr0531d.html&ID=3395&cat=COSATU%20Today)

20. (http://www.samwu.org.za/index.php?option=com_content&task=view&id=621&Itemid=1)

21. (http://www.thejc.com/news/uk-news/32579/unite-votes-boycott-israel)

22. (http://www.jpost.com/International/Article.aspx?id=179475)

23. (http://www.cicweb.ca/scene/2010/06/statement-by-the-histadrut/)

24. (http://www.labourstart.org/israel/Histadrut_on_Gaza.pdf)

25. (http://www.jpost.com/International/Article.aspx?id=177210)

26. (http://www.nrk.no/nyheter/norge/1.7148110)

27. (http://www.ynetnews.com/articles/0,7340,L-3898052,00.html)

28. (http://www.sfgate.com/cgi-bin/article.cgi?f=%2Fc%2Fa%2F2010%2F06%2F20%2FBA0G1E28CV.DTL)

29. (http://pwjcoordinators.blogspot.com/2010/06/peace-with-justice-coordinators_17.html)

30. Leading Christian Palestinian figures from various denominations issued "Kairos Palestine: A Moment of Truth" in 2009, adopting BDS as a form of non-violent resistance and calling on world churches to follow suit. (http://www.kairospalestine.ps/sites/default/Documents/English.pdf)

31. (http://www.tescdivest.org/news.php)

32. (http://www.pacbi.org/etemplate.php?id=930)

33. (http://pacbi.org/etemplate.php?id=315)

34. (http://www.pacbi.org/etemplate.php?id=869)

35. (http://www.guardian.co.uk/world/2010/jun/03/boycott-israel-iain-banks)

36. (http://www.huffingtonpost.com/stephane-frederic-hessel/gaza-flotilla-global-citi_b_612865.html)

37. (http://www.telegraph.co.uk/news/worldnews/middleeast/palestinianauthority/7795692/Gaza-aid-flotilla-Henning-Mankell-calls-for-sanctions-on-Israel.htm)

38. (http://www.independent.co.uk/opinion/letters/iiosi-letters-emails-amp-online-postings-6-june-2010-1992480.html)

39. (http://www.aftonbladet.se/ledare/ledarkronika/helleklein/article4164419.ab) and (http://www.aftonbladet.se/ledare/article7248085.ab)

40. (http://www.tribune.ie/news/editorial-opinion/article/2010/jun/06/a-boycott-of-israeli-goods-is-now-necessary/)

41. (http://mideast.foreignpolicy.com/posts/2010/06/10/israelis_speak_up)

42. (http://www.jpost.com/Israel/Article.aspx?id=129307)

43. (http://www.haaretz.com/news/national/klaxons-and-gorillaz-sound-system-cancel-israel-shows-apparently-due-to-gaza-flotilla-raid-1.294191)

44. (http://www.abc.net.au/news/stories/2010/06/06/2919568.htm?section=justin)

45. (http://www.devendrabanhart.com/news/2010/06/14)

46. (http://www.washingtonpost.com/wp-dyn/content/article/2010/06/21/AR2010062104706.html)

47. (http://www.billboard.com/news#/news/israeli-raid-on-gaza-bound-flotilla-draws-1004097608.story)

48. (http://www.pacbi.org/etemplate.php?id=1236&key=santana)

49. Launched in 2006 by the Israeli foreign ministry, the "Brand Israel" project aims at improving Israel's international image. "We will send well-known novelists and writers overseas, theater companies, exhibits," said Arye Mekel, the ministry's deputy director general for cultural affairs. "This way you show Israel's prettier face, so we are not thought of purely in the context of war." (http://www.nytimes.com/2009/03/19/world/middleeast/19israel.html?_r=3&hp). Also see: (http://www.israel21c.org/opinion/jewish-week-marketing-a-new-image)

50. (http://www.forward.com/articles/128185/)

51. (http://www.tadamon.ca/post/5824)

52. (http://www.pacbi.org/etemplate.php?id=415)

53. See (www.PACBI.org)

54. (http://www.pngo.net/data/files/english_statements/08/PNGO-THT-HP5208(2).pdf)

55. (http://boycottisrael.info/)

56. (www.PACBI.org)

57. (http://www.jmcc.org/news.aspx?id=1066)

58. (http://palestinechronicle.com/view_article_details.php?id=14921)

EXPEDITING THE DAY OF LIBERATION

Adam Shapiro

On the night of May 28, 2002, I sat with other internationals, Palestinians, and even an Israeli as we started talking about preparations for a likely Israeli attack on the West Bank in the wake of the suicide bombing of a hotel in Natanya the previous evening. As Israeli and American politicians took to the airwaves to outdo one another in calling for blood, we sat and tried to figure out what we—the International Solidarity Movement (ISM)—could do to protect Palestinian lives and to stand up to the coming aggression. Already we were deeply involved in trying to overcome aspects of the Israeli occupation and call attention to the brutalities suffered by Palestinians, but this was going to be something different.

In the early morning hours of the next morning, the invasion began in Ramallah. We gathered the fifty or so foreign volunteers we had on hand and started training and planning. Meanwhile one of my colleagues and I got aboard a Palestinian ambulance to provide international accompaniment for it as it made its rounds in the city. Over the coming days and weeks, Israeli tanks, soldiers, and helicopters would invade and attack all the major cities of the West Bank (except Jericho) and kill, injure, and detain thousands of Palestinian civilians. While the "cycle of violence" spun out of control, a new phenomenon was developing, as hundreds more foreign civilians came to an active battleground to join in solidarity with Palestinians, much to our surprise. The ISM had planned a two-week campaign for this time, but we fully expected most of the participants to withdraw once the images from Ramallah, Bethlehem, and Jenin were broadcast back home. However, by the middle of April, over 200 international civilians of all ages came to join in solidarity and to try to protect Palestinians.

In fact, since 2001 when the ISM was launched to engage in nonviolent popular resistance to the Israeli occupation in solidarity with Palestinians, more than 7,000 foreign civilians from over thirty countries have come to the West Bank, Gaza, and Jerusalem. Even after the brutal murders of Rachel Corrie and Tom Hurndall and the severe injuring of Brian Avery, Tristan Anderson, and Emily Henochowicz, volunteers continue to come to join the struggle in Bil'in, Budrus, Na'alin, Jayyous, Nablus, Silwan, the South Hebron Hills, and elsewhere. In addition to ISM there are many other locally focused groups that have sprung up, developing solidarity relationships with specific Palestinian communities and villages. Documentary films, books, art, and poetry have reported on and been inspired by these experiences and relationships, all serving to bring out of Palestine a more rooted understanding of what is happening on the ground than any media organization bothers to provide.

This international component of the struggle for freedom for Palestinians took on a new dimension when a group of activists organized the Free Gaza Movement and started sending ships to break the illegal Israeli blockade on Gaza in August 2008. Since the first two ships arrived in Gaza, eight missions have been organized, with the Freedom Flotilla being the largest and most significant. These efforts have required a whole new level of organization, fundraising, planning, and political strategy, even as the basic grassroots and civil society components of movement-building have added to existing efforts to support Palestinians.

The Freedom Flotilla headed on the last leg of the trip to Gaza on May 30, 2010, brought together 700 participants from over thirty countries, including MPs, doctors, lawyers, human rights activists, former U.N. officials, and journalists. Eight ships set off for Gaza, organized by a coalition of six groups, with dozens of other organizations, movements, community groups, and individuals contributing funds, cargo, and support in various ways. Two of the ships were sabotaged by Israel and one was ultimately unable to join the flotilla. When the Israeli commandos attacked the ships, they were attacking the international community as represented by the people from Chile to Malaysia, from the United States to Indonesia.

What brought these people together, and what has fueled a growing international movement to confront Israeli apartheid, is a combination of tiredness and frustration with the lack of progress for Palestinian human rights and freedoms, combined with a notion that Israel cannot be confronted by Palestinians alone and that it is incumbent upon all of us in the international community to stand up for justice. The flip side is that increasingly we are all aware of the ways in which the Israeli occupation and apartheid policies are propped up by international support at the government level. As such, all of us are indeed responsible for the situation in Palestine.

While the direct action component of this international activism for Palestine—a kind of global intifada—is manifest through the ISM, the Free Gaza Movement, Viva Palestina, the Gaza Freedom March, the International Women's Peace Service, and other such groups, the work back at home is taking off in new directions. For years, activists have returned home to conduct lecture tours, write, perform, and present photos and videos of their time and experience in Palestine. Building on expanded community awareness and increased acknowledgment of the devastation the Israeli occupation is causing to the Palestinian people, international civilians are seeking ways to make their voices heard and challenge these policies. In the United States, for instance, lobbying elected officials seems both impossible and meaningless, given the vast support for Israel from the U.S. government (and U.S. taxpayer money). Whereas groups like Stop U.S. Taxpayer Aid to Israel Now (SUSTAIN) emerged in 2000 and 2001 and ran out of steam in the middle of the decade, by 2009 there were vibrant and active boycott, divestment, and sanctions (BDS) groups emerging in communities, cities, and on college campuses around the United States.

The BDS movement is an international effort that in a mere five years has already earned major successes in a number of countries and on a number of fronts. From a Dutch bank that removed its investment in a French company building a rail link in occupied East Jerusalem, to a Canadian postal workers union that voted to endorse divestment; and from a U.S. university that voted for divestment from U.S. companies complicit in the Israeli occupation, to internationally renowned artists like Santana and Elvis Costello who have cancelled their concerts in Israel to boycott Israeli policies, BDS is showing real results. In fact, the BDS effort has been so effective that there are already news articles appearing regularly in the Israeli press calculating the costs to Israel's economy and prestige as a result of this nascent effort.

The BDS movement is a response to the call for such action by Palestinian civil society in 2005, but that could not have happened without the already prepped and ripe audience to receive that call. Through all of these efforts—the direct action and BDS, as well as countless other international works in film, art, music, and literature—the front lines of the Israeli-Palestinian conflict have shifted, and the discourse of the conflict itself has been reformulated. And this reconstitution of the conflict has the potential to deliver radical change toward freedom and justice.

Up until the 1980s, the PLO as a vibrant political-military-social organization was able to confront Israel primarily from abroad, including from neighboring states as well as in various international forums. And while there were always solidarity efforts to support Palestinians during this time, the locus of the conflict was between Israel and the PLO. As the PLO experienced a dramatic decline by the late 1980s, culminating in the decision to support Iraq in its decision to invade Kuwait in 1990, Palestinians inside the Occupied Territories launched an intifada which drew the attention and sympathy of the world, even as most international supporters could do little more than hold protest rallies or complain to their elected officials. When the Palestinian Authority was established, the confrontation against Israeli occupation not only was dampened; it was fully relocated inside the two cages that are the West Bank and Gaza. By the time the next intifada was launched in 2000, Palestinians were arguably at their weakest, most vulnerable strategic position since 1948.

The surge of international support for Palestinian rights and freedom, and against the Israeli occupation and apartheid policies has now reshaped the dynamic of confrontation and shifted the balance of power away from Israel. This is not to say that Israel does not maintain great power, particularly the ability to "create facts on the ground," but rather to suggest that there is a radical shift in momentum, in which Israel's power is on the decline while that of the anti-occupation/anti-apartheid camp is growing. The disparity of the starting points of each side necessarily means that while the moment has shifted, it will still be a long time before concrete results are materialized, but even before there is parity in terms of power, there will be a realignment and reconfiguration of interests by those who wield the power of oppression.

The Freedom Flotilla represented the largest manifestation yet to confront through direct action Israeli policies of oppression. More than the number of ships and passengers, there were thousands, if not millions, of people around the world organizing behind the scenes, preparing simultaneous demonstrations, calling their media and elected officials, tweeting, Facebooking, and otherwise engaged with supporting the mission. The face of this international movement is diverse, with people of all backgrounds, ages, professions, ethnicities, and religions; and it offers to the world a different narrative than the old notion of this being a blood feud between two irreconcilable foes. The story is no longer Arab vs. Israeli or Palestinian vs. Israeli; it is the whole world vs. Israeli apartheid and occupation and freedom vs. apartheid. And the front lines of this movement is no longer just Ramallah, Beirut, or Gaza but also New York, London, Stockholm, Istanbul, Toronto, Buenos Aires, Hong Kong, Kuala Lumpur, college campuses, sports stadiums, concert halls, and film festivals.

Indeed, as with apartheid South Africa, the cracks are starting to appear. Of course, as the old regime seeks to maintain its grip, it will undoubtedly use greater force, as that is the only language right-wing governments know how to use. The increased violence used to suppress the growing nonviolent movement in the Palestinian territories, the increased intimidation and silencing of second-class Palestinian citizens of Israel who dare to speak out and organize, and the undeclared war that Israel has launched against international civilians who take direct action against the occupation and apartheid should not surprise anyone, and it is something for which we must be prepared. But make no mistake, it also signals the unraveling of Israeli oppression and the regime and institutions built to support it.

As groups like Free Gaza and its coalition partners, the ISM and other groups in the West Bank, and the BDS movement internationally, take steps to escalate the confrontation, and as more and more Palestinian villages take to strategic nonviolent direct action to challenge the occupation, we must constantly work to make this transnational effort operate in harmony. The days of the oppression of Palestinians—whether in the Occupied Palestinian Territories, in refugee camps, or in the diaspora—are numbered. It is now in all our power to expedite that day of liberation.

ACKNOWLEDGMENTS

Putting this book together, particularly considering its accelerated publishing schedule, across several time zones, has been a formidable task. I would like to thank Colin Robinson of OR Books, who originally approached me with the project, and Anthony Arnove of Haymarket Books, who has been instrumental all along. My agent, Katherine Fausset, provided much needed help and guidance. This book would simply not exist were it not for the tireless efforts of Liliana Segura. Her astute judgment, marvelous editorial abilities, and keen political instincts have added so much wisdom and depth to this book. Many other people have also been helpful along the way, and I would like to thank all of them. They include: Huwaida Arraf, Frank Barat, my father, Mohamed Bayoumi (who graciously helped at the last hour with a needed translation), Phyllis Bennis, Michael Brown, Roane Carey, Lamis Deek, Katherine Gallagher, Dr. Hatim Kanaaneh (whose generosity is boundless), Rhoda Kanaaneh, Ceren Kenar, Sana' Odeh, Andy Pollack, Michael Ratner, Corey Robin, Adam Shatz, Muge Sokmen, and Kumru Toktamis. I would also like to acknowledge the organizers of the Gaza Freedom Flotilla and the volunteers on the ships for their courage and dedication along with the people of Gaza and Palestinians far and wide for their resolute steadfastness over generations of dispossession.

CONTRIBUTORS

Ali Abunimah is the co-founder of the Electronic Intifada and author of *One Country: A Bold Proposal to End the Israeli-Palestinian Impasse.*

Lamis Andoni is a veteran journalist and independent columnist and commentator on Middle East affairs.

Omar Barghouti is an independent Palestinian researcher and human rights activist. He is a founding member of the Palestinian Campaign for the Academic and Cultural Boycott of Israel (PACBI) and the global BDS campaign against Israel.

Moustafa Bayoumi is the author of *How Does it Feel to be a Problem? Being Young and Arab in America,* which won an American Book Award and an Arab American Book Award. His writing has appeared in the *New York Times,* the *Guardian,* the *Nation,* and the *London Review of Books.* He teaches at Brooklyn College, City University of New York.

George Bisharat is a professor at Hastings College of the Law and writes frequently about law and politics in the Middle East.

Max Blumenthal is an award-winning journalist and author of *Republican Gomorrah: Inside the Movement That Shattered the Party* (Nation Books). He is currently working inside Israel-Palestine.

Noam Chomsky is Institute Professor (emeritus) of linguistics and philosophy at MIT. He is the author of many books, including, most recently, *Hopes and Prospects* (Haymarket Books).

Marsha B. Cohen is a Middle East analyst specializing in Israeli-Iranian relations and U.S. foreign policy toward Israel and Iran. Her articles have been published by PBS/*Frontline*'s Tehran Bureau, the Inter Press Service

News Agency and its affiliate Lobelog, AlterNet, Payvand, and Global Dialogue.

Juan Cole is Richard P. Mitchell Collegiate Professor of History at the University of Michigan. His books include *Engaging the Muslim World* (March 2009) and *Napoleon's Egypt: Invading the Middle East* (2007) His blog, Informed Comment, is at www.juancole.com.

Murat Dagli studied international relations at Bilkent University, Ankara, and has a M.A. in political science from McGill University in Montreal. He is currently a Ph.D. candidate in Middle Eastern history at the University of California, Berkeley.

Jamal Elshayyal is a news producer for Al Jazeera English and one of the founding members of its specialized Middle East Desk. In 2006 he was the youngest ever candidate for a major political party in the British elections.

Sümeyye Ertekin graduated from Anatolian University in Turkey in 2006 and has been working as a correspondent for TVNET ever since, covering stories in Pakistan, Armenia, Syria, Lebanon, Israel, Gaza, Bosnia, and Egypt.

Norman Finkelstein is an independent scholar and the author of several books, most recently, *'This Time We Went Too Far': Truth and Consequences of the Gaza Invasion*.

Gisha.org is an Israeli not-for-profit organization, founded in 2005, whose goal is to protect the freedom of movement of Palestinians, especially Gaza residents. Gisha promotes rights guaranteed by international and Israeli law.

Neve Gordon is an Israeli academic and is the author of *Israel's Occupation* (University of California Press, 2008). His website is israeloccupation.com.

Glenn Greenwald, a columnist at *Salon*, is a former constitutional law and civil rights litigator and author of the bestselling *How Would a Patriot Act?* and *A Tragic Legacy*. His most recent book is *Great American Hypocrites: Toppling the Myths of Republican Politics*.

Arun Gupta is a founding editor of the *Indypendent* newspaper. He is a contributing writer for AlterNet, Truthout, and *Z* Magazine, and is a regular commentator on *Democracy Now!*, GRITtv, and Al Jazeera. He is a writing a book on the politics of food for Haymarket Books.

Amira Hass writes a regular column in *Haaretz* newspaper, and is the author of *Drinking the Sea at Gaza: Days and Nights in a Land Under Siege* and *Reporting From Ramallah: An Israeli Journalist in an Occupied Land.*

Nadia Hijab is an independent analyst, columnist, and senior fellow at the Institute for Palestine Studies. Her works include co-authorship of *Citizens Apart: A Portrait of Palestinians in Israel* (I. B. Tauris.)

Adam Horowitz is co-editor of *Mondoweiss*, a news website devoted to covering American foreign policy in the Middle East, chiefly from a progressive Jewish perspective. His work has appeared in the *Nation, Middle East Report,* the Huffington Post, Talking Points Memo, and TheHill. com.

Rashid Khalidi is Edward Said Professor of Arab Studies at Columbia University and author of *Palestinian Identity* (1997, rev. ed. 2010), *The Iron Cage* (2006), and, most recently, *Sowing Crisis: The Cold War and American Dominance in the Middle East* (2009).

Stephen Kinzer is an award-winning foreign correspondent and the author of *Reset: Iran, Turkey and America's Future.*

Paul Larudee is co-founder of the Free Palestine Movement and the Free Gaza Movement, whose boats broke a forty-one-year Israeli naval blockade of Gaza in August 2008. He works as a piano tuner/technician in California.

Iara Lee, a filmmaker, is founder of the Caipirinha Foundation. She is the director of the films *Synthetic Pleasures, Modulations,* and the forthcoming *Cultures of Resistance.*

Gideon Levy is an award-winning journalist who, since 1982, has been on staff at *Haaretz,* where he has served as deputy editor and is currently on the editorial board. His weekly column, *Twilight Zone,* covers the Israeli occupation in the West Bank and Gaza.

Daniel Luban is a doctoral student in political science at the University of Chicago. He previously worked as a reporter for Inter Press Service and currently blogs at www.lobelog.com.

Alia Malek is a civil rights lawyer who has lived and worked in Palestine and the author of *A Country Called Amreeka: Arab Roots, American Stories.*

She is currently editing a book of post-9/11 oral histories in the Voice of Witness series published by McSweeney's Books. Her website is www.acountrycalledamreeka.com.

Henning Mankell is one of the world's bestselling authors. His books have sold more that 30 million copies, perhaps most famous among them his Kurt Wallander detective series. In addition to his Gaza activism, he is committed to the global fight against AIDS.

Mike Marqusee is a London-based writer and activist, author of *If I Am Not for Myself: Journey of an Anti-Zionist Jew* (Verso, 2008) among other books. He is a columnist for the *Hindu* (India) and *Red Pepper* (Britain), and a contributor to the *Guardian*; see www.mikemarqusee.com.

Lubna Masarwa is on the board of directors of the Free Gaza Movement and was one of the organizers of the Freedom Flotilla. She is a Palestinian '48 activist who works as a community organizer fighting against the Israeli occupation, home demolitions, and forced displacement.

Yousef Munayyer is the executive director of the Palestine Center and the Jerusalem Fund for Education and Community Development and is completing doctoral work in government and politics at the University of Maryland.

Ken O'Keefe is a former U.S. Marine who served in the 1991 Gulf War and later led the Human Shield Action to Iraq in 2003. In 2001 he formally renounced his U.S. citizenship and has since naturalized as an Irish, Palestinian, and Hawaiian citizen. He is currently attending a fellowship program for the School of Social Entrepreneurs in London and is the managing director for Aloha Palestine CIC.

Kevin Ovenden is an organizer of the Viva Palestina solidarity group and veteran of two convoys to Gaza.

Ilan Pappé directs the European Centre for Palestine Studies at Exeter University and is the author of *The Ethnic Cleansing of Palestine*.

Doron Rosenblum is a senior correspondent for *Haaretz* and a member of the newspaper's editorial board.

Sara Roy is a senior research scholar at Harvard University's Center for Middle Eastern Studies who has worked in the Gaza Strip and West Bank since 1985. Her books include *Failing Peace: Gaza and the Palestinian-*

Israeli Conflict (2007) and the forthcoming *Hamas and Social Islam in Palestine.*

Ben Saul is co-director of the Sydney Center for International Law (SCIL) and a barrister. He has published widely in international law journals is the author of *Defining Terrorism in International Law* (Oxford University Press, 2006).

Eyad Al Sarraj is a psychiatrist and founder of the Gaza Community Mental Health Program and a commissioner of the Palestinian Independent Commission for Human Rights.

Adam Shapiro is a documentary filmmaker and human rights activist. He is on the board of directors of the Free Gaza Movement and was a co-founder of the International Solidarity Movement. He produced and directed the documentary film series *Chronicles of a Refugee.*

Raja Shehadeh is a Palestinian lawyer and writer. He is the author of several books, including *Palestinian Walks*, which won the 2008 Orwell Prize. His latest book is *A Rift in Time: Travels With My Ottoman Uncle.*

Henry Siegman, director of the U.S./Middle East Project, is a visiting professor at the Sir Joseph Hotung Middle East Program at the University of London. A former senior fellow at the Council on Foreign Relations, he was national director of the American Jewish Congress from 1978 to 1994.

Ahdaf Soueif is an Egyptian short story writer, novelist, and political and cultural commentator.

Raji Sourani is the director of the Gaza-based Palestinian Centre for Human Rights (PCHR) and vice president of the International Federation for Human Rights (FIDH).

Richard Tillinghast is the author of ten books of poetry, most recently *Selected Poems* (Dedalus Press, 2009), and three books of nonfiction. He has taught at Harvard and Berkeley, and is professor emeritus of English literature at the University of Michigan. He is a 2010–2011 Guggenheim fellow.

Alice Walker is a writer, poet, and activist whose writings have been translated into more than two dozen languages. Her books have sold more than ten million copies, among them *The Color Purple*, which won the Pulitzer Prize.

Stephen M. Walt teaches at Harvard University's Kennedy School of Government, where he served as academic dean from 2002 to 2006. He is the author of *Taming American Power: The Global Response to U.S. Primacy* (2005), and, with coauthor J. J. Mearsheimer, *The Israel Lobby* (2007).

Philip Weiss founded the website *Mondoweiss* in 2006. He has published two books, a political novel, *Cock-A-Doodle-Doo*, and *American Taboo*, an investigative account of a 1976 murder in the Peace Corps in the Kingdom of Tonga.

Haneen Zoabi is a member of the Israeli Knesset, representing the Balad party. She was the first woman to be elected to the Knesset on an Arab party's list.

CREDITS

Doron Rosenblum's "Israel's Commando Complex" was reprinted with permission from the June 4, 2010, edition of *Haaretz*. © 2010 Haaretz

Ilan Pappé's "The Deadly Closing of the Israeli Mind" was reprinted with permission courtesy of the author. Originally appeared in the June 6, 2010, edition of the *Independent* U.K.

Henry Siegman's "Israel's Loss of Moral Imagination" was reprinted with permission courtesy of the author. Originally appeared in the June 11, 2010, edition of *Haaretz*.

Lamis Andoni's "The Myth of Israeli Morality" was reprinted with permission courtesy of the author. Originally appeared at english.aljazeera.net.

Yousef Munayyer's "A History of Impunity" was reprinted with permission from the Palestine Center.

Murat Dagli's "Turkey After the Flotilla" was reprinted with permission courtesy of the author. Originally appeared on June 9, 2010, at the Electronic Intifada.

Marsha B. Cohen's "Smearing the IHH" was reprinted with permission by the author. Originally published under the title, "'Terror' smear against IHH springs from a familiar source," on June 4, 2010, by Mondoweiss.

Glenn Greenwald's "Victimhood, Aggression, and Tribalism" was adapted with permission courtesy of the author, from blog posts that first appeared on June 3, 2010, on *Salon*.

Stephen M. Walt's "Defending the Indefensible: A How-To Guide" was reprinted with permission courtesy of the author. Originally published on June 2, 2010 by *Foreign Policy*, at walt.foreignpolicy.com. © 2010 Foreign Policy

Stephen Kinzer's "Treat Israel Like Iran" was reprinted with permission from the Daily Beast. Originally published on June 2, 2010, at www.thedailybeast.com. © 2010 The Daily Beast

Arun Gupta's "The Victim That Is Israel" was reprinted with permission from an article adapted from a piece published by AlterNet on June 16, 2010.

Daniel Luban's "No Direction Home" was adapted with permission from an article first published on June 3, 2010, by *Tablet* magazine. © 2010 Daniel Luban

About Haymarket Books

Haymarket Books is a nonprofit, progressive book distributor and publisher, a project of the Center for Economic Research and Social Change. We believe that activists need to take ideas, history, and politics into the many struggles for social justice today. Learning the lessons of past victories, as well as defeats, can arm a new generation of fighters for a better world. As Karl Marx said, "The philosophers have merely interpreted the world; the point however is to change it."

.We take inspiration and courage from our namesakes, the Haymarket Martyrs, who gave their lives fighting for a better world. Their 1886 struggle for the eight-hour day reminds workers around the world that ordinary people can organize and struggle for their own liberation.

For more information and to shop our complete catalog of titles, visit us online at www.haymarketbooks.org.

Also from Haymarket Books

Gaza in Crisis
Noam Chomsky and Ilan Pappé

**Boycott, Divestment, and Sanctions:
The Struggle for Palestinian Civil Rights**
Omar Barghouti

The Israeli Left and the Struggle for Palestine
Tikva Honig-Parnass

The Palestine Communist Party 1919–1948
Musa Budeiri

**Between the Lines: Readings on Israel,
the Palestinians, and the U.S. "War on Terror"**
Tikva Honig-Parnass and Toufic Haddad

Diary of Bergen-Belsen: 1944–1945
Hanna Lévy-Hass, foreword and afterword by Amira Hass